THE GRAPHIC DESIGN READER

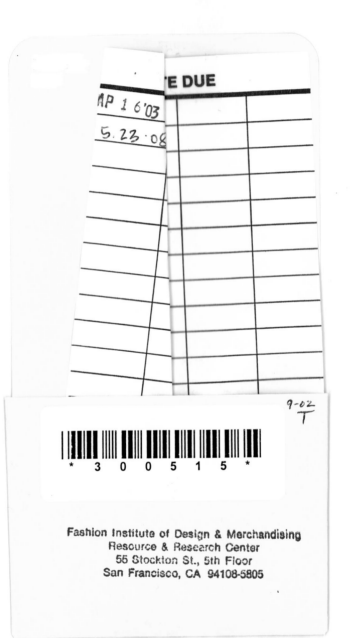

9-02
T

*3 0 0 5 1 5 *

THE GRAPHIC DESIGN READER

BY

STEVEN HELLER

ALLWORTH PRESS
NEW YORK

06 05 04 03 02   5 4 3 2 1

Published by Allworth Press
An imprint of Allworth Communications
10 East 23rd Street, New York, NY 10010

Book design by Christoph Niemann

Page composition/typography by SR Desktop Services, Ridge, NY

Library of Congress Cataloging-in-Publication Data
Heller, Steven.
    The graphic design reader / by Steven Heller.
        p.   cm.
    Includes bibliographical references and index.
    ISBN 1-58115-214-0
    1. Graphic arts—United States.   2. Commercial art—United States.
3. Popular culture—United States.   I. Title.
NC998.5.A1   H438 2002
741.6'0973—dc21   2001006464

Printed in Canada

CONTENTS

DEDICATION

This book is dedicated to the people
who have given meaning to my life.

Nicolas Heller, son
Louise Fili, wife
Seymour Chwast, best friend, East Coast
Dugald Stermer, best friend, West Coast
Brad Holland, mentor
Lita Talarico, collaborator
Paula Scher, confidant
Tom Bodkin, boss
Art Spiegelman, good friend
Marian Rand, good friend
Martin Fox, good friend
Rick Poynor, good friend
Tad Crawford, good publisher
Milton Heller, dad
Bernice Heller, mom

ACKNOWLEDGMENTS

Thanks to all the editors at the magazines who edited
and published some of these articles and essays:

Julie Lasky, *Interiors*
Joyce Rutter Kaye, *Print*
Nancy Bernard, *Critique*
Marty Neumier, *Critique*
Martin Pedersen, *Metropolis*
John Walters, *Eye*
Hans Dieter Reichert, *Baseline*
Tom Zeller, the *New York Times*
Andrea Codrington, *Trace, AIGA Journal*

Also thanks to friends and colleagues who have given me
support and succor:

Silas Rhodes
David Rhodes
Marshall Arisman
Art Chantry
Mirko Ilic
Barbara Kruger
James Victore
Richard Wilde

Thanks again to the crew at Allworth:
Bob Porter, associate publisher
Nicole Potter, editor
Jamie Kijowski, production editor
Liz Van Hoose, associate editor
Kate Lothman, associate editor

And finally, but not least, thanks to
Christoph Niemann, for his witty design.

READ ME

INTRODUCTION

The author (middle) looking for a job.

INTRODUCTION

I never wanted to be a plumber. Although I have a healthy respect for good plumbers, the idea of performing a task where I follow rote procedures is definitely not for me, and I am sure I would fail at it anyway. So, by singling out plumbers I mean no disrespect.

Plumbing is akin to graphic design because, in a sense, a graphic designer plumbs communications problems using a finite number of tried and true solutions. The difference between the two professions is that to be a proficient plumber demands years of apprenticeship, but to be a great graphic designer requires innate talent. This certainly does not diminish the proficiency a designer garners over time, nor minimize the talent of a plumber, but it introduces the distinction between service provider and commercial artist. It implies that, given talent, a graphic designer potentially contributes to culture—which is not to say that the plumber does not benefit society. But, although they intersect, society and culture are not the same thing.

Culture is the product of a society's collective and individual actions manifest in art, literature, music, sports, and politics. The plumber's job is to maintain society's infrastructure. Graphic designers, serving as both primary and supporting creators, help build cultural objects.

This book is a paean to their achievements, large and small, good and bad. It is also a reflection of my varied, obsessive interests in popular culture. Frankly, I cannot think of anything I would rather be doing than working every day as an art director, except maybe writing about the influence of visual culture. That is, unless a really easy plumbing job came along.   —Steven Heller

CRITIQUES

SECTION I

(P) **plazm fonts**™

ARS FONTS, By Angus R. Shamal $385/All ARS FONTS

Censor Sans Regular ABEGHJSTVXYZabcghjstvxyzl234567890
Censor Sans Slanted ABEGHJSTVXYZabcghjstvxyz123456789
Censor Sans Bold ABEGHJSTVXYZabghjostvxyzl234567890
Censor Sans Bold Slanted ABEGHJSTVXYZabcghj234567890

$90/Four

Censor Serif Regular ABCEGHJSTVYZabceghjstvyzl234567890
Censor Serif Slanted ABCEGHJSTVYZabceghjstvyzl234567890
Censor Serif Bold ABCEGHJSTUVYZabceghjstvxyzl234567890
Censor Serif Bold Slanted ABCEGHJSTVYZabceghjsl234567890

$90/Four
$150/All eight faces

CODE STEADY ABCEGHJKLNOSTUVXYZABCEGHJOSTUVXYZl234567890
CODE HEAVY ABCEGHJKLNOPRSTUVXYZABCEGHJSTVXYZl234567890

$60/Pair

HUMAIN GRAPHICA abCEGHIhLMNOPRStUUWXYZ123456781©
HUMAIN SYNTHETICA abCEGhhLMNStUUXYZ1234667891©

$90/Pair

Platrica Gothic ABCGHIKTVXZabcghjstvyzl234567890
PLATRICA HARMONIZED ABCEGHIOSTVYZl234567890

$60/Pair

Roscent Regular ABCEGHJKOPRSTUVYZabceghjostvxyz1234567890
Roscent Italic ABCGHJKLMNPRSTUVYZabcdefghjkstvyz1234567890
Roscent Semibold ABCGHJKLMNPSTVYZabcghjkstvyz1234567890
Roscent Bold ABCEGHJKLMNSTVXYZabcghjstvxyz1234567890

$90/Four

OPULUX SERIES 2000 FONTS, By Dave Henderleiter $165/All OPULUX FONTS

DIZZY SPELL ABCEf9HJKLOSTVXYZAbCEf9HJKLMl234567890 $40

Dogboy Split Home ABCEHJOSTVXYZabceghiostvxyz1234567890 $40

DoeMan ABCEFGHJKLNOPSTVXYZabcefghjkLmnopstvxyzl234567890 $40

PULSITALLIA ABCEGHJOSTVXYZABCEGHJOPSTXYZl234567890 $40

Sygarlift ABCEFGHJKhrOSTUVXYZabceghjkmnostvxyzl2@456789l0 $40

Detail of a 1999 specimen sheet for contorted and distressed typefaces from Plazm Fonts.

THE ME TOO GENERATION

"Thank god it's over," said Milton Glaser, responding to my question, "How do you feel about the self-indulgent, designer-as-artist-above-all-else era of graphic design that we just passed through?" What else could he say? "I miss it already?" or "Too bad sobriety has returned?" But despite the loaded question, the fact is, during the past decade there has been a fervent desire among many young designers to be considered independently hip. Exhibit one: the many showcase design books with the words "hot," "cool," and "killer" in the titles, mostly about type, typography, and Web sites, that reinforce by reward the notion that novelty and slavish idiosyncrasy is somehow a virtue.

What constitutes hot-cool-killer design? I would characterize it as a clash of new technologies and old styles with novel conceits and faddish fashions. Timely labels for these—like Grunge, New Wave, Techno, Post-Punk, New Minimalism, and even Neo-Modernism—have added to the era's edgy cachet. But perhaps "Me Too Design" is a better catch phrase. For this was an era when popular acceptance (or at least acknowledgment) of graphic design by the mass media (e.g., the *New York Times, Time, Newsweek,* etc.) encouraged designers to become relentlessly expressive. Many graphic designers, however, found their means of expression in the same basic sources: supermarket signage, twentieth-century Modern art, futuristic fantasies, computer programming quirks, and even a little of that old-time corporate

Modernism. The end product (or byproduct) was a pre-proto-neo-post stew, tasty but hard to digest.

Nineties graphic design began to evolve in the early eighties, when a rebellion against sterile corporate Modernism and slick opulent professionalism erupted. Designers attacked the Swiss style that ordered and clarified information and replaced it with type and image that literally collided on a single page. Once sacrosanct rules of form and function were expunged through the use of distressed or distorted letterforms that resulted in dissonant compositions. So-called post-Modern graphic designers from progressive design schools in Holland, Switzerland, England, and the United States borrowed the language of poststructuralism from highbrow French literary critics. This allowed them to "talk about themselves, expose their own mechanics, and hold a dialog or discourse about their own constructs," explains Katherine McCoy, the former co-chair of Cranbrook Academy of Art, once the wellspring of graphic design's deconstruction movement.

Deconstruction theorists at Cranbrook and elsewhere proposed to transform graphic design from a mere commercial tool to a rich cultural language. They believed that a participatory audience interpreted information in an individual way. Therefore, everyday messages were not to be taken at face value simply because they were set in official typefaces and printed on fine papers. Deconstruction questioned the authority and morality of all kinds of propaganda—a worthwhile goal, although somewhat detached from design problems for common businesses, like annual reports, ketchup labels, or mail order catalogs.

Deconstruction would probably have remained behind the academy's walls if not for the almost simultaneous introduction of the designers' best friend, the Macintosh, in the mid-eighties, which caused the most profound stylistic *and* attitudinal changes since the 1920s, when European Modernists put forth the notion of design universality and formal purity. In fact, digitization was the first major revolution in graphic arts, particularly in how graphic design is produced and distributed if not conceived, since old man Guttenberg moved his earliest type slugs around in fifteenth-century Mainz. Even the shift from hot metal to cold type during the 1960s did not give individual graphic designers the same opportunity to directly control the setting and printing of content while dabbling with form. Faceless technology, paradoxically, made personal expressionism possible for everyone.

A few intrepid designers quickly experimented in the early 1990s, realizing that the opportunity for unfettered exploration would disappear once marketing geniuses caught on to their discoveries. In the print arena, *Emigre* magazine, the clarion of digital typography, lead a charge that inspired the likes of *Beach Culture, Ray Gun, Bikini, Blur, Speak,* and scores of other outlets of "new design," where digital type jockeys galloped over the status quo. Similarly, *Fuse,* founded by Neville Brody and John Wozencroft, was a petri dish of type culture— a digital "magazine" and an international conference that encouraged conceptual type-play around such themes as politics, sexism, and pornography. *Fuse*'s conceptual, digital alphabets expressed burning social and cultural issues, rather than simply addressing the functional demands of type—that is, easy reading. Type became difficult to decipher and a metaphor for whatever issue required metaphors.

Emigre's Rudy VanderLans and Zusana Licko created unprecedented typefaces and layouts that pushed the limits of traditional design into that netherworld between art and functionality. They intuitively understood the potential power of the new tools—and they were not afraid to take risks that annoyed orthodox Modernists like Massimo Vignelli, one of their more vocal critics. But their influence was on other designers rather than on the mass market. Following close on their heels, however, David Carson, art director of *Ray Gun,* introduced typographic antics that evolved into the more widespread code of 1990s youth culture. He exploited the computer's mistakes to make design that looked more like abstract canvas than readable pages. Computer programming glitches provided an endless supply of graphic tricks that challenged legibility. It was not entirely new—having been done decades earlier under the banners of Dada, Merz, and Surrealism—but when revived in the digital age, it became symbolic of the new rebellion.

Rebellion against what, you might ask? Against the status quo, naturally—and, of course, against everything that could never be done prior to the computer. Digital freedom was Carson's license to be "me," and for so many acolytes it was an invitation to be "me too."

Having so much power on the desktop ushered in a wave of narcissism and self-indulgence. The idea that a designer was an *artiste* first and a communicator second (or third) was quaint at the outset, but offered diminished returns over the long term. Although individual personality routinely plays a key role in visual communication, it must be the result, not the goal, of solving design problems. Confusion ensues when the desire to express that singular "me" overpowers the client's message. When everyone is conducting experiments, no one is really experimenting—everyone's just following fashion. Design itself should not be the sole message, although in the "me too" era it was often mistaken as such.

Experimentation became a fashionable style. Carson's work, as idiosyncratic as it was, fostered "The End of Print Style." In fact, the desire to be "me" evolved, consciously or not, into the need for others to be "like me too." Cranbrook's grads spawned a style of layered typography, and even VanderLans's efforts resulted in an "Emigre Style." It was unavoidably predictable.

Emigre was, however, the first to question its own role in this vortex of style, and by the mid-1990s VanderLans had admitted that its methods were being mimicked (perhaps even abused) by lemming-like acolytes. He refined his work by shifting over to a more uncluttered manner built around Emigre's signature typefaces, proving that behind all his experimentation was a skillful designer. Nonetheless, the controlled chaos that had been unleashed was now tried, true, and stylish, too. The herd of me-too-ers could be seen in design competitions and showcase books. Anything with smashed, blurred, or contorted type was a shoe-in.

In the 1990s, graphic design emerged as a look-at-me profession. Neville Brody, David Carson, and others were celebrated in the style sections of mainstream newspapers and magazines, and graphic design earned a lofty cultural status. Yet with status came commodification. Commercial entrepreneurs (and their art directors) appropriated the scourge-of-Western-civilization methods and mannerisms—dumbed down, of course. "Me design" became an identity—a hook—for products like soft drinks, jeans, and tampons aimed at tweens, teens, and Gen X-, Y-, and Z-ers. Yet, as Glaser said, "It's over," and graphic designers today seem to be in a reactive mode, less expressionistic, more objective, somewhat detached (even bland corporate Modernism and Helvetica type are making a comeback). The idea that graphic design should be responsive to society's needs also appears to be on the rise. Perhaps this could be the dawning of the age of "You Too Design"?

Poster for an AIGA competition by Michael Mabry influenced by Russian Constructivism.

HISTORY LITE

When American type designer Frederic Goudy declared back in the early 1900s that "those old guys stole some of our best ideas," he had no clue that many decades later this ironic phrase would be quoted as one reason for the ambivalence among young designers toward the serious study of graphic design history. But, the fact is, young designers always prefer to find their own pathways, even if in the end they return to inventions of the past. And I'm not talking about the distant past, either.

History is rarely esteemed by youth because it is construed as something that occurred way-back-when (say, before the advent of DVDs), regardless of how few or how many years have actually passed. Even the term, "that's history," implies *uncool, passé,* and *boring.* Only with a modicum of maturity (say, by the mid- to late-twenties) can one really begin to appreciate the past (old movies, old books, *and* old graphic design) as a cultural resource rather than burdensome tradition. However, another theory suggests that reverence for the past usually skips a generation. Invariably, a current generation rejects the previous one while admiring the one immediately before it. Of course, in graphic design terms, generations are measured not by long decades, but rather by a few short years. Hence, I have observed that the current generation of design students (of the late 1990s) has little interest in (and indeed a modicum of derision for) David Carson's early 1990s "End of Print" style of cacophonous layering, but is fascinated by

Neville Brody's late 1980s dyptho-Modern post-*Face* style. I've also found that this interest is manifest in a kind of hybridization of forms, resulting in a growing number of student and young professional works invoking or sampling Modernist simplicity with a contemporary edge in layout and type selection, such as in *Wallpaper* magazine.

It is axiomatic that when one dominant mannerism transcends its usefulness, an alternative method emerges—which is why, currently, designers are leaning toward more Modernlike elementary values, rejecting grunge typefaces and Photoshop pyrotechnics in favor of white space and grid-inspired formats, among other attributes. The question becomes this: Are these values drawn from philosophical traditions with deep-rooted histories, or are they just knee-jerk reactions to shifting trends? Has the study and practice of graphic design history played a significant or incidental role in our evolutionary progression?

Over the past two decades, graphic design history has definitely been more consequential in design education. There have been an increased number of history courses and more books, articles, and conferences attempting to integrate history into practice. In addition, more original historical research has been encouraged, which uncovers unknown facets of individual designers and new relationships between design and the broader culture. Just a decade ago, few trade publishers were willing to invest in historical and critical biographies, anthologies, and analyses of graphic design culture, whereas today they are modestly competing for this material and for the limited pool of accomplished writer-researchers who engage in it, suggesting that design history has an audience.

But what is the essence of this audience? I propose that over the past decade, design history has gone in and out of being "cool" as a stylistic resource and that the audience is less interested in the issues raised by historical pursuit than the material artifacts it offers for widespread sampling. In other words, rather than validating its own design continuum, what might be termed "history chic" validates today's fashions and fads.

In the late 1970s, however, I argued that "retro" design was a means of introducing historical precedent to those designers who were unschooled in formal design history. I also reasoned that with the paucity of legitimate history courses at that time, history used as style was like a trigger-point injection that stimulated further discovery.

And I believe today that despite some stylistic monstrosities developed under the retro banner, young designers were nonetheless introduced to the Bauhaus, Constructivism, Futurism, and other Modern design movements through work that was borrowed from these sources. Copying historical forms was similar to those lessons learned from redrawing great-master paintings. But, ultimately, history as style offers diminishing returns, because style exists for ephemeral purposes only. Using Bauhaus style today and Swiss International tomorrow only serves to trivialize the value of history.

During the late 1980s and the early 1990s, hothouse institutions, like Cranbrook Academy, used history as a linchpin in the development of a theoretical approach to design. Students were introduced to a variety of historical figures and movements in order to provide context for their own revolutionary deconstructivism, which resulted in a uniquely contemporary palette of design methods. Now, in a post-deconstruction era, the reactions to these phenomena have forced certain designers to take refuge in another kind of retro that references 1950s' late Modern methods as practiced by Paul Rand, Ladislav Sutnar, and Alvin Lustig, among others.

However, in a recent seminar where I talked with graduate students about the intricacies of graphic design history, very few of them had ever heard of Sutnar or Lustig. Rand was an exception because at least one of his books was required reading during their schooling. Although both Sutnar and Lustig are featured in Roger Remington and Barbara Hodik's *Nine Pioneers in American Design,*[1] when asked about their references, a few of these students did recall having seen reproductions of Sutnar's and Lustig's works but could not put proper names to them. One student said that her particular project was influenced by Sutnar's graphical information design in his 1950 book, *Catalog Design Progress,* but at the time she was unaware of who the designer was. "I saw a bunch of these pages reproduced somewhere, maybe in *EYE,*" she admitted. "And I liked the way they looked, so I copied them for my own project."

In the mid-1980s, during the AIGA's first national conference in Boston, author and critic Tom Wolfe referred to graphic designers in a post-Modern sense as deriving inspiration from the "Big Closet" of history. At that time he was commenting on retro pastiche, and implied that many graphic designers (as well as architects) are prone to appropriate the past without understanding its context or larger ramifications. His words had resonance for many, and after his talk it seemed that the stock in serious design history went up a notch. Among the pioneers, so to speak, Keith Goddard and Warren Lehrer lectured and addressed conferences; Philip Meggs wrote the first edition of *A History of Graphic Design* (now in its third edition);[2] and other serious historians, including Roger Remington, Victor Margolin, Lorraine Wild, Katherine McCoy, and myself, were beginning to publish articles on history. Soon after, Ellen Lupton and J. Abbott Miller began working on historical exhibitions and catalogs at the Herb Lubalin Center in New York. History itself became a subject for critical analysis, as practitioners discovered new perspectives—feminist, Marxist, connoisseur, etc.—and delved into uncharted realms of design history, both pro- and anti-cannon. Thus began serious historical pursuit, in the United States at least, which momentarily put graphic design history on the front burner—so I thought.

Presumably, the flurry of activity in the early 1990s begot a well-functioning design history discipline with various young historians (from deep within and outside the field), numerous educative programs at art schools and colleges, and increased awareness (and interest) among students and young professionals. Indeed, there are more resources and references today than over a decade ago (including Internet sites), but after this initial surge there has been a marked tapering off of activity. And this curious decline in progress seems related to the very real fact that history is an adjunct to design practice—an elective, not a prescriptive.

Despite interest by some (if not most) schools in having design history courses, there are no courses devoted to training graphic design history teachers in theory, criticism, or research. I recently was asked by a prestigious institution to recommend a history teacher for a tenure track position and could not think of one person with the necessary qualifications (who was not already ensconced). To be frank, there are no real incentives: No viable monetary reward awaits those who want to dedicate themselves to research, writing, and teaching design history; the book industry pays little in relation to the amount of work that is involved in serious historical research; full-time teaching positions are rare; and grant money is paltry yet requires considerable effort for one to obtain it. In short, design historians must at best be part-timers in order to survive. Hence, most schools rely on ad hoc courses. They are lucky to have a strong teacher; otherwise such courses are history-lite: a potpourri of anecdote, canonical history, guest speakers, quirky facts, and so on. Even with the best intentions, history is ultimately not taken as seriously as studio, lab, or portfolio courses that produce quantifiable professional results. So when students are exposed to historical materials, these materials are often in the form of object lessons (i.e., copying historical styles), which invariably encourage decontextualization and appropriation.

There is no immediate solution to this problem. Graphic design history is just too low down in the priorities of undergraduate and graduate educational institutions, especially as the parameters of the profession are changing to include new media and multiple disciplines. But I do believe that graphic design history is too important to be shunted off either to the realm of theoretical arcana or copycat portfolio classes. While a mature history curriculum can integrate theory and practice, for the most part design education has not succeeded in doing this well enough to see qualitative results.

For history to be more than just a stylistic touchstone, students should not be encouraged to make their own Bauhaus or Dada designs. The technology has so radically changed since the original forms were introduced that this mimicry serves no useful purpose, anyway. Instead, students should be told stories (which is the essence of history) that inspire and excite. Design is only one part surface. The other parts are the stories and contexts that derive from the cultures that produced the designs and the designers. Design history is ultimately a collection of stories embodied in artifacts and individuals. Furthermore, graphic design history is a process of unearthing lost objects and ideas for the purpose of building a cultural and professional legacy. So for history to be more than style, it must be about intense exploration and reflection. And ultimately it must be an integral discipline that serves to bind all aspects of design practice together.

---

[1] Remington, Roger, and Barbara Hodik. *Nine Pioneers in American Graphic Design.* Cambridge, Massachusetts: MIT University Press, 1989.

[2] Meggs, Philip B. *A History of Graphic Design.* New York: John Wiley & Sons, 1998.

Cover of the East Village Other *by Vaughn Bode from 1969, when hippie culture influenced mainstream marketing.*

THE UNDERGROUND MAINSTREAM

Commercial culture relies on the theft of intellectual property for its livelihood. Mass marketers steal ideas from visionaries, alter them slightly, if at all, then reissue them to the public as new products. In the process, what was once insurgent becomes commodity, and what was once the shock of the new becomes the shlock of the novel. The avant-garde is usurped when eccentricity is reduced to acceptability.

In the 1920s, Earnest Elmo Calkins, a progressive American advertising executive, argued that everyday packages and advertising must mimic avant-garde European Modern art. Cubistic, Futuristic, and Expressionistic veneers, he argued, would capture the consumer's attention better than a hundred clever slogans. In the post–World War I era, renewal was touted and new-and-improved-ness was the commercial mantra. But why waste time, Calkins reasoned, inventing something when the most experimental artists and designers of the age were already testing the tolerance of new ideas on their own dime? Calkins encouraged commercial artists to simply appropriate and smooth out the edges of Modern art, add an ornament here and there to make it palatable for the consumer class—voilà! Instant allure and immediate sales. He further proposed the doctrine of forced obsolescence to keep the traffic in new products constantly flowing. He rightly believed that frequent cosmetic changes to everything from a soap box to a radio receiver cabinet would encourage consumers to discard the old, purchase the new, and replenish the economy. Of course, this required a food chain comprising true visionaries, skillful acolytes, and capable mimics. The dichotomy between "fine" and commercial art reached a crescendo at this time. Commercial artists are indeed in the knock-off trade.

Even when intrepid commercial artists attempted to push the boundaries of visual communication, they had to be cognizant of what industrial designer Raymond Loewy called MAYA (Most Advanced Yet Acceptable). It fell, therefore, to fervent avant-gardists to create truly unprecedented form, the kind that drives the public crazy because it does not have points of reference from which to judge merit. After all, when no one is telling us what to like, we reflexively dislike what is radically new until we're made to feel comfortable. When avant-gardisms become familiar, a kind of trickle-down occurs. What begins with a subculture that emerges out of rebellion against an establishment then follows a predictable trajectory from societal revulsion to popular embrace.

Take the 1960s psychedelic movement. It was born in a small community that shared a proclivity for sex, drugs, and anarchic behavior—all threatening to mainstream America. Kindred visual artists, musicians, and designers developed means of expression that helped define the culture's distinct characteristics. Psychedelic art and design comprised a vocabulary, influenced by earlier graphic languages, that overturned the rigid rules of clarity and legibility put forth by the once avant-garde Moderns. Through its very raucousness and raunchiness, it manifested the ideals of the youth culture. For a brief time it was decidedly a shock to the system. But as additional adherents were quickly drawn to the music, art, and lifestyle, it turned into a code that could easily be synthesized by marketers.

"Synthetic *psychedelia*" was manufactured when the visions of the originators were co-opted by the profit motives of entrepreneurs. And what began as a pact of mutual self-interest turned into acts of cultural imperialism. Underground bands led the way in a commercial whirlpool. They were given record contracts by labels owned by major corporations that wanted significant market share. In turn, the record labels advertised and packaged these bands using the very codes that signaled "alternative" to the growing youth market. Psychedelic design was this code. At first the look was fairly consistent with the original vision and motivation of the avant-garde pioneers. Many album covers of the period are today "classic" examples of true psychedelic design. But within a very short period, as profits began to roll in, youth culture trend-spotters expanded the range, thereby dulling the edge, of the psychedelic style. Psychedelic was no longer an alternative language: It was the confirmation of conformist behavior, a uniform of alienation. The establishment still disapproved of the aesthetics, but it was difficult to be terrified of something that was becoming so integrated into the mass marketplace. Drugs were still bad, but psychedelia was just decorative. The avant-garde was mainstreamed and the result was a mediocre, self-conscious rip-off—a hollow style that denoted an era remained.

During the ensuing decades, the emergence of other confrontational art and design movements—including Punk, Deconstruction, Grunge—as well as schools and movements that sought to unhinge dominant methods and mannerisms, were ultimately absorbed into the mass culture. It has become axiomatic that fringe art, if it presumes to have any influence, will gravitate to, or be pushed toward, the center. All it takes are followers and followers of followers to cut a clear path to the mainstream. Indeed, the mainstream embraces almost anything edgy, because once the label is applied, the movement is effectively no longer on the edge.

Punk, an emotionally taught expression of disaffected youth, gave way to New Wave, or "sanitized punk." It is hard today not to find aspects of Punk fashion, music, and graphics in establishment environs—even certain degrees of self-mutilation have earned acceptability. Likewise, the avant-garde graphic languages that caused such an uproar in the 1990s among typographical purists (and plain old reactionaries)—including the influence of *Emigre, Ray Gun,* and *Fuse*—have entered the mainstream as specimens of official quirkiness. One cannot open the children's magazine *Nickelodeon* without seeing pages of advertisements for national brand-name candies, games, and clothing that use Grunge and other distressed typefaces—the same types that were once condemned as scourges of the Western world.

Very little emanating from the so-called underground does not turn up in the mainstream. Even explicit pornography, once the bane of proper society, is used by the advertising industry to great effect. Despite the occasional blasts by religious groups, all manner of publicly taboo sexuality appears in magazines and on billboards. Homoeroticism, the most closeted of all unacceptable behaviors has come out with a vengeance as a stylistic manner. Likewise, popular tolerances have increased to a level where shock in any realm is hard to come by. In this environment, graphic design is the least shocking of all the communications media. Less than a decade ago, hackles were raised by typographic improprieties. Today this is one of the many fallen taboos. As long as the marketplace hungers for newness, undergrounds and subcultures will feed the insatiable hunger for cultural novelty, whether they want to or not.

Cover of Maxim For Men, *softcore sex that sells on the newsstand.*

THIS IS NOT A LIBRARY

Rudolph Giuliani spent the better part of his two mayoral terms transforming Manhattan's squalid peep show–video parlors into permissible family-oriented video emporia. I personally felt that the triple-X shop on my block blighted the neighborhood. And yet, since there was nothing ambiguous about the neon words "NAKED GIRLS LIVE" on the store's marquee, I never mistook it for Blockbuster. But now, according to new city council ordinances that proscribe a ratio of nonsexual to sexual material throughout the store, if it wants to remain in business, this instructive illuminated signage is all but eliminated. In fact, a few months ago, believing that a new local establishment was a "party" store as advertised in its front window, I entered with my then–eleven-year-old son looking for favors, only to find a few goody-bag items nestled among the leather "love-making" paraphernalia. Apparently, other residents had the same problem, and recently the shop was replaced by a pet store (although I intend to make extra certain that there is absolutely no ambiguity here).

Nonetheless, in his zeal to eradicate pornography (and boost property values), Guiliani failed to realize that community standards have significantly changed from when he was a federal prosecutor to now. These days, one needn't be a peep show parlor habitué to be titillated on demand. Thanks to the intense competition within the field of men's and women's fashion and lifestyle magazines, one merely has to frequent the numerous news shops located in most Manhattan residential and commercial neighborhoods to get a good dose of salaciousness.

Although many proprietors continue the venerable practice of veiling *Playboy, Penthouse, Hustler,* and *Big Boobs* magazines in brown paper wrappers, they do not conceal **Maxim, GQ, Details, Stuff, Gear, Cosmopolitan, Vibe,** and countless other "mainstream" magazines that routinely feature extremely sexy, thong-underwear-bikini-clad or semi-nude female models on their covers. What was once sequestered in the "adult" section or behind the counter of a smoke-shop or luncheonette is currently displayed on brightly lit racks for all to see. And on any given month there is an eyeful—especially during last winter, when five magazines featured women with almost completely uncovered breasts all during the same month and when, the next month, a few magazines showed women in fetching, S and M leather ensembles.

Call me old-fashioned, but the porn-chic that is acceptable on magazine covers today is kind of scandalous, particularly given my own experience. Over three decades ago, when I was seventeen, I was the first art director of *Screw: The Sex Review* and subsequently copublished and designed the *New York Review of Sex,* both "underground" tabloids. It was extremely difficult back then to get newsstand owners to display a publication with even a telltale hint of sexual explicitness. The dealers rightfully feared that the "morals squad," the name given to the NYPD's vice cops, would swoop down, arrest them, and confiscate the contraband. It required a huge amount of monetary promises and legal assurances to obtain a reasonable showing. And, believe me, the covers of these things were not anywhere near as sensual (or seductive) as the average lifestyle magazine is today. Regardless, the cops issued summonses and made arrests on charges that ranged from indecent exposure to pandering to whatever other trumped-up statute could be used to harass. It turned out, however, that the New York State Supreme Court deemed such actions unconstitutional, and within a short period three-quarter frontal nudity evolved to full frontal nudity from the waist up—which eventually prompted *Playboy, Penthouse,* and *Hustler* to become more fleshy, too.

European periodicals, including weekly "news" magazines such as *Der Stern* and *Paris Match,* were traditionally more liberal in terms of cover nudity, or of what one might call "incidental breasts," where the subjects in photos just incidentally happened to be nude. This is always more tantalizing than self-consciously posed nudity, anyway. In the late 1960s, *Twen,* a popular glossy German monthly aimed at teenagers, featured beautiful nude nymphs romping on the covers of every issue. But in those days there were very few international news shops in New York, so a store like Hotalings in Times Square was the destination for avid aficionados. Today, every news shop contains a large quantity of imported publications fighting for both impulse and loyal consumers. It is, therefore, not surprising that American magazine publishers feel the pressure to up the ante on sexual allure if only to keep their native audiences.

The netherworld between soft- and hardcore porn is called cheesecake. In the sixties even cheesecake was taboo, but today, news shops are like Junior's, the famous Brooklyn restaurant known for its creamy confections. So for those who are satisfied with soft pleasures, mainstream magazine covers have certainly become a form of stimulation. What began with the libidinous annual *Sports Illustrated* swimsuit issue has burgeoned into a publishing genre. For example, *Maxim,* the slick and raunchy guide to manly pleasures, is among the hottest of a new breed. While its covers push the limits of prurience through a regular diet of models wearing tight-fitting, nipple-punctuated lingerie and leathers, it does not show full nudity either on the cover or inside. It has thus set a new cheesecake standard that other magazines have adopted. Photos featuring abundant cleavage, thigh, and buttock with a hint of outlined nipple appear to be the common fare for magazines like *Gear* and *Details,* although men's magazines are not the only showcases. Both old and new women's (and teenage girls') magazines offer a runway full of semi-dressed models in come-hither poses. And even some of the shelter magazines, including an occasional issue of *Wallpaper,* have their share of temptresses on their covers.

News shop dealers used to scream, "This is not a library!" at those who loitered around browsing the covers and pages of magazines. But today, they seem to welcome it. It has become something of a ritual. News shops in New York do not have flashing signs announcing GIRLS GIRLS GIRLS, or barkers herding lonely soldiers behind beaded curtains to feast on fleshpots, but their shop windows are usually filled with the sexiest covers of the week. (I rarely see *Time* or *Newsweek* in the windows). Once inside, there is little to distinguish them from triple-X shops. Sexy covers are lined up in rows like a meat market. But is it just me? Has anyone else noticed this phenomenon? Maybe I'm a prude. Or maybe people just aren't acknowledging it, lest the mayor spend the rest of his term trying to transform news stores into family-oriented video emporia, too.

A Digital leaflet from ilovebacon.com, issued after the 2000 election.

YOU'VE GOT SPAM

During the dark days of the 2000 presidential election, the limbo period following cast votes and dangling chads, the only bright light was on the computer screen. Internet sites and e-mail queues were flooded with GIFFS, TIFFS, STUFFITS, and JPEGS of digitally manipulated photographs and graphics poking fun at, indeed often skewering, the presumptive president-elect for his real and exaggerated intellectual, anatomical, and verbal deficits.

An energetic digital leafleting or spam campaign (the widespread e-mail distribution of missives, usually advertisements, sent to harvested e-lists of innocent recipients) goosed the body politic—well, at least this body's politic. Such digital communiqués continue the tradition of satirical cartooning and protest-poster sniping that has been in the forefront of visual polemics. Owing to the current widespread use of digital cameras, Photoshop software, and Internet distribution, a new era of visual hijinks was launched, with George W. Bush as its virtual poster boy.

The election may be over, but for a large percentage of the television media map's "blue zone," the states that went for Al Gore, Dubya's lack of a clear mandate is an issue that continues to prompt anti-Bush e-mail. These usually come in the form of forwarded attachments, since people find copying existing messages that express their personal feelings easier than creating original ones. The senders engage in a sort of barter relay. "The more you send to others the more they send to you," explains Nathan Felde, a graphic designer and sometime e-sniper. "I presume that people resend the ones that they identify with most closely, thereby acting as filters—like kids trading baseball cards."

There is not, however, a sinister international conspiracy at work here—no dirty-tricks clearinghouse with a retinue of scheming propagandists. Immediately after the Florida butterfly ballot controversy, copies of the misleading form and a few homemade comic parodies hit the e-waves. It was quick but not orchestrated. Actually, the majority of today's virtual leaflets are resolutely ad hoc, with most of them produced by erstwhile amateurs and few professional graphic designers. Given the availability of sophisticated software and the need to maintain a level of unpretentious simplicity, the professional and amateur approaches are usually indistinguishable. A specimen distributed a week before the inauguration, designed by Felde (and unsigned), is a wordplay that removes the last two letters in each of the stacked words "Bull Shit" resulting in the word "Bush." It was created on the spur of the moment with an untutored air about it. "I designed it for my wife, who needed a sign to take to the inaugural protest that succinctly expressed her feelings," says Felde. And so finessed typography was eschewed to maximize its ultimate impact.

Felde sent this e-flyer to thirty friends and acquaintances on his personal e-mail list. Thus the chain began. In addition to receiving Felde's original mailing, I also received the same attachment from two other sources, not on his list, each showing between thirty to fifty names in the "send to" fields. Add to that the forty or so names that I forwarded the attachment to on my "intimate friends" list, and the result was a fairly sizable number, which my then–twelve-year-old son estimated to be around 5,000 recipients. Consider that at least half of those are likely to forward it to their respective e-lists, and, exponentially, the potential distribution over the course of a month (the usual time frame for saturation) is considerable. While some people get only momentary chuckles from what pops up on their screens, others print out and literally post the leaflet for offline display.

The anti-Bush e-mail barrage tapered off after the Supreme Court decision, but the specimens created since Dubya was selected president are bitingly ridiculing. David Vogler, a graphic designer and chief creative officer of Mutation Labs, Inc., an Internet content creation company, recently distributed a short QuickTime movie that was passed along to him by a fellow anti-Bush pal in Los Angeles. The twenty-second film, called "Geo Bush Picks a Running Mate," captures Duyba, then president of the Texas Rangers baseball franchise, sitting in his stadium box aggressively picking his nasal cavity with forefinger and pinky. The whereabouts of the original film is being kept a secret, but the invasive camera is a great political tool. Furthermore, "This is a nice demonstration of the power of iMovie and a Mac," says Vogler. "It's desktop video "'sniping'" for the Web, and this sort of media is wonderful guerilla communication."

Of course, the "bushpic.mov," as it is slugged, like many other digital leaflets, is not in the same league as the artfully caustic graphic commentaries of nineteenth- and twentieth-century master caricaturists Honoré Daumier, George Grosz, or David Levine, but it does serve the same purpose: to "out" political folly by ridiculing those in power—the more venal the politician, the more biting the caricature. In Bush's case, venality at this stage of his presidency seems to be less of a hook than inanity, so anti-Dubya leaflets tend to be more like pranks than exposés.

Yet taken en masse, like any effective advertising campaign, the cumulative effect of these digital leaflets in the public's mind reinforces the perception of Bush's natural shortcomings. The missives highlight his ties to Poppy (a.k.a. George, Sr.) and his cronies ("I Will Call Him Mini-Me") and wed this concept to his difficulties with the mother tongue ("Duh, um, huh, Mitha-Cheny . . .") as well as to his uncanny resemblance to a beloved simian ("Curious George"). Some of the satires are sobering ("Bush Didn't Win, America Lost" and the *Castaway* parody that shows Tom Hanks writing on a stone, "Have Been Here 1500 Days Heard Bush Stole Election—Have Decided to Stay"). Others focus on past misdeeds, including drug and alcohol abuse ("MasterRace"). Some are just silly ("Moe Bush").

Digital leaflets are mostly anonymous—the attacks are hit and run—so attempting to track down the originators is usually futile. Nonetheless, repository sites for e-missives have sprung up, and one of the most inclusive is *ilovebacon.com,* a daily, updated Web site for digital image postings, and some of the anti-Bush material is archived there. Rob Glenn, founder of ilovebacon.com, is a graphic designer who once worked for a political paper called *The Washington Wit* and now devotes all his time to this site. He says that he has no great mission: "It's just a place where you can find all the goofy crap that gets circulated around the Internet via e-mail." Glenn admits that during and immediately after the election he saw an influx of anti-Bush postings,

A Digital leaflet sent anonymously through email before the 2000 election.

but it was pretty equal on both sides. "I only posted about 10 percent of the stuff I got. Most of it wasn't all that funny, and personally I think political humor is a bit too easy. Lately it's mostly been Bush stuff, but I'm sure I'd be getting Gore stuff had he won."

Glenn edits the submitted postings based on quality of wit and other standards of acceptability. "We try to stay somewhere around a PG-13 to R rating," he says. Most of the postings are by people who have digital cameras "and notice weird stuff," but he allows that anonymous professional image-makers contribute too, like Moe Bush and VP Curly at *www.ilovebacon.com/jokes/012601.shtml* and *www.ilovebacon.com/jokes/021601b.shtml*. As for intellectual property rights, Glenn reports, "I don't ask for exclusive rights. Some of the stuff, like jokes, are just retold and retold and are pretty much impossible to figure out where they came from."

Illegally wheat-pasting posters, however, remains the confrontational activity of choice for many veteran graphic protesters, because in addition to getting a message onto the street, poster sniping is an act of civil disobedience. Sniping on the Web is legal, safe, and free of consequence. Yet Robbie Conal, known for his "Art Attacks" in major American cities with his posters against Jesse Helms, Clarence Thomas, and anti-abortion advocates, has recently engaged in digital leafleting to augment his campaigns. "I used to just be annoyed by e-mail leaflets, until my eighteen-year-old intern from USC taught me how to do them," admits Conal. After he learned how to do Photoshop "remixes" of conservative mainstream images and text, he says, "I got excited. It's like being a hip-hop DJ doing dance party versions of standard tunes. We made a few of Bush and John Ashcroft, and I started e-mailing them around to annoy my friends and enemies around the Internet. It works! Of course, the streets it ain't! It's still limited to people who have the equipment and the inclination."

Nonetheless, Internet technology has breathed new life into the venerable art of alternative satire. Okay, digital leafleting may not change the world, but it has opened a channel for Dubya opponents to exercise their democratic right to be pissed.

Cover of The Rings, *a British Punk "do-it-yourself" fanzine, 1977, produced on the cheap.*

CHEAPSKATE DESIGN

Paul Rand scribbled handwritten headlines on his 1940s covers for *Direction* magazine because he was too frugal to buy type. Alex Steinweiss scrawled curvilinear script on his record covers for CBS because he lacked funds for typesetting. And Ben Shahn drew block letters on his posters and book covers because there was no budget to do otherwise. The results, while decidedly unique and wonderfully expressive, prove that frugality is one of the mothers of invention—particularly in graphic design, which for the first forty or fifty years of this century was definitely a cheapskate profession.

Fees for design and layout were low, even by the standards of the early 1900s. In the 1930s, book jackets, for example, paid between $10 and $25. That fee included imagery (typically a painting or drawing), hand-cut color separations, and typesetting. Advertisements and show-cards went for between $5 and $10, depending on size. Layout people earned between $5 and $15 per job in an economy where a good meal cost $.25 and weekly rent averaged about $5 to $10. Therefore, it was often incumbent upon graphic artists to create their own lettering (which is why calligraphy was so common) and ornament rather than share their meager fees with typesetters. And since photostats were usually dear, designers often hand-rendered whatever images they needed. For a freelancer to make a viable income, high volume, production shortcuts, and being a jack-of-all-trades were not just options; if one wanted to bring home bread, no less bacon, these were necessary strategies.

Economic conditions also determined who would become a graphic artist. Typically, people from immigrant families chose design as an alternative to lesser trades. Before World War II, women played a surprisingly prominent, though routinely anonymous, role in illustration, lettering, retouching, and layout. In the *1928 Graphic Design Yearbook* (a precursor to *The Black Book*), roughly 35 percent of freelancers listed were women; many were hand-letterers working in ambient styles. Since clients thought of these women as temporary workers on the road to permanent careers in motherhood, women were paid even less than men, and so represented an even better bargain. (After World War II, the number of women in design dropped significantly, for two reasons. First, the number of freelancers dropped overall in direct proportion to the rise of in-house art departments and independent design firms. And the postwar baby boom further cut the "secondary" feminine workforce, leaving women designers in the minority until the 1980s.)

Pre–World War II freelance designers—young and old, male and female, from the United States and Europe—were not as savvy about budgets as their counterparts are today. The 1930s ledgers of the Swiss-born graphic designer Erik Nitsche show typical earnings. Before immigrating to the United States in the 1950s and becoming the celebrated design director of General Dynamics, he freelanced as an illustrator and typographer in Germany and Switzerland. His thick, ink-stained ledger chronicles a decade of working on hundreds of cheap commissions, from magazine spot illustrations to large posters, for fees ranging from the modern-day equivalent of $10 to $50. The ledger profiles a tireless, underpaid designer who "did many jobs simply to eat," Nitsche recalled shortly before his death in 1998. "Some of the designs were definitely mediocre. Nonetheless, considering the speed with which I made them, a few were infinitely better than even my best, and highest-paid, work."

Early in his career, Nitsche cut corners by using the fewest possible elements, making airy layouts with simple lines of sans serif type. He later used the same methods on higher-budgeted record albums for Decca Records and advertisements for Orbachs department store in New York, eventually becoming one of the masters of the Modern "less-is-more" idiom. His technique was directly influenced by paltry fees. "Learning to cut corners when I was poor gave me a real appreciation for materials when I was better off," he said.

Like Nitsche, Paul Rand began with few resources beyond his wit and talent. His covers for the independent, antifascist, arts-and-culture magazine *Direction* earned virtually nothing (although he did exchange his design for a few Le Corbusier drawings that later increased in value). Instead, he was given total creative freedom—only one out of thirty covers was killed by the client—and developed a signature approach that relied exclusively on his own hand. He drew the lettering in a distinctive, lightline script (he hated calligraphy), and either sketched the images or made montages by sandwiching negatives on a copy camera himself. Not counting the time a cover took to produce, he spent only a few dollars on film and paper for each job; and that bought him the rare opportunity to experiment in public.

In another public experiment, the first original cover art for record albums was invented by Alex Steinweiss. Although his boss at Columbia Records encouraged him to push the boundaries, the money allotted to design each cover went directly into the printing and production, leaving nothing for the art. Hence, Steinweiss painted all his own cover images, made his own color separations on overlays, and rendered the type and lettering by hand. Some of the lettering he designed to fit the theme or genre of a specific record was painstakingly intricate. But like Rand he introduced a utility curlicue script called "the Steinweiss Scrawl," which could be used as a tophead or subhead for virtually any theme. Naturally, Columbia didn't pay for their distinctive house font; but later, in the 1950s, Steinweiss licensed the Scrawl to Photolettering, Inc., and earned royalties on its frequent sales.

Ben Shahn was a committed artist who took any opportunity to make imagery, experimenting with paint, ink, and photography. He also took any opportunity to express social and political messages in such vehicles as posters against fascist atrocities in Eastern Europe and WPA announcements for the Farm Administration's good works at home. Being a painter trained in lettering, he routinely cut corners by doing everything himself—as much for economy as to satisfy his own aesthetic. Shahn developed a lettering style with square block capitals that made his work instantly recognizable: It was well suited to the decidedly nonlucrative book covers he did in the 1950s (not even prestigious trade books for reputable publishers paid well). But Shahn's total control of every facet of design and production resulted in distinctive, timeless work.

Destitution is an obstacle for some, but in design it can also provide the impetus for innovation. The members of Europe's early twentieth-century Modern design movements, for instance, were more concerned with ideological expression than with budgets. The radical designers of Dada, Futurism, and Constructivism took little recompense, focusing instead on the freedom to serve their cultural-political agendas. The rule-breaking, asymmetrical compositions that defined the New Typography of the 1920s have been characterized as a rebellion against antiquated bourgeois notions of acceptability, which is, doubtless, true. However, the emblematic Modern method was determined as much by monetary and material constraints as by conviction.

In post–World War I Europe, hot metal typesetting was expensive; in post-revolutionary Russia, paper and ink were extremely scarce; the young activists had to find other ways to convey messages to a mass public. So they used print shop "leftovers"—old printing cuts and discarded, hellbox type slugs. The anarchic Dada aesthetic relied on being able to use disparate fonts in single lines of type, or to make page ornaments from old, random typecase materials. Rather than making and reproducing paintings or drawings, they made mechanical photomontages of existing materials. Forms that signaled antibourgeois rebellion also saved money. The radicals would probably have challenged convention, even if standard printing had been available for free, but the economic limitations certainly stimulated the transformation of the ordinary printed page into a vessel for radical convention busting.

Similarly, the ascetic, less-is-more Modernist philosophy—which evolved into the functional design of the Bauhaus and related schools—originally expressed economy of means as well as thought. But, ultimately, reductive Bauhaus-inspired design became the profit-driven Corporate Modernism of the 1950s and early 1960s. Multinational corporations prized the less-is-more aesthetic for its ability to project identity through a universal, if bland, graphic vocabulary. Visual austerity, once an adaptive strategy for the financially challenged, became a popular international style, and design systems that eliminated all but the most functional elements ironically cost thousands to produce.

Thus, in the 1960s a backlash movement emerged. This time, however, despite limited means, the radical idea was to fill the printed page with as much minutia as possible—"more for less"? "Hippie," "psychedelic," and "underground" members of the 1960s counterculture published leftwing newspapers and broadsheet posters announcing anti-Vietnam protests, civil rights demonstrations, and rock 'n' roll concerts that curiously echoed the aesthetics of the Dada onslaught fifty years earlier. The new generation was not necessarily familiar with Dada—in fact, the fundamental politics were different—yet the economic factors were similar. Neither had money. And the lack of funds forced designers to decide what they'd pay for with cash, and what they'd borrow, co-opt, or steal.

This was the age of the flea-market aesthetic, in which old type and ornament from Victorian and Art Nouveau sources, vintage wood engravings, and antique decoupage images, were pasted together into vibrant, unified compositions. The work was designed to appear as elaborate as possible at the least possible cost. For their psychedelic posters, Victor Moscoso, Rick Griffin, and Wes Wilson drew intricate ornamental lettering and made multiple acetate color separations painstakingly by hand to circumvent stripping fees. Alternative techniques, such as split fountain inking (blending two or more colors on a single roller or screen to give the impression of many more), solarization (a darkroom technique giving the illusion of three dimensions), and high-contrast palettes, added visual depth without cost. Underground newspapers may have been less artful, but they conformed to the basic aesthetic by using collage, split fountain, and vibrating color combinations. Though their layout artists routinely used transfer type, Typositor, or Address-O-Graph lettering, resident cartoonists and illustrators more often drew the headlines to give underground newspapers a homemade veneer. Handwork not only saved money—it accentuated the era's anarchic, anti–mass-commercial-culture graphic look.

But psychedelic "innocence" was short-lived. Within a few years, the originators were co-opted by the marketplace, and the hippie sensibility became a profitable fashion. Psychedelic lettering, the cheap, if time-consuming, alternative to commercial typesetting, was reproduced as Photolettering Inc. fonts; hippie tropes showed up on TV backdrops for Sonny and Cher; and the fashion industry discovered "Cheap Chic." In the end, as with the earlier Modernist aesthetic, it took heaps of money to produce authentically cheap-looking hippie stuff.

The tides of fashion invariably ebb, and another wave of a reaction was rising. In the early 1970s, Punk emerged as the next generational sensibility to be built on frugality. If the 1960s feeding frenzy taught any lessons, it was to avoid developing design styles that could be swiftly co-opted: Clichéd psychedelic graphic motifs had been built on vibrant colors and organic forms, epitomized by Peter Max's highly polished, saccharine supergraphics. The hippie style had been co-optable because, once it had been stripped of its context, its aesthetics were comfortable enough, and pretty enough, to be easily exploited.

This was not to be the case with Punk. Punk was dreary, cruddy, and untidy—in short, everything amateurish. Taking Dada a step further: Punk was so contemptuous of conventional beauty that it rose to haute-ugly. There was little temptation for mainstream trendsetters to mine Punk for profit. Or was there? To the astute observer, the primitive torn-and-tattered style, especially the ransom note typography and anarchic collages on publications, record covers, and posters, suggested a usable—indeed, a co-optable—style. Again, what began as an inexpensive means to address an exclusive audience became shorthand for youth culture. In fact, precisely because the visual materials and design tools were so cheaply accessible to anyone with a pair of scissors and a glue pot, Punk, so tied to sampling, became a prime target for sampling itself.

Perhaps the most flagrant samplers were the Condé Nast fashion magazines in the early 1980s under Alexander Liberman, a publication designer who believed that elegant design had become too frou-frou. He spent millions making *Vogue, Self, Mademoiselle,* and *Travel and Leisure* (among others) look cheap—or at least look as though they'd been scraped together from the same materials used by the Punks. The result, however, was disingenuous: Punk worked because it was real, without artifice, as were Rand's script and Shahn's block letters and Moscoso's vibrating colors. Liberman's design was a manufactured cheap—the apotheosis of cheap—on slick paper, with expensive photography, and buckets of color, its art directed by highly paid professionals.

Now, at the end of the century, design fees range from unimaginably high to obscenely low—but the computer is a great equalizer. It can give low-budget projects expensive veneers, and it can make high-ticket jobs look cheap. Where designers once had to use wit and craft to maximize low or nonexistent budgets, today the cost-cutting methods are keystrokes away. Today Steinweiss could simply make the Scrawl with Fontographer (then put it on the Web and earn a bundle in six weeks); the Dadas could select from thousands of typefaces with ease (there is even a typeface called Dada); and Punks could use Photoshop to collage any scrap material they might find, free, on the Internet. Anyone can make the work look as slick as he or she desires, and no one has the budget or time to craft anything by hand.

If cheap no longer serves as the mother of invention, what will push the next style backlash? Maybe hand-drawn designs have had their charming day, and that's okay. Maybe the next generation will go beyond reacting to surfaces and techniques, and begin to challenge their elders—ourselves—through the meanings they create.

Detail from comic book about the Korean War using stereotypes of the evil enemy, 1952.

HATE THY ENEMY

A dirty little secret about graphic design is that it promotes hatred. In fact, the graphic language of loathing is every bit as pervasive, if not as universal, as the International Style. While the aesthetic of enmity may not be rooted in any one particular typeface or composition, the rhetoric is fairly consistent. It includes verbal and visual hyperbole, caricature and stereotype, and threat and agitation, all given concrete graphic form by designers and illustrators. More disturbingly, not only are derogatory messages the product of extremist and fringe groups—the vast majority of hate propaganda is government sanctioned and professionally produced.

"In the beginning we create the enemy," writes Sam Keen in *Faces of the Enemy: Reflections of the Hostile Imagination* (Harper and Row, 1986), about the art and psychology of state coercion. "We think others to death and then invent the battle-axe or ballistic missiles with which to kill them." Propaganda precedes technology as a means to soften otherwise rational minds into malleable clay. Hot and cold wars on a battlefield or in hearts and minds cannot be fought without the collaboration of people of conscience. Therefore, the process of demonic manufacture, wherein the object of abhorrence must be thoroughly stripped of its human characteristics is essential in securing mass hostility toward one group or another. "The war of icons, or the eroding of the collective countenance of one's rivals," noted Marshall McLuhan in *Understanding Media: The Extensions of Man* in 1964, "has long been underway. Ink and photo are supplanting soldiery and tanks. The pen daily becomes mightier than the sword."

Since the sixteenth century, when Martin Luther, the father of propaganda, was portrayed as the devil in church-sanctioned cautionary prints, the archetypes of visual terror have progressed unabated. Summoning the Prince of Darkness may now seem outdated, particularly since devil worship is accepted as pop style, yet Satan, say his adversaries, appears in numerous guises. Vilification is often accomplished in the twentieth century by references both banal and nefarious. Through the visual lexicon of hate, artists and designers employ the devil as the main text, or subtext, in allegories transforming individuals and groups into beasts, criminals, torturers, rapists, defilers, and even death itself. The clichéd predictability of these unnerving symbols is what gives them sustained power. Even those who believe that Lucifer is little more than superstitious mumbo-jumbo are somehow conditioned to revile deadly sins and sinners, in part because they represent our repressed personal transgressions. As Walt Kelly's Pogo once said, "We have seen the enemy, and he is us."

Fear triggers hatred and inflames ignorance, which the skilled propagandist converts into manifestations of terror. Whether in picture or word, the specter of unspeakable harm cannot help but wreak havoc on the psyche. When wed to a particularly repellent depiction of a foe, it is impossible for the susceptible to avoid being dragged into a state of antipathy, much in the same way that well-crafted, villainous literary or film characters evoke intense animosity. Repetition becomes the artist's primary tool in this process. The more an image or epithet (or visual epithet) is repeated, the more indelible it becomes. The big lie is synthetic truth.

Of course, real truth is necessary to bolster extreme exaggeration. Wicked political leaders are expedient and justifiable prototypes, and violent organizations beg to be exposed as such. But purveyors of hate imagery routinely latch onto the lowest common denominator and overgeneralize a particular people or nation on the basis of a single characteristic or trait—as in all Jews are rapacious, all Palestinians are terrorists, or all blacks are drug addicts. In U.S. propaganda of the 1950s, Joseph Stalin, a real scoundrel, represented all Soviets—not merely the regime over which he lorded—because the United States was engaged in a cold war against the entire Soviet system and, by extension, its citizenry. Not surprisingly, in Soviet propaganda Americans were, tit for tat, portrayed as corrupt, corpulent money-grubbers, often given the composite features of "typical" capitalists. In the litany of hate, everyone, irrespective of individual persona, is tarred with the same brush. When seen only as a mass of faceless types, the enemy becomes even more terrifying. So in the design of hate, condemning the guilty demands slandering the innocent.

At the outset of World War II, U.S. propagandists, including designers and illustrators from the advertising industry, were drafted into the paper war against Axis Germany, Japan, and Italy to create and propagate odious stereotypes that subverted tenets of peacetime civility. The Office of War Information in Washington, DC, helped define the parameters of the depictions being fed to civilians at home and to soldiers overseas. The methods were similar, but the goals were different. Civilians had to be constantly reminded of the ruthlessness of the enemy, while soldiers had to be encouraged to kill them without remorse. This was only accomplished through relentless dehumanization—the ends justified abominable graphic means. Yet the harshness of caricature was insidiously different between German/Italian and Japanese representations.

While both approaches were justifiably harsh, the propaganda aimed at white Europeans was less vicious than at yellow Asians, who were depicted as having exaggerated, sinister, racially distinct features. The Nazis and fascists were alternately illustrated as buffoonish (Hitler and Mussolini as clowns) or menacing (saber-rattling warriors), but the Japanese, whether presented as buffoon or menace, invariably appeared more subhuman as presumably befitted their race. In fact, in times of war, racist depictions are more endemic to the rhetoric of hate than any other form—the more stomach-turning the better.

A postcard issued in 1942 by the U.S. Forest Service cautioning campers against accidentally igniting forest fires was typical of how the racist approach was introduced in all manner of public media. In this textbook study of visual enmity, Smokey the Bear is replaced by the quintessential Japanese demon: He was a buck-toothed, four-eyed (as though thick-lens glasses somehow indicated inferiority), low-browed, and pointy-eared soldier threateningly holding a lighted match. When placed in a number of other cautionary scenarios, this archetype underscored the duplicity and savagery ascribed to the yellow race. The marriage of the grotesque to the immoral in this portrayal was as powerful as a planeload of bombs and left similar scars. The "Japs" could not be made to look any more preternatural. But since war is hatred run amuck, it gives license for pent-up atavistic animosities that surge like a shot of adrenaline through the body politic. Extreme caricatures of the Japanese plumbed the depths of fear.

A poster from 1943 for the "Beast of the East," a film about America's World War II enemy—the Japs.

Designers and artists who perpetrated these stereotypes were themselves caught up in mass hysteria, and their work reflected prejudices born of indoctrination. Some were opportunists while others were patriots. Some worked to fight evil—some perpetuated it. When Arthur Szyk, a Polish-born illustrator working in the United States, produced various horrifying caricatures of Japanese Emperor Hirohito and War Minister Tojo during World War II for mass-market magazines like *Colliers,* he believed that he was justly attacking the principal scourges of war through ridicule and derision for which racism was a tool. When Joseph Goebbels, the Nazi minister of propaganda, ordered his German Propaganda Studio to twist vulgar anti-Semitic stereotypes into subhuman (Untermensch) depictions, his motive was to incite callous treatment and justify extermination.

A now infamous poster for the pseudo-documentary film *Der Ewige Jude,* ("The Eternal Jew"), directed by the Nazis' "anti-Jewish

GROSSE POLITISCHE SCHAU IM BIBLIOTHEKSBAU DES DEUTSCHEN MUSEUMS
ZU MÜNCHEN · AB 8. NOVEMBER 1937 · TÄGLICH GEÖFFNET VON 10-21 UHR

Poster for The Eternal Jew exhibition.

*A poster advertising "The Eternal Jew," an anti-Semitic
Nazi propaganda film.*

expert," Dr. Eberhard Taubert, portrays a heinous caricature of a
generic Chasidic Jew in long coat and skullcap (the garments that for
centuries distinguished this devout sect from more assimilated Jews)
presented as an avaricious, cowardly fiend poised to devour the world.
When pitted against high German culture, the obvious message was
that the Jew was a defiler, and therefore the target of permissible mal-
ice. Hitler expounded, "The Jew has destroyed hundreds of cultures,
but built none of his own." Goebbels's propagandists derived certain
Jewish stereotypes from myths like The Golem, taken from Jewish
lore,[1] in the same way that many derogatory racial stereotypes were
inspired by venerable and indigenous tales and stories elsewhere. The
Jew was portrayed as barbarous and perverted in the most infamous of
all Nazi hate propaganda, an SS booklet titled *The Subhuman,* a manual of hatred and loathing that viewed its victims as vermin.

"Civilization is a constant struggle to hold back the forces of barbarism," writes Sam Keen, observing that ". . . the barbarian, the giant running amok, the uncivilized enemy, symbolize power divorced from intelligence." So the graphic lexicon of hate abounds with metaphor and allegory in which the barbarism of any opponent is made concrete through images of vicious anthropomorphic beasts—polemical werewolves—the embodiment of bloodthirsty wickedness. Never mind that in wars each side resorts to barbarism to achieve its aims. Never mind that the vocabulary of hate invariably uses barbarism to "fight" barbarism. In the propaganda war, the victor is the nation that claims God is on its side and that invents the most mnemonic and horrific image of its enemy. During World War I, the U.S. artists and designers, under the watchful art direction of Charles Dana Gibson at the Committee on Public Information, invented images (bolstered by rumors of German savagery against civilians) that depicted German troops as even more venal than those portrayed later in World War II. The "Hun," an ape-like beast with blood-soaked canines clutching young female hostages (implying that rape was an instrument of policy), was the veritable poster child of hate. This model existed until the 1960s, when, ironically, superhero cartoons like the *X-Men* turned similarly frightening creatures into sympathetic antiheroes.

War is not the sole rationale for institutional, graphic hatred. In fact, there is no greater motivator than apprehension of "otherness," and no more effective imagery, once again, than ethnic and racial stereotypes that exacerbate the suspicions of insecure people. Absurd racial stereotypes have historically been (and still are) used as benign commercial symbols in comics, advertisements, packages, and even logos, but when similar caricatures are tweaked with just a hint of menace—such as a lustful gaze or dramatic shadow—they switch from benign comedy into vengeful attack. It takes very little effort on the part of designers to open the Pandora's box of offensive graphics. In recent years, given oil crises and terrorist bombings, Arabs have been caricatured in the United States in a manner recalling anti-Semitic cartoons of earlier times. Such images have doubtless influenced a common view of these people as a whole. The single derogatory picture often negates a thousand positive words.

"Hate-driven imagery cannot, by definition, be produced by groups open to debate or transparency," says Dan Walsh, director of the Justice Project, which uses graphics to teach freedom and tolerance. Yet not all images designed to elicit hatred are lies or exaggerations. Though always odious, in certain paradoxical instances hate messages expose reality to elicit protest against evil. Depending on where one stood along the ideological divide in the late 1960s—for or against the Vietnam War—the graphics that offered evidence of U.S. atrocities against civilians provoked enmity toward American leaders (and sometimes even soldiers in the field). The famous news photograph by R. Haeberle of the aftermath of the massacre of twenty-one women and children in the remote hamlet of Mi Lai— vividly showing lifeless bodies lying in a ditch after troops led by Lieutenant William Calley cut them down—was produced as an antiwar poster with the headline, "Q: And Babies . . . ? A: And Babies." Because it so totally contradicted the civilized image that Americans held of themselves, the poster became a call to pity the victims and hate the perpetrators of the war. Similarly, photographs coming from Vietnam and published in underground periodicals, showing soldiers holding severed Viet Cong heads as trophies, were intended to foster the same rage as did the pictorial evidence of World War II atrocities. These visuals of demonic acts did not have to be designed or manipulated in any way—supposedly the camera did not lie. Yet designers had to intervene with the material so that there would be no ambiguity in the message.

"Hate/rage/revolt imagery is often the most graphically charged because there is no operational code of conduct in place between the combatants—no taboos are recognized," argues Dan Walsh. Nor is there any mystery, allusion, or subtlety in this form of address. The language of hate leaves no room for interpretation. It is good or bad, black or white. It is never neutral. "Propaganda allows us to exteriorize the battle," writes Sam Keen, "project the struggle within the psyche into the realm of politics." The design of demonic representations is a battle rooted in obsession, and perhaps more insidious than what Marshall McLuhan had called "the old hot wars of industrial hardware."

---

[1]Goebbels maintained a huge library of books about Jewish mythology and required that his propagandists study Jewish lore, which they twisted into the most vicious stereotypes.

1/16th SCALE
WORLD FIGURE SERIES
GERMAN WEHRMACHT
TANK CREWMAN
★ READY TO ASSEMBLE PRECISION MODEL KIT
★ MODELING SKILLS HELPFUL IF UNDER 10 YEARS OF AGE

1/16 ワールドフィギュアシリーズNO.1
ドイツ国防軍戦車兵
接着剤別売

Package for a ¹⁄₁₆ scale model Wehrmacht Tank Crewman.

G. I. FRITZ

When I was a kid, girls had Barbie dolls and boys had super-annuated Kens called G. I. Joe "action figures" with facial hair, World War II uniforms, and weapons (additional battle ensembles sold separately). Hasbro introduced the original G. I. Joe in 1964, and in 1966 he issued a World War II German "Joe" in its "Soldiers of the World" collection. Guiltily, I preferred G. I. Fritz, as I called him, for reasons that I will reveal later.

Fritz looked fairly benign—indeed, he resembled Joe in all but his blonde hair and snappy black Panzer officer's uniform (sans swastika)—but he was a Nazi and, therefore, was usually sold through model collectors' shops rather than in toy stores. I bought mine, however, in an Upper East Side shop owned, ironically, by the son of a Holocaust survivor. As far as I know, in the subsequent thirty-four years Hasbro has not issued another German soldier. In fact, until recently, it was virtually impossible to find any World War II action figures in everyday toy emporia, long ago replaced by more *au courant* cyber-cop, sci-fi hero, and movie tie-in figures. During the past couple of years, however, World War II has made a comeback in the action figure market, marked in particular by an increased number of German soldiers, some representing elite SS military units.

Battling for its share of preteen consumers with Hasbro, is 21st Century Toys in Alameda, California, creators of the Ultimate Soldier. At stores like Kay Bee, Toys 'R' Us, Target, and Kmart, the toy maker sells two lines of World War II twelve-inch and 1:18-scale figures, including Luftwaffe, Wehrmacht, and Panzer Corps troops and accessories, some wearing small Nazi-era military markings. The first time

I saw these at the Toys 'R' Us on Union Square in New York, I was drawn to the detailed quality of the figures yet decidedly repulsed by what they represented. By virtue of where they are sold, these toys are aimed at youngsters who have no idea about the Holocaust but have been conditioned to play with heroic action figures. Other than German helmets that look similar to those worn by Darth Vader's storm troopers, nothing distinguishes the heroes from the villains. For all the kids know, these are simply two opposing factions of equal weight, and they are encouraged to "collect 'em all."

Older collectors, so-called re-creationists (teens starting at fourteen and adults) who build dioramas of documented wartime scenes and are presumed to know good from bad, are the prime consumers for an even newer type of authentically detailed twelve-inch figure sold at card and model collector's shops. Two years ago, Dragon, a Hong Kong–based model company, started producing highly developed German soldier action figures precisely detailed down to the iron cross, SS runes, and swastika worn on a wide array of jackets, helmets, and belt buckles. The same emblematic details that give incredible allure to this precisionist generation of figure nonetheless causes profound emotional discomfort, at least in me, as it begs the question: Should the Nazi army be commemorated in any way? Remember Bitburg? Moreover, are we becoming so detached from the horrors of the Nazi era that Wehrmacht and Waffen SS soldiers, decidedly the military instruments of the Nazi regime, are now reduced to innocuous playthings?

Re-creationist action figure enthusiasts argue that their obsession is not play. And I am told that the largest segment of action figure collectors focus on World War II and possess in-depth knowledge of battles and campaigns. The dioramas and vignettes they make are visible displays of what they've learned about a particular machine gun or uniform, not paeans to Nazi military might, explains Ken Smolinsky, proprietor of Goodstufftogo.com, an online collector's site. "I may be fooling myself," he asserts, "but the collectors do not seem to be closet neo-Nazis. Rather, they have an interest in German military history that goes back to the Prussian Empire, when every unit had a different kind of uniform. Likewise, the World War II German figures in uniforms are more interesting to collect than G. I.s."

Okay, I understand that German action figures are props for amateur historians, and Smolinsky says emphatically that "so far the figures have only been military-oriented, and, when representing the

SS, they have largely been the Waffen, or military side, of the SS." Nevertheless, the potential for trivializing Nazism is a very real concern when its indelible symbols are reduced to accessories on doll clothes. Some years ago a company called Cotswold in Washington State (which produced replacement parts for G. I. Joes) issued the black SS uniforms used by Hitler's Nazi police (whose duties included the maintenance of death camps) and were sold to a small segment of collectors who design "custom figures." While accuracy is the watchword for collectors—and these uniforms were not sold in Toys 'R' Us—even Smolinsky, who insists that Cotswald's products "never became a national thing," agrees that selling SS uniforms steps over the line.

What is this line? Politics and ideology are *verboten,* explains Scott Crawford, spokesperson for Dragon Models. Dragon's line of World War II action figures is military in character, with emphasis on the individual, generic soldier. And to underscore this, each box includes a brief history of the unit or battle from which the soldier is taken. The figures come in boxes that portray soldiers in what Crawford calls "a neutral military context," neither heroic nor barbaric, most of them in color illustrations by a well-known military artist, Ronald Volstad. "Our World War II German figures are neither designed nor intended to be a glorification of Nazism or the Third Reich." He adds that while Dragon's collector fan base is "keen in the military aspect of World War II Germany—its fighting men, its equipment, its vehicles—the vast majority also consider the politics of Nazism to be repugnant in the extreme. That is a view, incidentally, which Dragon Models as a company also shares. Consequently, you will never see an Adolf Hitler or Heinrich Himmler action figure from Dragon—only real soldiers engaged in military operations." Of course, Dragon cannot control how the individual figures are portrayed or displayed, but Crawford persists, "Our military figures are intended to be soldiers fighting honorably in the defense of their country, although not necessarily always in defense of their country's ideology."

And I take these sentiments as truth, yet how can the swastika, the twentieth century's most blatant symbol of evil, which appears in various iterations on Dragon's German uniforms, be presented in a neutral or non-ideological way? Indeed, how are young collectors informed that these accoutrements are icons of hate rather than badges of glory? Crawford refers to a declaration printed on all packaging of Dragon World War II military action figures:

This product represents a subject from a specific period in history. It contains details, equipment, uniform and/or vehicles that include insignia or marking that some may find offensive. All insignia and emblems are included to maintain complete historical accuracy. The inclusion of these insignia and emblems/markings is no way an endorsement or approval of the activities associated with the subject matter at any time or manner.

But is the disclaimer enough? Shouldn't it be more emphatic that these soldiers fought *honorably* in the service of a regime void of honor?

While Dragon has steered clear of making figures in the traditional pre–World War II black SS uniforms, the Gestapo, or the "Brown Shirts" of the SA, not all model companies are this circumspect. Two makers of 1:16 resin models—Legends and Lore, and Jaguar—sell statuettes of Adolf Hilter and Reinhard Heydrich, the deputy chief of the SS and architect of the "final solution," at model and comic book shops. Admittedly, the resin models appeal to a very different audience than action figures, what Smolinsky calls model builders who are more interested in making "an art piece" and who, according to the fine print on the Hitler model package, represent an age range from fourteen years and older. Yet, given the benign poses of the models, it appears that no value judgments are placed on these "art pieces," leaving their function up to the user.

World War II was a just war, and the defeat of the Nazis was valorous. The soldiers who fought Nazi troops deserve to be commemorated in many ways—action figures are just one of them. But as survivors of the Nazi crimes die and as new generations become more detached from the truth of the Holocaust, there is a real peril that these toys and models replete with Nazi emblems and insignia may neutralize, or worse, distort reality. When I was a kid I preferred G. I. Fritz because I didn't even know what a Nazi was, and he was dressed so much cooler than G. I. Joe. Kids don't read William S. Shirer's or Stephen Ambrose's histories of the Third Reich. They play with action figures and make models because they are fun—the cooler they look, the better—and Nazis had better uniforms.

COMMERCIAL ARTS

SECTION II

The "Move Our Money" bus designed by Stefan Sagmeister as part of a grass roots campaign to reduce Pentagon expenditures.

ICE CREAM AND HOT ISSUES

Known for such ice cream confections as Cherry Garcia and Chunky Monkey, Ben Cohen, cofounder of Ben & Jerry's Homemade, Inc., of Burlington, Vermont, went into severe meltdown when he heard that in 1997 Congress was balancing the national budget by whittling funds for social programs while increasing Pentagon appropriations. "Congress had added $9 billion more onto the military budget than the Pentagon had even requested," he said incredulously. "And they were going to slip it by in the middle of the night, at the very end of the legislative session." In retaliation he founded an activist group called Business Leaders for Sensible Priorities (BLSP), which has become the spearhead of a concerted strategy to alert the public to the budget imbalance as it lobbies Congress for a more equitable distribution of tax dollars.

The former hippie-turned-capitalist is no stranger to social advocacy. After Ben & Jerry's inception in 1978, Cohen began using his company to promote social causes, from environmental protection messages printed on every recycled-paper package to the creation of the Ben & Jerry's Foundation,[1] which funds models of systemic change and examples of creative problem solving, with emphasis on children and families, disenfranchised groups, and the environment. At this stage of Cohen's business career, he sits on Ben & Jerry's board of directors but is no longer responsible for daily operations, which leaves him plenty of time to help carve 15 percent away from the military budget for reallocation to social and educational programs.

"Mission" is actually a better word to describe the Sisyphean task Cohen has given himself. It takes that kind of zeal to rouse the support necessary to win the hearts and minds of America's lawmakers who refuse to sacrifice 15 percent of their sacred pork. Yet this is one fight that Cohen has carefully reconnoitered in preparation for the ultimate victory. "Our analysis of the situation is that the problem is inside the Beltway, and there's no way that we're going to change the way Congress people vote until we're able to generate grass-roots support and get this to be part of the national public debate," Cohen says in a mild-mannered cadence. "But at the moment, the issue hasn't even been on their radar screen. So we feel that before we can get Congress to act, we need to get the public educated."

The education process began when several executives funded a full-page ad in the *New York Times,* which was signed by around thirty business people (including the CEOs of Hasbro, Quad Graphics, Bell Industries, and Stride-Rite), and has burgeoned into a long-term campaign that consumed Cohen's energy at least through the Y2K election. "Since we realized that one advertisement wasn't going to solve the problem," Cohen acknowledges, "we decided to make an effort over the next few years, leading to the presidential election [in 2000], to gather support for changing federal budget allocations." The guiding principle in founding BLSP is rooted in the proposition that business is an incredibly powerful voice. "Business leaders are able to get the attention of the media, politicians, and the public," says Cohen. "They are viewed as quite credible. Yet in this area of speaking out in favor of putting more money into social needs and taking it out of the military, [CEOs] are not the usual suspects."

After the first *Times* ad, Cohen called a press conference to announce further action. However, the offensive was launched inopportunely at the moment Monicagate broke, which thwarted BLSP's momentum. "Nobody showed up to the conference," Cohen recalled. So presuming that BLSP was not going to slip through the Washington press corps' then-current obsession, Cohen decided to launch a more proactive campaign, which he calls "Move Our Money" and which is distinguished from the three-piece-suit-type aspect of the main organization, as a "hipper, cooler consumer brand of the BLSP corporation." BLSP does the arm-twisting, "Move Our Money" the public outreach.

The current Move Our Money campaign began on April 14, 2000, in Washington, D.C., to coincide with tax filing day with an agit-prop bus tour that attacked "media markets" throughout the United States, with stops in New England—particularly New Hampshire—New York, Pennsylvania, and other Atlantic Coast states to hit that year's presidential caucuses and primaries. Dave Nelson, the BSLP bus coordinator, reported that they moved west to Iowa, Nebraska, Kansas, and on to the Children's Defense Fund Conference in Houston, Texas, then making a California swing to Los Angeles, Oakland, and San Francisco. The idea was to partner with local activist and community events to garner local and national media coverage through various carnival-like attractions, which employed large inflatable charts and graphs, including one twenty-foot rubberized infant emblazoned with the world's infant mortality rates.

The Move Our Money bus was a retrofitted Greyhound, colorfully painted with charts and graphs explaining where tax dollars are currently destined. A troupe of Move Our Money performers, who traveled on the bus, combined entertainment with facts on the issues. The bus was manned by three young activist/performers: CM Hall of Oregon, Ivy Paisner of New York, and Eric Lee (as Uncle Sam) of Des Moines, Iowa. Other volunteers conducted what Cohen calls "you slice the pie" activities, as an interactive means to educate the citizenry about how the federal budget pie was sliced up, contrasting Pentagon appropriations with health care, education, and aid to children's programs (Head Start, for example). "At the end of this, the [participants] are given the opportunity to slice up the budget pie as they think it should be done." The outcome of this was tabulated and entered into a large database (and on the Move Our Money Web site) for eventual presentation to congressional leaders. Over the course of the year, Move Our Money intervened in whatever the public debate was about—over a particular expenditure or weapons system—"to add in the idea that for this same amount of money that we're talking about for this weapons system, we could renovate, say, 200,000 schools," says Cohen.

While in Des Moines, Iowa, when the bus was parked by the river during a dress rehearsal, Nelson reports that the crew was visited by the blues rocker Bonnie Raitt, who not only invited them to her own concert that evening, but also plugged the tour from the stage in front of a standing-room-only sellout crowd of over 2,700 Iowans. "She endorsed our efforts and dedicated a song to us 'and all the other activists who walk the walk and not just talk the talk.'"

The bus tour was financed by members of BLSP; by socially conscious philanthropic foundations; and by sales from the Move Our Money products, which included T-shirts, coffee mugs, and a credit-card-sized slide chart of this data for easy reference (all designed by Stefan Sagmeister). The T-shirts and mugs serve as "opportunities for the people who are wearing them to discuss the subject matter with people they run into," says Cohen.

Cohen met Sagmeister when both men lectured at the 1998 TED [Technology, Entertainment, Design] Conference. "I was incredibly impressed with Stefan's theories and philosophies of design," Cohen recalls, "so I sought him out because I wanted to get to know him better, and also because I thought that there would be a way for him to help us on this project." Sagmeister, who is best known for his in-your-face conceptual CD album covers for the likes of David Byrne and the Rolling Stones, stylistically restrained himself for this campaign. "Our scheme is very simple," Sagmeister reports. "The numbers involved in all this are so incredibly impressive (such as 50 percent of all the money that Congress spends goes to the military) that we decided to make graphs, pie charts, etc., into the logo for Move Our Money." The result is a graphic format that serves the information.

Cohen insists that little is going to happen in Washington until there is some public demand, "So the first part of this campaign [was] designed to stimulate that demand," he says. "Then once we've gotten it on the map as an issue, our efforts end up moving toward Congress." The four charts designed by Sagmeister address military spending since 1990; the comparative number of jobs created in the military, health care, and education sectors; global military spending; and "how Congress spends $1 million of your income tax." Cohen argues that "the public has no conception of the idea that Iraq is spending $8 billion a year on their military, and we're spending $270 billion, and that this is totally out of proportion."

Since Move Our Money was a fairly traditional crusade and since BLSP's CEOs must maintain their credibility, Cohen rejects civil disobedience. Nevertheless, he tacitly supports a spinoff guerrilla poster–sniping campaign that uses Move Our Money as its inspiration.

Air filled balloons with data and statistics showing where federal money is allocated, designed by Stefan Sagmeister.

During the 1998 election, large-scale posters, which were funded, printed, and sniped anonymously and designed by Seymour Chwast and DK Holland of the Pushpin Group, appeared in Washington and New York. They show brightly colored, side-by-side photos of President Clinton and former House speaker Newt Gingrich, the faces of whom are defaced, graffiti-style. Clinton with devil horns and Gingrich with a pig's ears and snout appear under the headline (set in blown-up typewriter type): "The Real Scandal: Bimbos or Bombers," with the subtitle under Gingrich that reads: "Billions of our tax dollars wasted on military pork while 1 in 5 kids live in poverty." A companion poster showing the head of Clinton next to one of a small child is headlined: "The Real Scandal: Oversexed or Underfed"; and under the picture of the child, a sub-head reads: "4,000,000 kids go hungry each day in the USA, the world's wealthiest country." A smaller poster proposed that a part of the bloated military budget be allocated to children's causes. "Our concept was to put issues in perspective," says Chwast. "The press is so obsessed with the president's scandals that they ignore real issues." Cohen claims that he was not involved with this campaign but adds, "We always expected that other groups, once they heard about this, were going to take matters into their own hands, and I think they did a rather nice job of it."

In Washington the posters were removed immediately. Likewise, in New York the posters lasted for only a short period, owing to Mayor Rudolph Giuliani's zealous poster police. Yet Cohen guarantees that the Business Leaders for Sensible Priorities and the Move Our Money campaign are not only going to stick around for a long time, but will have the desired influence on Congress.

Of course, only time will tell whether Ben Cohen will succeed in selling this idea as well as he's sold ice cream, but he promises that the fight against inequitable budget appropriations will be his hot issue.

---

[1]The Ben & Jerry's Foundation offers competitive grants to not-for-profit organizations throughout the United States, which facilitate progressive social change by addressing the underlying conditions of societal or environmental problems. The

Ben & Jerry's Foundation was established in 1985 through a donation of stock in Ben & Jerry's Homemade, Inc. These funds are used as an endowment. In addition, Ben & Jerry's Homemade, Inc., makes quarterly donations at its board's discretion of approximately 7.5 percent of its pretax profits. The foundation receives a portion of those funds. (An additional portion is earmarked for employee Community Action Teams. The CATs distribute small grants to community groups within the state of Vermont. Please write to the Community Action Teams, c/o Ben & Jerry's Homemade, Inc., 30 Community Drive, South Burlington, Vermont, 05403-6828, call (802) 846-1500, or visit www.benjerry.com/foundation, for more information.)

Cover of Eros *magazine, 1962, designed by Herb Lubalin.*

HARD COVER SEX

Evidence that the petitioners deliberately represented the accused publications as erotically arousing and commercially exploited them as erotica solely for the sake of prurient appeal amply supported the trial court's determination that the material was obscene under the standards of the Roth case [*Roth v. United States,* 354 U.S. 476]. The mere fact of profit from the sale of the publication is not considered; but in a close case a showing of exploitation of interests in titillation by pornography with respect to material lending itself to such exploitation through pervasive treatment or description of sexual matters supports a determination that the material is obscene.[1]

This 1966 opinion, delivered by Supreme Court Justice William Brennan, in the matter of *Ginzburg et al. v. United States* hammered the final nail in the coffin of Ralph Ginzburg's *Eros* magazine. It was the first time in American history that a publisher was sentenced to and served a federal prison term for producing and distributing a magazine that was judged to have abrogated the moral values and standards of society. Given today's permissive climate, however, *Eros* was a thousand times less salacious or risqué than *Maxim* or *Cosmo.* But in 1963, when prosecutors first charged that the federal obscenity statute, 18 U. S. C. § 1461, was violated "by mailing an expensive hard-cover magazine dealing with sex . . . " and that it was "obscene in the context of their production, sale, and attendant publicity," the word "pregnant" was forbidden on the airwaves, television moms and dads slept in separate beds, and bras could be shown in print or TV ads only on head-less dummies. As far as sex went, Americans were dummies, too. On the surface, the nation was still unrepentantly puritanical, and in the most elegant way, *Eros* dared to challenge society's hypocritical mores.

Despite its indictment, *Eros* number 1 (1962) and the three subsequent issues were surprisingly tame. It was neither a tawdry porn rag nor a faux-artistic nudist periodical, both of which were routinely sold under adult store counters in plain brown wrappers. In fact, this subscription-only quarterly was one of the most tastefully designed magazines produced in its day, perhaps ever—certainly on a par with Alexey Brodovitch's legendary *Portfolio* magazine. Art director Herb Lubalin infused *Eros'* pages with exquisite typography, and sensual metaphoric type-image compositions that were as enticing as the contents of the magazine itself. No detail was too small, no nuance too unimportant, and each layout was designed and paced for its aesthetic impact. If there was indeed titillation, it was in the lushness of the production.

Playboy, which began in 1955, used partial nudity, particularly women with ample, airbrushed breasts, to lure male readers into its cosmopolitan lifestyle coverage and entertainment. Conversely, *Eros* did not exploit or objectify women in this or any other way. There were no Playmates, pinups, or gatefolds of any kind—no gratuitous nudity whatsoever. In the four issues that were published, eroticism was addressed as an integral fact of life. The magazine did not take the name Eros, the "bastard" son of Aphrodite and the god of love, in vain. The marriage of love and sex that was routinely ignored in publications that pandered to voyeuristic male appetites was sanctified in *Eros.* "To me they often combine," explained Ginzburg in an interview. "Speaking from personal experience, the erotic in my life has always been richest, most fulfilling, when intertwined with love, with the romantic. The investigation and portrayal of this summital combination is what *Eros* was all about."

Eros explored the full spectrum of sexuality—from passion to humor, as art and culture, both past and present. Articles like "My Quest for a French Tickler in Japan" by restaurant critic Mimi Sheraton, "Patent for the Chasity Belt," and "Q: How Do Porcupines Do It? A: Carefully!," were witty peeks at socially taboo themes. Conversely, "The Plea for Polygamy" by Albert Ellis, "A Study of Erotomania" by Dr. Theodor Reik, "Love in the Bible" by Rufus Mott, and "The Sexual Side of Anti-Semitism" by Shepherd Raymond, examined how sex is endemic to all segments of mass culture. Excerpts from such works as Madame Teillier's Brothel by Guy de Maupassant and Lysistrata by Aristophanes reprised the banned parts of classic drama and literature. The feature, "We All Loved Jack" by Faye Emerson, reported on the much whispered but never overtly discussed sensual appeal of JFK. And the surprising "President Harding's Second Lady" by John Hejno, Jr., examined the role of Harding's mistress long before the "Starr Report" revealed the sexual quirks that were unearthed during the Clinton/Lewinsky affair. Remember, the details of Clinton's peccadilloes were published for all to read and hear in every major magazine and on TV throughout the world.

Instead of prurient photo spreads, *Eros*'s art and photography portfolios explored eroticism through the historian's and journalist's lens. Among them "The Brothel in Art" looked at two centuries of how artists through to Picasso addressed the world's oldest profession. "Me and the Male Prostitutes of Bombay" by Art Kane and "The Mesdemoiselles de la Rue St. Denis" sensitively examined the underbelly of sex as a business. *Eros* was the first national magazine to publish a feature revealing intimacy between a black man and a white woman. Ralph Hatterseley's stunning portfolio, titled "Black and White in Color," caused more consternation because it busted the biggest of all taboos—interracial love. Even the portfolio of photographs by Bert Stern of Marilyn Monroe naked, the last studio portraits of MM taken six weeks before her tragic death, was tastefully presented (and remains one of the few documents that shows the natural beauty of this tormented "official" sex goddess). Although Stern's portfolio was declaimed as obscene, movie stars today pay dearly for the same kind of exposure in national magazines, not to mention on the screen.

Yet this was the early 1960s. America was reeling from McCarthy's anti-Communist witch-hunts and Congressional investigations into cultural transgression (even comic books and rock 'n' roll lyrics were investigated by elected officials). With the consequential exception of *Playboy* and its clones, sexuality was still taboo, and the gatekeepers of moral decency looked for any constitutional loopholes to repress any challenge to its hegemony. "The Uptightniks felt that something—anything! for god's sake—had to be done to quash this rampant sexuality," says Ginzburg. "And I was an irresistible target. Bobby Kennedy was persuaded by certain religious interests to attack me. Attempts to suppress magazines of Hugh Hefner and others had failed. Their rights were upheld in the courts, but mine were not."

The First Amendment guaranteed Ginzburg the right to publish *Eros* free from judicial restraint. Certainly when compared to *Playboy*'s overt photography, there seemed to be little debate that *Eros* would be safe from prosecution. But as Ginzburg notes, "The crime of 'obscenity' or 'pornography' is a crime without definition or victim. It is very much like the crime of witchery in centuries past. It is a bag of smoke used to conceal one's own dislikes with regard to aspects of sexual portrayal or behavior." Whereas *Playboy* had earned considerable popularity—and with it legal immunity—*Eros* had a rarified subscription base, which left Ginzburg vulnerable. As he reports,

> The very closest I can come to documentation for [why *Eros* was targeted] is a book written by . . . either a Supreme Court Justice's clerk or a member of the Justice Department and perhaps even by a U. S. Attorney General whose name was something like Nicholas deKatzenbach in which (on about two pages of the book) he describes the meeting at which it was decided to indict me. According to that account, Bobby Kennedy feared that a feature in *Eros* depicting a pair of nude dancers (no genitals showing) consisting of a black man and white woman would undermine the Kennedy Administration's racial integration efforts.
>
> This has always seemed bizarre to me but I'm giving you facts as I recall having read them in that book. My own personal belief is that Bobby (now, ironically, known to have been an energetic whoremonger—and I point this out not to put him down on moral grounds but to underscore his religious and legal hypocrisy) acted at the instigation of a New York priest named Morton Hill, head of a local Catholic-front antipornography outfit, and a man in Cincinnati who headed a national antipornography unit of the Church called something like Citizens for Decency in Literature. I believe his name was Keating and that he was later imprisoned for major crime during the savings and loan association scandal.

From a contemporary perspective it is difficult to comprehend why *Eros* caused such a furor. The sex act was never shown, and nudity comprised, one might say, a disappointingly minor percentage of the entire magazine. Today there is more explicitness on the covers of newsstand magazines and on cable TV than ever appeared in *Eros*. But the government felt the pressure to attack, and Ginzburg's constitutional protection was lost when he decided, wittily, to send out subscription mailings from the towns of Blueballs and Intercourse, Pennsylvania. This prompted the postal authorities to petition for Federal prosecution on the grounds of pandering and solicitation through the mails. Like Al Capone, who was found guilty of tax evasion rather than racketeering, Ralph Ginzburg was sentenced to prison for posting materials deemed to be obscene. He served nine months of his yearlong sentence, and, he says, "I became a social outcast as a result of my conviction and imprisonment—a U.S.-Supreme-Court-certified felon, at that—and very few established businesses would deal with me. Thus my publishing potential after release from prison was severely circumscribed. I have always felt that I might have become a major force in American publishing had it not been for my conviction. Instead, I'm just a curious footnote."

The four issues of *Eros* may be only a footnote in the annals of free speech, but in the history of graphic design, they speak volumes. *Eros,* and later Ginzburg's *Avant Garde* and *Fact* magazines, was the proving ground for Herb Lubalin's typographic experimentation, which influenced magazine layouts and advertising for the next decade. The design was helped by the fact that *Eros* did not take any advertising and thus became a masterpiece of pacing and flow. Lubalin was expert at modulating text pages in relation to pictorial matter—this and his metaphoric typography were hallmarks. Although what Lubalin spawned now has a period flavor, *Eros* is nonetheless graphically timeless, and after all that has passed—all that has been revealed about sex—its content and presentation are surprisingly original.

---

[1]No. 42 Supreme Court of the United States 383 U.S. 463 (Argued December 7, 1965. Decided March 21, 1966.)

Ralph Steadman's 1980 depiction of President Ronald Reagan on the cover of the British New Statesman.

PRESIDENTIAL CARICATURE: RITUAL MUTILATION

JFK was too handsome; Carter too nice; Bush, Sr., too bland; Reagan too Teflon; and Clinton, well, too cute. But Richard M. Nixon was a caricaturist's ideal. A ski-slope nose, bulbous jowls, five o'clock shadow, and a widow's peak—these were cartoon exaggerations waiting to erupt, and his misdeeds further added to the allure.

At this writing, early in the new administration, George W. Bush's caricature appears complete. The drooping lip, ample ears, and smallish head, as well as a diminutive intellectual reputation, seem to have crystallized among the nation's editorial artists into a cross between Ross Perot and Sad Sack—or perhaps into something more primitive: "It's hard for me not to hear the call of the chimp in these features," says Steven Brodner, whose political caricatures appear in *Esquire* and the *New Yorker.* In the narrowness of the president's eyes ("one is slightly deformed the other turned in," according to Brodner) along with the large overhanging lip and ears, caricaturists have seen in the forty-third president everything from a man-child to a chimpanzee. And if Nixon is remembered as much for the caricatures drawn by Herblock, Levine, and Sorel, as for his tenure as president, so too might Mr. Bush be remembered for sketches by Peters, Deering, and Gorrel. Such is the ability of caricature to make an already ubiquitous public persona, the American president, into an indelible graphic icon. What caricaturists hate to admit, however, is that the objects of their derision have learned to embrace the lampoon.

Philip Burke's 1986 caricature of Presidents Reagan and Nixon.

Ever since the fifteenth century, when Leonardo da Vinci sketched the warts of clerics and nobles, the "charged portrait," as caricature is known, has been a vehicle for political and social criticism. In the late nineteenth century, Thomas Nast's acerbic depictions of New York's Boss Tweed in *Harper's Weekly* established Tweed in the popular consciousness as a bloated, corrupt politician. Similarly, Frederick Opper's drawings helped turn public opinion against McKinley by portraying him as the leader of a buffoonish minstrel show.

What made these caricatures so effective? From a strictly technical standpoint, the success of a caricature derives from a mixture of physical truth, a perceived inner essence, and an astute interpretation of the historical moment—a tall order that is satisfied, for instance, when a floppy-eared Bush (physical truth) is drawn as a child (perceived inner essence) sitting on Dick Cheney's knee (the historical moment).

Of course, some artists might explain it much more simply. "In truth our presidents really look like what they are," says Edward Sorel, who has been creating scabrous caricatures since Kennedy. "Bush I and II and Gerald Ford really looked stupid, and Nixon and Clinton really looked like sleazeballs." One of the most enduring caricatures in Sorel's repertoire portrayed Nixon as Richard III, capturing the venality of the presidential reign. Similarly, for a cover of the *National Lampoon,* Robert Grossman, whose caricatures appear in the *New York Observer,* made Nixon into Pinocchio with a nose that extended onto a foldout gatefold.

Biting portraits like these have traditionally provided "a way to vicariously and bloodlessly tear down or deface a public figure," says Bernard Reilly, former curator of prints and drawings at the Library of Congress and currently director of research and access at the Chicago Historical Society. "This function was fulfilled in earlier societies by burning or hanging the king, the Pope or the tax-collector in effigy. Our own ancestors prior to the American Revolution resorted to tarring and feathering the representatives of the Crown. Something from these earlier practices survives in a more civilized form in caricature."

No surprise then that artists like Ralph Steadman, the English satirist, once believed that their distorted drawings could amount to a graphic assassination. "I actually thought I was going to bring down the culprits and surge forward with a whole new and a better world," he said of his barbed political portraits during the 1960s and 1970s, "but, it wasn't to be."

That may be because, as the twentieth century wore on, politicians and other targets of caricature became increasingly savvy to the rhetorical benefits of self-deprecation—a tack that included embracing caricatures of themselves. "In a way, they are a form of validation for their subject," said Reilly, "a sort of perverse Mount Rushmore." Most presidents (or at least their librarians) have become ardent collectors of political cartoons about themselves, which is perhaps the greatest insult to the caricaturist. Sorel reports that the White House wanted to buy his 1992 *New Yorker* cover of the Clinton inauguration, but he had already sold it. And Lyndon Johnson seemed to like seeing himself in cartoons so much that he didn't mind whether they were flattering or not. "Judge Bork's son bought what I thought was a devastating caricature," Sorel said of a caricature he made of the former Supreme Court nominee. "But his check didn't bounce."

Still, for his part, Ralph Steadman refuses to sell his cartoons to objects of enmity, and at times he feels disheartened about the raw materials coming out of Washington these days. "Now, politicians are boring," he said. "But," he added, "the one you have now may get me going again."

Chris Ware hand letters his Acme Novelty *comics with precision and wit.*

MORE THAN *WHAM! BANG! BOOM!*: THE ART AND DESIGN OF COMICS LETTERING

Culture snobs bifurcate art into high and low, creating polar opposites within everything from literature to graphic design. High design, for instance, is given classical or Modernist pedigrees, while low is crass and populist, like the comics. Even within the hierarchies of art schools and professional circles, designers are considered saints, and comics artists are placed a notch above greeting card illustrators. Although graphic novels have earned serious critical attention, thanks in large part to Art Spiegelman's Pulitzer Prize–winning *Maus,* comics are still situated in the design culture's pecking order as the bastard offspring of a sordid *ménage à trois* between art, literature, and design. In reality, comics are the first real multimedia, a co-mix of these three disciplines and something more—comics are fonts of typographic innovation.

More than mere *Wham!, Bang!,* and *Boom!,* decorated and metaphorical comic strip typography has been inspired by, and is the inspiration for, myriad visual artifacts from billboards to tattoos. And yet, comic lettering's origins date back to illuminated manuscripts. In fact, a comic strip is a kind of sequential manuscript in which word and picture have equal weight. Comic lettering also has roots in nineteenth-century sign painting, known for contoured letters with colorful dramatic drop shadows, and in circus poster alphabets made from ornamented Tuscans and Egyptians. Vintage twentieth-century film title cards and movie foyer posters are also among comic lettering's forebears. Today, with such easy access to digital typefaces, comic book–style hand lettering offers more than a historical grounding—it is a dynamic alternative to rote typography.

The introductory frame of a comic strip, known as the splash panel, is a marquee designed to dramatically announce the visual narrative and is thus invested with more graphic bravado than, say, a common book title page. And while the elegant typographic nuances found in book type composition are negligible, there is, nonetheless, a quirky bookishness in comics lettering insofar as it establishes a visual tone for the strip or comic book. Comic lettering, usually designed to echo either the drawing style or thematic thrust of the strip, is perfectly complementary and purposely composed. "Comic lettering is a unique form of typography because it is incredibly specific and functional," says Peter Girardi, founder of the multimedia design firm Funny Garbage and a former graffiti artist whose approach to Web creation is inspired by the art and design of comics. "I always loved when comic lettering and titling became part of the story. I could tell who lettered a comic in the same way I could tell who inked and penciled a comic." In fact, what to some may seem like generic lettering is for others filled with the personality, character, and nuance endemic to all fine typography, if not more so because it is so uniquely individual.

Comic lettering evokes mood. While splashy words illuminate the stage on which a comic strip drama, comedy, or fantasy takes place, speech balloon lettering underscores the narrative's timbre and verbal identity. "Like other traditional forms of typesetting," Girardi continues, "comic lettering has a very specific task that couldn't be accomplished by traditional typographic means. Look at word balloons. That is an incredibly specific form of typography that has become part of the comic book vocabulary. EC comics used the Leroy Lettering kit that really influenced the feel and impact of the comics. Comic typography is not secondary to the image in the way that most graphic design is."

In the world of traditional strips, superhero comics have their own style suited to the subject matter—loud, demonstrative, and masculine. The same is true for war, horror, and sci-fi, while romance comics use "feminine" letters with swashes and curlicues. Certain lettering styles are emblems for their themes, but since the advent of Underground Comix in the late 1960s, there is even more to comic lettering than obvious, metaphoric relationships. The lettering is indeed art.

Looking back to antique forms of typography, the San Francisco Underground artists—including R. Crumb, Rick Griffin, and Victor Moscoso—were passionate about slab serif wood type and curvilinear Art Nouveau motifs. These applications were not simply copied verbatim but were manipulated and massaged into a comics form. The late Rick Griffin was among the most innovative—and visionary—of all the Underground letterers. In addition to designing the original psychedelic curlicue swash logo for *Rolling Stone* (no longer used), he developed hand-drawn typography that was more beautifully eccentric than most of the recent crop of expressive digital alphabets. His intricately inked, meandering words and phrases, virtually sewn into a complex mélange of in- and outline alphabetic forms, are artworks as much as type-works. The typography for his opus, a hybrid comic called *Utopia,* is a veritable commentary on the function and abstraction of letterforms. In this episodic graphic book, some of the comics are sequential images, while others are just gibberish (a kind of highly advanced Greeking) that rises to the level of pure expressionism. Griffin was a master of what might be called the Rorschach school of calligraphy, with page after page of letter drawings that have mysterious, multiple meanings.

There are no multiple interpretations of this kind to be found in Gary Panter's scratchy scrawls. But neither are they meant for passive viewing. Panter, known for his postapocalyptic *Jimbo* comics, builds on a rough-hewn drawing style comprised of ratty lines and crooked masses. His alphabets—including Donkey and Phosphic Acidsome, which have recently been digitized by Funny Garbage— echo and complement his rough-hewn, figurative renderings. While somewhat dopey in form, they are seriously effective on the printed page. Panter also enjoys reprising the quirky classics of nineteenth-century commercial culture. His Western-style Panterosa (a wink and nod to the legendary Ponderosa ranch from the TV show *Bonanza*) is a purposely flawed hand rendering of this exaggerated slab serif, which during the 1960s was, incidentally, one of the mainstays of psychedelic poster lettering.

The stylistic range of comics lettering is as diverse and personal as the comics artists are idiosyncratic. Art Spiegelman's title lettering for his first comic strip anthology, *Breakdowns,* is a craggy and shaky block letter, vividly alluding to psychotic episodes. When juxtaposed with the cover of a repeating pattern of Spiegelman self-portraits in

Specimens of Gary Panter's "ratty" hand lettering as digital typefaces.

which he is depicted sitting at his drawing board slugging down a bottle of India ink, the typography has even more gravity as a signpost. Similarly, Spiegelman's earliest lettering for *Maus,* a scrawl of blood, is "Lettering Parlant" that speaks volumes about the strip. Such a violent design may have been an obvious choice—like type with icicles on an ice machine—to introduce a visual narrative about the Holocaust, but it functions perfectly in context. And it was but one stage during a long evolution of lettering before he settled on the most emblematic style for this opus, which was slightly less overt but just as expressive. A student of comics, Spiegelman builds a lettering vocabulary on icons of the past. His logo for the mid-1980s and early 1990s comic magazine *RAW* continually changed, because it was drawn by different artists and because it was intended to reflect the multidimensional comics within the magazine.

Some sage—or maybe it was a curmudgeon—once said that comics artists who cannot letter should not draw comics. Lettering is endemic to the art form, and the lettering-challenged have no business in the business. The comics of Ward Sutton, a poster artist and cartoonist, exemplify total integration of picture and letter. His references include everything from album covers to book covers to old comic books, packaging, and posters. "I often look at these examples and create my own hand-drawn version of the type or a composite of different type styles combined into one," he explains. "And, of course, I also just make up type styles as well." Sutton says that comics lettering is wonderfully organic. "In this computer age where fonts seem to come a dime a dozen, hand-lettering is what stands out to me. Of course fonts can now be altered to make them look unique within a design, but I can tell when things are hand-lettered."

Not all comics lettering is sinuous or freehand. Richard McGuire's is precisionist and architectonic, although it is unmistakably lettered by hand. An admirer of advertising display types from the 1920s and 1930s Deco, electrical circuitry, hand-painted signs, and cut paper, McGuire once used a variety of draftsman's tools to achieve geometric effects, but now the computer aids in his quest for the perfectly proportioned, quirky letterform as he shifts from angular to globular, depending on the mood and meaning. Chris Ware's extraordinary typographic homage to turn-of-the-century novelty and mail order catalogs also falls into the realm of tightly rendered verisimilitude. Ware's Acme Novelty lettering could fill a veritable catalog of boisterous dis-

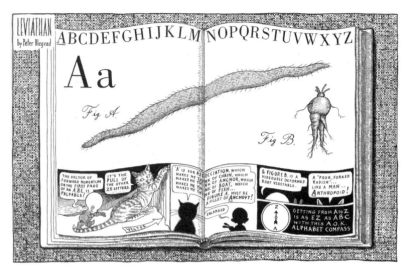

Peter Blegvad's lettering for his comic strip Leviathan *is elegant and classical.*

play, or show-card, writing. He lovingly recreates a world of now from the visual lexicon of the past through letters that complement his sublime drawing style.

No absolute paradigm of comics lettering exists. Simply compare the typography of comics artists and illustrators Jonathon Rosen, Steven Guarnaccia, and Peter Blegvad to see that lettering is a fingerprint. Rosen's type is like automatic writing; Guarnaccia's is more stylized in a 1930s Deco-like script manner, but no less fluid; Blegvad draws upon Dürer's *Of the Just Shaping of Letters* and other sources: "I love the look of crude hand-lettering as exemplified in the photographs Ben Shahn took of storefront signs," he says, "or in the work of Isidore Isou (founder of the Letterist movement), or of the Rev. Howard Finster, etc. In an era of expedient digital conformity like ours, hand-lettering—expressive and charged with idiosyncratic character—has become an endangered species."

Endangered? Not as long as comics artists continue to use pen and ink or brush and paint—or as long as expression and emotion are valued over Modernist objectivity. Last time I looked, the hand was not yet a vestigial appendage. And yet there are scores of "original" comics typefaces available as fonts on the Web, and even the originators of alphabets have digitized their work for mass consumption. Why spend all the time lettering by hand, goes the logic, when they can get the same result with an existing typeface that someone else has drawn? And this is nothing new. In 1936 Howard Trafton designed the brush-letter Cartoon, long accepted as the quintessential comics typeface. As hand lettering makes a comeback to offset digital perfection, comics-derived faces will become increasingly available to anyone looking for a quirky character. But the quirkiness will never come straight from the box; it's got to come from the hand.

Der Stürmer, *the Nazi's most vicious anti-Semitic periodical, even made some Nazis squirm.*

SHOCK OF THE VILE

Having long studied the propaganda of the Nazi era, I was well aware of *Der Stürmer* (The Stormer), the rabid, anti-Semitic weekly newspaper edited by the infamous "Jew-baiter" and Nuremberg war criminal, Julius Streicher. Yet nothing could prepare me for the surprise—and indescribable sense of defilement—that I experienced when I held a copy in my own hands. This was not triggered by simply looking at *Der Stürmer*—if one does not understand German, it looks like one of the conventional newspapers of the day. But when my translator read each terse story (and the same themes were often repeated numerous times throughout a single issue) about the crimes of Jews, including ritual murder and savage rape, I could feel the black, spiky *Der Stürmer* masthead dripping like blood onto the front page. Its incendiary motto, "The Jew Is Our Misery," printed at the bottom of the cover in red ink and repeated on at least eight of its sixteen pages, left no doubt that I was holding depravity incarnate. It is impossible for one who has never turned the pages of *Der Stürmer* to viscerally experience the magnitude of its evil, just as during World War II it was difficult to accept the horrors of the Holocaust, until the vivid evidence was made public.

Der Stürmer, a semiofficial organ of the Nazis, lasted for twenty-three years until the final weeks of the Third Reich, its sole purpose to slander the German Jewish population, who, it argued, debased German morals. Its message was conveyed through gross pornographic tracts and hideous caricature. At its height it printed over 2 million copies per week and was posted in public display cases in every German town and city. Yet it fell victim to its own success; its circulation began to plummet around 1940, when Jews were eliminated from every walk of German life and none of *Der Stürmer*'s enemies were left to be slandered.

The last page from Seymour Chwast's The South, *a testament to the American civil rights movement.*

LOOK AWAY, DIXIELAND

Martin Luther King, Jr. was assassinated in 1968. Yet as tragic and senseless as this act of violence was, it was just another in a long legacy of racial injustice. The civil rights movement in the United States, which began with the abolitionists in the mid-nineteenth century, and reached catharsis with the March on Washington in the mid-1960s, was met with forceful resistance matched only by those willing to die for freedom. In the Deep South—Alabama and Mississippi—civil rights workers who fought to end well over a century of institutionalized racism were brutalized or killed. When in 1964 three young civil rights workers, Andrew Goodman and Michael H. Schwerner, both white middle-class New Yorkers, and James Earl Chaney, a Southern black man, were murdered in Philadelphia, Mississippi, by Ku Klux Klan members (including sheriff's deputies), each brutally beaten, shot, and mutilated, Americans began to take notice. Martyrs make a revolution, and the civil rights movement had plenty of them.

In 1969 Seymour Chwast paid homage to these martyrs in issue no. 54 of the *Push Pin Graphic,* the monthly promotional publication of New York's Push Pin Studios. The *Graphic* printed only three to five thousand copies, but it was highly influential in its unique approach to visual form and content among graphic and advertising designers. Push Pin Studios was the wellspring of visual eclecticism during a period when cold Swiss Modernism was the reigning style. The *Graphic* not only showcased Push Pin's overarching sensibility and its individual members' talents—it covered a wide range of issues and themes, some of them controversial.

Chwast has always been politically aware. During the 1960s he demonstrated against the Vietnam War, stood on peace vigils, and produced posters and flyers for social causes. When it was his turn to develop the decade-ending issue of the *Graphic,* he looked back: "I remember segregation," he explains. "I remember being on a picket line in front of Woolworth's [the chain of stores that refused to serve blacks at its soda fountains, even in the "integrated" North]." He was angry. "There had been a succession of killings that we all knew about. Especially the three civil rights workers, it affected us all. It was in the news for a long time because they couldn't find the bodies." He was also moved. "The March on Washington was a very important, enlightening event for the nation, and for me personally."

"The South" issue of the *Push Pin Graphic* was a response to his feelings toward civil rights. Although the North could, in fact, be just as segregated, violence emanated from the South. Moreover, it was where the trappings of slavery and laws of intolerance were maintained. Chwast conceived of the *Push Pin Graphic* as a catalog of benign Southern stereotypes countered by grim social realities. He believed that this was a war to expunge intolerable Southern values. Each right-

A page from The South.

hand page featured a large color image of Southern "virtue" with an inset picture of Southern injustice, the photographs of civil rights martyrs. On the verso side were lyrics from traditional Southern songs (such as "Rose of Alabama") offset by a short biography of the slain individual. As the *coup de grace,* a small hole was shot through the *Graphic.* The photographs were positioned so that the hole (which forms the "o" in South) pierced the heads of each victim—the penultimate picture shows Martin Luther King with a hole through his eye. But there is a twist on the final spread. The large image is of the March on Washington with the inset picture of a Southern Belle. On the verso side, the hole shoots through the lyrics of "Dixie," the Confederate anthem—marking the symbolic death of the old South.

Chwast reports that he received a few letters at the time criticizing him for "always picking on the South." Nonetheless, it took another decade or so of civil protest and federal government intervention before racially prejudicial voting restrictions in the South ended and blacks rose to leadership roles in local governments. In the United States, racial inequality still persists, the Ku Klux Klan still exists, but the old South is rapidly disappearing. Curiously, though, "The South" issue of the *Push Pin Graphic* is not simply an artifact of bygone days, but rather a reminder of what it cost to come this far.

A spread from The South *illustrating the stereotypes of the old south and the martyrs of the civil rights movement.*

Cover of The Inner City Mother Goose *designed by Lawrence Ratzkin.*

THE INNER CITY MOTHER GOOSE

The term "inner city" was coined during the mid-1960s to indicate the new urban ghetto, a small city within a large city, a place where the poor congregate, surrounded by walls of prosperity. Racial tensions and social hostility boiled within the inner city. And when the euphemism "inner city youth" was used, it was clear that it referred to young people of color and all this suggests. Inner city habitats and inhabitants were doomed by virtue of what sociologists called "benign neglect" by the power elites. This very hopelessness is what also, paradoxically, spurred hope through an increased number of progressive social programs designed to build economic and educational bridges connecting the inner city to the outside world. Yet it took considerable effort to convince people that the inner city was worth salvaging. The result has never been totally achieved.

When published in 1969, *The Inner City Mother Goose,* a collection of poems by Eve Merriam and "visuals" by Lawrence Ratzkin, took ironic and satiric jabs at inner city prejudice. It was not the first book to lampoon the powerful or criticize squalid conditions, but it was one of the first "trade" paperbacks on this theme to be published by a major New York publishing house, Simon & Schuster. In the tradition of Marshall McLuhan and Quentin Fiore's *Medium is the Message,* Ratzkin used photography and typography to communicate a poignant social message and frame Merriam's Mother Goose send-up.

Ratzkin, then a thirty-six-year-old book cover and jacket designer, was originally given the poet Merriam's manuscript to illustrate. "To be perfectly honest," Ratzkin recalls, "when I saw it I said,

A spread from The Inner City Mother Goose.

'What am I going to do with this?' The text in typewritten form was weird." But he had never had the opportunity to work on a complete book, so he accepted the job.

Ratzkin was sympathetic to the civil rights struggle yet admits that he felt it was "presumptuous to be two white bleeding-heart Jewish liberals doing this thing." Nonetheless, he pushed ahead, taking photographs of the street, which started percolating ideas. "I did not think that a linear way would work, so I addressed myself specifically to each text," he explains. "Some of the pages are more unambiguous but others really allude to larger issues." Indeed the ninety-four short poems tackled poverty, illiteracy, drug and alcohol abuse, as well as police brutality and the Vietnam War. While following the basic format of a conventional illustrated children's book, Ratzkin also broke out with expressive typographic treatments when the poems were verbally demonstrative, such as "Hark, Hark, the Dogs Do Bark," a noise poem that through a cacophony of words in bold gothic type evokes the tumult of the ghetto streets. "I owe that approach to Paul Rand's children's book, "Sparkle and Spin," Ratzkin confides.

Merriam, who died in 1992, only met Ratzkin from time to time because she apparently accepted that his "visuals" were not simply

A spread from The Inner City Mother Goose *that typographically simulates the sounds of the ghetto.*

graphic interpretations of her words but commentaries that spun off from them. "She was not critical of what I did," states Ratzkin. "But there was one picture that she objected to, a black street person wearing a blonde, braided wig that was plunked onto her head. To me it said something about her condition, but Eve felt it was somehow demeaning. So I took it out."

Merriam referred to *Inner City* as "just about the most banned book in the country," because its sale was indeed limited to a few large urban centers and because it was often misplaced in stores that did carry it. Merriam was known as a children's book author, and although this book was designed for adults, it found its way onto children's shelves. Nonetheless, sales were as high as 75,000 copies in this particular form. It was also later repackaged for children with drawn illustrations and was the basis for a 1971 Broadway musical, *Inner City.*

The impact of *The Inner City Mother Goose* cannot be underestimated as both a polemic for the civil rights cause and a model of expressive, conscience-driven design. Over thirty years later, it still speaks truth about the conditions of the inner city.

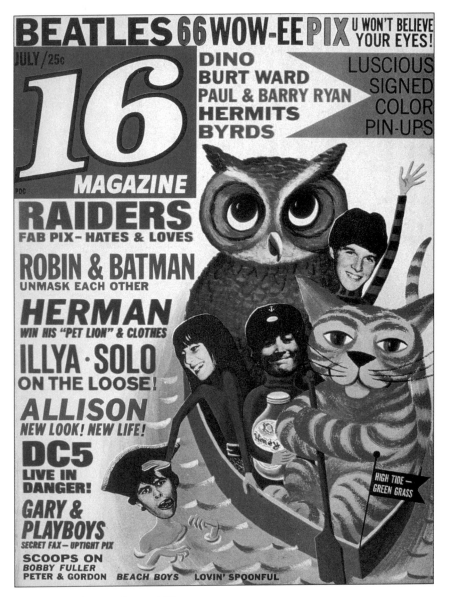

16 Magazine, *the teeny-boppers bible.*

THE TEEN MAGAZINE FAME MACHINE

I have a confession. During the mid-1960s I read *16* magazine, which targeted star-struck adolescent girls but also appealed to a minority of star-wannabe teenage boys—like myself. Edited by former fashion model and pop idolmaker Gloria Stavers, *16* was the first bona fide American teenage fan magazine and hype engine for the popular music and television juggernaut thrusting its way into the hearts and minds of America's baby-boom, teeny-bop generation. As a magazine, *16* defined a graphic style that spoke directly to this audience. It was also a voyeur's cornucopia, replete with "oodles" of never-before-seen "wow-ee" publicity pix of "adorable" blemish-free stars, candid canned gossip about pop's leading heartthrobs, and probing interviews revealing their favorite colors, girls, food, girls, longings, girls, etc.—all presented without an iota of irony.

Newly pubescent girls suffering from Barbie-and-Ken withdrawals found that *16* was a dream machine of unattainable, yet imaginable lovers. Hormone-awakened boys used it as a guide to what the coolest cats wore, which was what you (I) should be wearing if you (I) were feeling that tingly feeling and you (I) longed to make out with a *16* reader of the opposite gender.

Stavers, hired in 1957 as *16*'s subscription clerk but in just one year promoted to editor-in-chief, understood that celebrity was an addictive drug. Regardless of a star's talent (or lack thereof), a familiar face and a well-known name could vicariously seduce impressionable young girls—and not simply influence their choice of acne cover-ups, either. Stavers's idol-making agenda was simple: Identify popular or rising TV, record, and radio personalities, then hype the hell out of them. This was accomplished by publishing countless cute 'n' cuddly (often signed) pinup photographs and "exclusive" articles (e.g., "The Dave Clark 5 Live in Danger") that ran in successive issues as long as the fickle finger of fame did not point downward. However, the basic formula was not original. Since the 1920s, *Photoplay, Silver Screen, Movie Star,* and other pulp fan magazines had mythologized, canonized, and otherwise deified Hollywood movie stars in order to turn fame into a commodity. Yet these magazines were not specifically aimed at young teens.

By 1957, when the first issue of *16* premiered with a picture of Elvis Presley lounging on the cover, the teenager as a consumer group was also in its early adolescence, and like the complexions of those who read *16,* it was about to erupt. Stavers realized that the first wave of preteen and teenage baby boomers were starving for a place of their own, where their fantasies were pampered. So she invented a design format that wed *Highlights for Children* (brightly colored type covers with cute, comic illustrations on which the heads of stars were pasted) with the *Police Gazette* (provocative teaser headlines and doctored photos). This was not "good" graphic design in any sophisticated understanding of the term. Typefaces were indiscriminately selected for boldness and color in the manner of sensational newspapers—not for balance or harmony. Layouts were suffocatingly packed with text and pics that were either publicity handouts or artless snapshots. But the design package was unmistakable and is still more or less copied by *16*'s imitators. When *Rolling Stone* premiered with its classical format— oxford rules and Times Roman headlines—it was a direct graphic attack on *16*'s visual immaturity.

Nonetheless, Stavers used graphics and text to develop a voice—a big sisterly one that was sympathetic to young desires as she exploited them. The magazine was the ultimate vicarious thrill. It allowed a reader to virtually hug heroes without fear of rejection. Think of it as a reliquary for pop saints, a shrine at which the impressionable paid homage as they flagellated themselves. And the illusion seemed to work, because girls sent countless love letters (care of the magazine) to their fave raves, and boys emulated the looks of these raves. Stavers was a genius and a pioneer at giving adolescent girls— and boys like me—what they wanted.

And yet, prior to World War II, those aged thirteen to nineteen were not collectively referred to as "teenagers." They were trapped in a netherworld between childhood and adulthood, not treated as a distinct demographic entity. Teenaged people were either portrayed in the movies as precocious youngsters (Andy Hardy) or delinquent thugs (the Dead End Kids, which now sounds like a boy band). At best they were mini-men and little women who imitated adult tastes and values but who were not officially adults. They couldn't legally vote or drink. However, with parental permission a seventeen-year-old boy could go to war to be killed.

After World War II, teens—particularly girls—were at last foisted into integral roles in the consumer society. In the late 1940s the mainstream magazines *Charm* and *Seventeen* helped launch the teenage fashion, cosmetic, and product industry. Girls, who develop faster than boys anyway, were targeted as beneficiaries of these exclusive gifts and wares. With the floodgates open, *Junior Bazaar, Ingenue for Teens,* and *'Teen,* among other mainstream magazines, advised adolescents on how to be "in" or glamorous and desirable—recommending the best deodorant (Arrid), hair color (Toni), and acne cream (Clearasil). They offered tips on how to meet the right guys and get modeling jobs. Punctuating the stories about "cutting, setting, and comb-out" and "Dazzling Duds," all these magazines published a requisite number of celebrity features, frequently about child stars who precariously stepped over the chronological Maginot line into their twenties. In a 1962 *'Teen* magazine piece titled "We're Grown Up Now!" Annette Funicello (the most famous of the 1950s Mouseketeers and darling of the fan magazines) "reluctantly admitted that her loyal fans really don't want to accept the fact that she's grown up." Actually, these articles frequently balanced the glamour of fame with its downside. "Her record career has boomed then fizzled," continued the article. "In her glory days as a big record seller she was grateful. In these dry days of no big disc hits, she remains relaxed and self-assured that there will be brighter sales in the future."

At the same time, kids were starting to embrace their own culture of music (rock), clothes (leather), and art (comics), much of it frightening to adults. Flames were fanned by "teensploitation" films that portrayed youth culture as bawdy and rowdy—boys as hoods and girls as tarts, all under the influence of rock 'n' roll, the drug that released uncontrolled urges. So begins the schism between the clean teen and the juvenile delinquent (the latter also included the subcategory of the sensitive rebel).

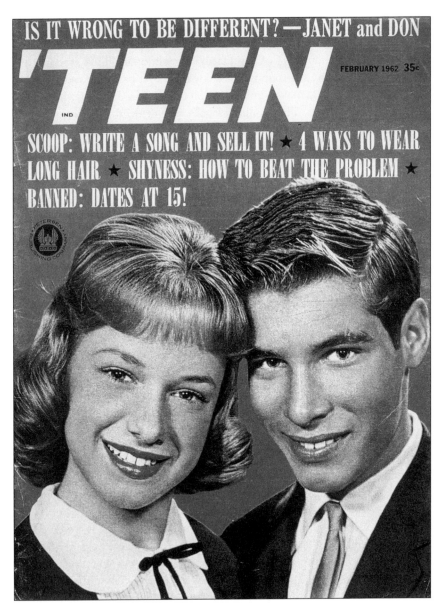

'Teen *celebrates two fave clean teens of the early sixties.*

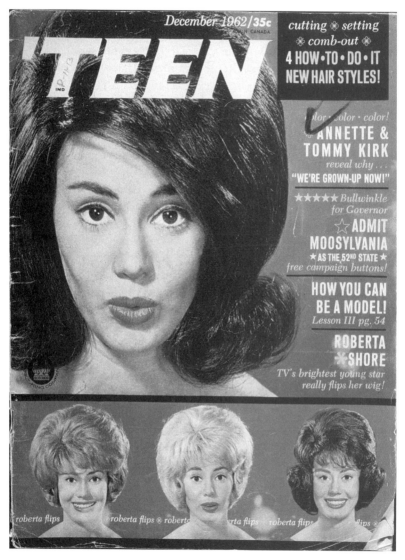

'Teen *displays the hottest hair styles of 1962.*

Graphics used to exploit the delinquent teen copied the sensationalist mannerisms of the raunchy tabloids. It was Punk long before the advent of the Punk Movement, the real thing, so to speak. Countless mass market paperbacks, B-film posters, and other pop ephemera visually portrayed gritty youth as backstreet thugs (boy bands, again?) drenched in hair grease, framed in tableau that included "torn-from-the-headlines" type treatments, and a variant of social realist painting that emphasized sex and violence.

On the other hand, the clean teen was bolstered by magazines that fixated on personal "development" by setting common standards of beauty promoted by the famous. The delinquents did not have a national magazine on their side—yet the purveyors of popular culture always rise to meet trend and fashion; and since rock 'n' roll, the scourge of Western civilization, was such a potentially huge profit center, the raucous musical rebels who propagated the stuff found that they were being co-opted by a celebrity industry that created its own sanitized celebs. While this industry could not reconfigure some of the true originals (like Elvis), it did everything industrially possible to make these icons acceptable to the masses. The theory was that impressionable teens would spend their meager allowances on teen products, but if their parents felt comfortable with their idols, many more dollars would be spent on the kids' behalf. Millions were invested in growing and harvesting a crop of adult-friendly celebrities who were showcased on TV (from *American Bandstand* to the *Ed Sullivan Show*) and in films (from *Beach Party Bingo* to *Gidget*).

When it came to celebrating these unthreatening celebrities, *16*—and later its imitators, *Tiger Beat, Rave, Dig,* and more—was preeminent. It worshiped the singer, not the song. And during the late 1950s and early 1960s, when such cleansters as Fabian, Frankie Avalon, Paul Anka, Bobby Rydell, Annette, the Lennon Sisters (no relation to John), and Ricky Nelson were riding the crest, *16* propelled them even further. After the Beatles and the British Invasion hit American shores between 1963 and 1966, *16* reinforced the mop-top myth rather than the subsequent psychedelic revolution that emerged during the 1967 Summer of Love. There would be plenty of time for that when *Rolling Stone* premiered in 1967. For *16* and its ilk, the famous could not also be infamous. Even such protopsychedelic bands as the popular Lovin' Spoonful were positioned as benign through omission of their drug sins. As a high school student, I personally knew two stars hyped in

16—and believe me, they were no saints. Indeed, some of *16*'s fave raves were eventually savaged in the tabloids.

But Gloria Stavers was the queen of clean. Her graphics never pandered to the psychedelia, even after it was mainstreamed by such teen magazines as the Hearst Corporation's *Eye.* She held sacrosanct the virtual innocence of her teeny-boppers, despite the increasingly "negative" publicity of her heartthrobs in the press and through the underground press.

Stavers did her best to promulgate the faith of her younger audience. Foresaking the older raves for fresh beefcake (as these youths with hairless chests were called) like Davey Jones, Bobby Sherman, David Cassidy, Donny Osmond, Leif Garrett, Shaun Cassidy, and John Travolta, by the mid-1970s *16* was resolutely teeny-bopper fodder.

Rolling Stone was the diametrical opposite of *16,* but it was no less a bulwark of the institution called fame. In 1969 I was art director of *Rock* magazine, a *Rolling Stone* wannabe, which also sought to elevate the bar of pop-culture journalism. Despite the pretentiously written, cerebral articles on such themes as the Rimbaud-like poetry of Country Joe and the Fish and the elegant typographic layouts, the magazine's covers flogged the hottest groups and singers of the day. Fame in *Rolling Stone* and in *Rock* may not have been as fetishized as it was in *16,* but it was a centrifugal force that sucked teens into its pages.

Today's teen magazines are still hyping stars, but the firmament is shorter now because the universe is larger. Surprisingly, given all that has changed in pop culture, the *16*-inspired teen mags are designed in much the same way as the original, only with slicker paper and more color photographs. Stavers, by the way, left *16* magazine in 1975, just as disco was rearing its faceless head, because she believed that the teen-idol cult was phasing out. If only she had stuck it out until the '90s, she would be back in the groove (and groovy), having a ball with Britney, Christine, N'Sync, and the Backstreet Boys. *Plus ça change . . .*

Cover of Gentry, *a very sophisticated magazine for men, art directed by William Segal in 1952.*

FOR 100,000 GOOD MEN

In the 1940s and '50s, *Gentry* set the standard for men's lifestyle magazines and became a cultural icon. Its innovative creator, along with his creation, are barely known today.

William C. Segal, who died in 2000 at age 96, is not nearly as well known an art director as his contemporaries Alexey Brodovitch or Alexander Liberman; his name does not appear in so much as a footnote in any design history textbook. Yet his influence on—if not his larger vision of—fashion magazines during the late 1940s and '50s equaled that of his more famous peers. Segal was not just a magazine art director and designer; he was the founder and managing director of Reporter Publications in New York City, as well as publisher and editor of its stunningly elaborate flagship periodicals, *American Fabrics* and *Gentry*. The former was an elegant "trade" magazine that combined articles on fine art and commercial textile manufacture aimed at elevating the "rag trade"; the latter was a general-interest quarterly men's lifestyle magazine that, owing to its broad themes and graphic special effects, rivaled the likes of *Esquire* and *Playboy*.

Segal's lack of recognition is confounding. Perhaps the fact that he held both the business and artistic reins somehow cancelled out his contributions in either realm. Or, perhaps, since he hired art directors and designers to work on projects, notably Alvin Lustig, he takes on the appearance of a client rather than a creator, and the number of clients cited in design histories is minuscule. But if the term "auteur" applies at all to graphic design, and arguably it does, then Segal's total participation in all aspects of his publications (from founding them, to selling ads for them, to laying them out) has certainly earned him that accolade. If he'd done little else but produce the quarterly *Gentry,* that feat of design stewardship alone should have ensured him a place in the design pantheon. But *Gentry,* which ran from 1951 to 1957, has been relegated to obscurity, while a similar periodical, Fleur Cowles's short-lived *Flair* magazine, was recently commemorated in an expensive facsimile collector's edition.

Magazines are ephemeral. To rise above its particular time, to be remembered and studied as a milestone, a magazine must be irrefutably unique. In that regard, the case for *Gentry* can easily be won on visual evidence alone: It was both daring and beautiful. But Segal's personal passion is what made it a paradigm of innovative publishing. As its editor, he belongs among an illustrious circle that includes Arnold Gingrich of *Esquire,* Diana Vreeland of *Vogue,* Hugh Hefner of *Playboy,* and Clay Felker of *New York,* all of whom imposed their wills, ids, and egos on their respective publications and, in so doing, shaped readers' tastes and perceptions.

Although Segal was this kind of editor, he was also somewhat different from the others in that he lived a remarkable parallel existence apart from his publishing life, which further informed *Gentry*'s content beyond the conventions of men's fashion. As a follower and confidante of G. I. Gurdjieff, the Armenian-born mystic who led an esoteric movement aimed at joining the wisdom of the East with the energy of the West, Segal devoted much of his time and energy to raising the spiritual level of everyday existence. He used *American Fabrics* and *Gentry,* in part, as outlets for personal exploration that he felt could help others cope with their lives. Segal practiced Buddhism[1] and sought out themes for magazine articles that delved deeper into human experience than was typical of the fare usually found in fashion publications.

But Segal was also a pragmatic businessman who found ways to align his humanistic and artistic pursuits with the constraints of trade publishing. "When we launched *Gentry,*" he said in an interview shortly before his death, "we visualized it as a magazine that could have a great cultural influence. At that time in the U.S., we were largely a nation of hicks. There was no culture. People did not know how to dress well, how to eat well, how to order wines or what to read. They were unfamiliar with the world of art. We thought we could have a civilizing influence through this publication." His practical goal was "to allow people to see the esthetic element that was a factor in choosing clothing. The importance of *Gentry* was to make the clothing part of the fine art of living."

Thus, he bolstered features on men's wear of the day with articles on a host of other subjects—art, history, philosophy, travel—as well as with short fiction pieces by leading authors. His wife, Marielle Baucou, in an unpublished biography of Segal, recalls the premiere issue of *Gentry:*

> All of Bill's life and interests were in that first issue: a riding lesson, building around his daughter Margaret; a page of music by Thomas de Hartmann, who arranged Gurdjieff's music; several pages on how to build a sauna, based on his own sauna; two pages devoted to twenty of Rembrandt's self-portraits; the first publication in America of *Siddharta* by Hermann Hesse. Already there was Bill's interest in Buddhism [in the following passage]: 'He strove in vain to dispel the conception of time, to imagine Nirvana and Samsara as one,' an idea that pleased Bill immensely. Finally, there was a section called 'Gentry Fashion,' addressed to men [who were] as elegant as the editor.

The son of Romanian immigrants, Segal was born around 1904 in Macon, Georgia (he couldn't give the exact date of his birth since his mother never celebrated or kept records of birthdays). His father moved the family from the South to Johnstown, Pennsylvania, and eventually to New York City, where Segal took business courses and studied Elizabethan theater at New York University. After graduating, he worked for a few years on a magazine called *Plastic and Wire* before he decided to start his own publication—in the menswear field. This initial publishing venture, in the late 1930s, was *The Neckwear Reporter,* a newsletter. Its success enabled him to expand his company, which ultimately produced six publications.

In 1946, with the help of his first wife, writer and editor Cora Carlyle, Segal started *American Fabrics,* envisioning a magazine that was more ambitious than his other trade journals. He chose an extra-large format and included a generous number of tipped-in fabric swatches, similar to textile catalogs, as a means to give tactility and dimension to an otherwise two-dimensional form. He also hired famous artists, including Salvador Dali, to create covers and interior spreads, believing that "such a magazine would at least have an artistic life, and would intrigue a number of people. Much to my astonishment," he later recalled, "the magazine took off immediately—there evidently was a market for a quality publication."

Five years later, when Segal founded *Gentry* because he wished to do on a broader scale what he had done for the trade, he used similar production techniques and expanded the range of special effects. He was determined, from *Gentry*'s very first issue, "to have a very top publication physically . . . the printing, paper, and production of all the material would be first rate."

But at two dollars a copy, it would have to be more than "first rate" (the cover price of most magazines in 1951 averaged twenty-five cents). Segal's challenge was to imbue *Gentry* with an allure for the affluent. He hired Alvin Lustig, who had designed Segal's spacious residence in Manhattan and cramped offices in the Empire State Building, to create *Gentry*'s first cover (now difficult to find), which he illustrated with a dramatically cropped photograph of a Greek head to symbolize the high level of its content. But what really caught the public's attention was a prelaunch subscription advertisement in the *New Yorker* that defined Segal's prospective *readers* as "first rate," implying that they would be less than elite if they passed up this magazine. The headline read:

> In October a new type of magazine will be published.
> It will either elate the top 100,000 thinking men in this
> country, or be a miserable flop. Frankly, we don't
> know which.

The text that followed was a hard-pitch sell to his status-conscious would-be constituents:

> You are one of the 100,000 men (we honestly don't
> believe there are more than that number) who are a
> blend of certain characteristics . . . These are men who
> have matured in their thinking: who have reached an

economic niche above the mass stratum; but, more important, who are ever in quest of a better way to live with themselves as well as with others . . . It is always *why, why, why,* with these 100,000 men who look no different from all the others; who may have more or less wealth than many of the others; who may do any kind of work, or no work at all, for their daily bread. They want always to *know* more, so that they may *contribute* more to people near them and to the world in which they live; they want to *give* more so that they can *gain* more from each breath, each hour each day, each year of their lives.

The rest of the ad described the contents of the magazine:

It is hard to give a picture of *Gentry* for the reason that there is nothing in the world like it. For example, when *Gentry* prints a story on fishing, our technique calls for the swatching of an actual trout fly in the book. Or, perhaps we talk about smoking; in this case it is quite natural for *Gentry* to enclose a tobacco leaf. . . . We do not believe that the best magazine reproduction in the world, full color or black-and-white, can do justice to a fine tweed fabric. So, when *Gentry* illustrates a new coat, an actual swatch of the fabric will be tipped alongside the photo to make it come to life. . . .

Much like the legendary *Portfolio* magazine (art-directed by Alexey Brodovitch from 1949 to 1951), *Gentry* incorporated surprises in each issue: booklets, limited prints, die-cuts, half-sheets, fabrics—even a flattened bag of oats to accompany a story about horses. It seemed as though money were no object.

"His constant aim was to humanize the design, never to make it slick, mechanical or merely pretty, never to lose communication with the reader, always to assist the eye and the mind with a change of pace, an ingenious interruption to break the expected sequence of visual images," said Cecil Lubell, whom Segal hired as editor-in-chief of *American Fabrics* and *Gentry*. "He has an unerring eye for scale and

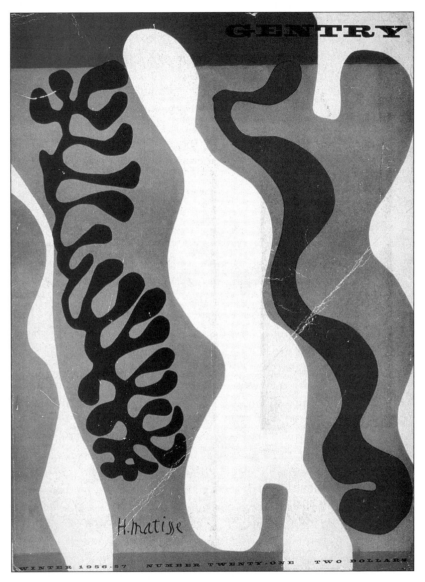

Gentry *with a cover by Henri Matisse, 1956.*

contrast, a rare talent for selecting just the right photo to enlarge and the lesser ones to take secondary place. The layout always came alive under his hand."

The demands of the business eventually forced Segal to cede some of the art directorial duties on *Gentry* to others, but he continued to monitor the visual content of the magazine. Though not listed on the masthead as art director for one of the final issues, Winter 1956–57, he was certainly instrumental in publishing a cover by Henri Matisse (as well as interior insert of Matisse's graphic art), an article illustrated by graphic journalist Felix Topolski, and another insert featuring drawings titled "Toscanini Conducting," by David Fredenthal.

"*Gentry* was a phenomenal success in one sense," Segal recalled, "in that it received reams of publicity . . . and truly had a superior audience. But the magazine itself was much more costly to produce than I thought. And perhaps while we had a great deal of advertising, we did not price per page sufficiently high." Even so, Segal was so consumed with *Gentry* that he sold off *Men's Reporter,* one of his successful trade magazines under the Reporter Publications imprimatur, to Fairchild in order to obtain needed capital. But when Time-Life czar Henry Luce offered to acquire *Gentry,* believing it would fill a vacancy in his publishing portfolio as a rival to *Esquire,* Segal refused.

Segal remembered a meeting with Luce that he had arranged in order to seek publicity in the Luce publications for a book by P. D. Ouspenky, Gurdjieff's prime disciple: "I noticed [Luce] kept pushing the book aside, and he kept wanting to speak about *Gentry.* And finally he brought the conversation around to the fact that he would like to publish *Gentry.* I would become one of the vice-presidents of Time-Life, and he would take over the magazine." While the offer was flattering, "Bill could imagine the array of business advisors, accountants, circulation managers, advertising managers and editors who would control the content and direction of his fledgling," said Robert Riley, a Segal friend who was curator of the Brooklyn Museum. "He ended the interview with an abrupt smile. [Bill] was amused. Mr. Luce was not."

For its readers, *Gentry* was a rich, sensuous experience—everything Segal had promised he delivered. For Segal, *Gentry* was a mission almost religious in nature to acculturate his audience. For Reporter Publications, however, *Gentry* was a financial albatross. "I kept putting more and more of the money we made on *American Fabrics* and other publications into *Gentry,*" Segal explained. "I suppose it fed my vanity, and my egoism." In 1957 he put *Gentry* up for sale. The buyer was the son-in-law of the owner of the Superman comic books, who had his own publishing company. Segal thought he did a very good job with the few issues he produced. "Nevertheless, they lost a million very quickly. The Superman publisher was discouraged, and eventually he asked me to take *Gentry* and *American Fabrics* back, which I did." *Gentry* folded shortly thereafter.

A few years later, Segal literally gave *American Fabrics* to a noted fabric artist and friend, Sheila Hicks, who struggled to keep it afloat. She sold it in 1980, some forty years after Segal had begun his publishing career. Ultimately, the magazine disappeared.

Today, various magazines, notably *Nest, Visionaire,* and *Flaunt,* continue in the Segal tradition of the devoted iconoclast editor flying in the face of convention. How the design history books will treat these magazines can't be predicted. If *Gentry*'s obscurity is any indication, they may well go unrecognized, even though the history of design has become more inclusive. One thing seems certain: If Segal had started *Gentry* today, he would be celebrated for his independence—and the buzz on *Gentry* would be deafening.

---

[1]A short documentary film by Ken Burns, *Vezelay: Exploring the Question of Search with William Segal,* made in 1996, examines this aspect of Segal's life.

Cover of Nest *with holes punched through it and the entire magazine, 1999.*

A MAN'S HOME IS HIS MAGAZINE

Nest, A Quarterly of Interiors, is a cacophony of visual excess and unrefined typography, the brainchild of its neophyte publisher/editor/art director Joe Holzman, a self-taught interior designer and decorator, who four years ago, untrained and inexperienced in the magazine and graphic design fields, switched from "chintz-slinging" to publishing. Despite its amateur beginnings, *Nest* has become one of the most daringly innovative and audaciously progressive new publications to hit the newsstands in recent years.

How does this square? *Nest*'s content and design derive from a curious logic that defies conventional standards. How else can one explain drilling four symmetrically placed holes through an entire issue (ads included), or wrapping another issue that has a full-frontal female nude on its cover in a buttoned-down fabric belly-band designed by Todd Oldham, or publishing a cover showing seven cat litter boxes filled with sparkling copper ink?

Nest is nothing like the leading establishment shelter magazines, *Architectural Digest* and *House and Garden,* or even the hip *Wallpaper.* Although *Nest* is printed on the same slick paper stock, it does not conform to the predictable canons of aesthetics (Modern or post-Modern) or accepted tastes. Nor does *Nest* exploit fashionably bawdy popular culture simply to inveigle its way into the youth market. *Nest*'s feature stories are not formulaic, nor are they presented in rigidly proscribed or repetitive layouts. The back cover, usually a magazine's prime commercial real estate, is never given over to an advertiser (sometimes it only contains a pattern or abstract design). And there is no such thing as a traditional front or back of the book (i.e., columns, reviews, factoids, or service features). Instead, the entire magazine, with the exception of the advertising sections in the front and back that sandwich the editorial well, is comprised of self-contained yet dissonant visual essays that are jarringly juxtaposed, both in terms of content and design, to disrupt the reader's complacent expectations.

Nest is also idiosyncratically personal, the unabashed expression of the forty-something Holzman's lifelong immersion into the history and practice of decorating interior spaces. *Nest* is a scrapbook of discovery wrapped in a magazine's skin, which is not to imply that it is a desktop fanzine (despite the fact that it is produced in an excruciatingly cramped apartment adjacent to the editor's apartment). In fact, nothing could be further from the truth! *Nest* is as slick and glossy as today's magazines come, but its design is purposely raucous, sometimes unkempt, to underscore Holzman's passionate obsession with the stuff that people compulsively, obtrusively, and eerily use to dress up their abodes, be they castles, igloos, or prison cells.

Holzman's own abode, a one-bedroom apartment, half a block from Central Park on New York's Upper East Side, resembles the visual essays in his magazine. Each small, claustrophobic room is crammed from floor to ceiling with bizarre, esoteric, and timeworn furniture, vases, paintings, frames, wallpapers, and ornament representing a clash of periods and an implosion of styles. Like the quirky magazine layouts and disorderly photographic settings, these rooms are stuffed with the homey and homely objects of a flea-market devotee, a reverie of boisterous ostentation. Yet, like his layouts, each individual accoutrement has a distinct purpose in the overall decorative scheme. Each thing deliberately contrasts with or complements the other objects in the environment.

One might say that this man's home is not merely his castle—it is the essence of his magazine and the personification of his editorial personality. *Nest* is predominantly influenced by its editor's first vocation, not by other contemporary magazines (which he says he rarely reads). In fact, he funded the first issue of *Nest* on earnings from the sale of his own apartment in Baltimore, where he was born in 1957, which had taken him five hermetic years to decorate because he had obsessed over every nook and cranny. The stories in *Nest* are developed with the same compulsive intensity, focusing almost exclusively on the concept of surface. Instead of worrying about the cut of a particular typeface or the kerning of a text block, Holzman agonizes over the placement of accoutrements on a page in order that his magazine exude the look and feel of a great interior. "I want a photograph to reveal the quality of the surface," he explains. "If it's really *velvetish* it will reflect light like velvet, and not be washed out and homogenized like so many architectural photographs that we're used to looking at." Holzman strives to simulate an actual physical, three-dimensional presence on each page. "The way I usually go about designing these pages," he continues, "is to find a background color or pattern that I think makes the whole idea more dynamic and makes the photograph sing." Yes, just like one of his rooms.

Although a magazine is not the best medium for this kind of virtual experience, Holzman's ingenious application of material and paper tip-ins, die-cuts, and foldouts contribute to Nest's tactility, which supports the reader's sense of being there. Since Holzman was not schooled in graphic design, he is not inhibited by its rules. He designs only for himself, not for any graphic design peers, pundits, or critics. And since he is own boss, he answers to nothing but his own taste. Having practiced a manner of interior decoration where oddity is a virtue, he has given himself the freedom to create a print environment in which anything goes. That is *anything* that conforms to his principles, which he believes ultimately contribute to the quality and appreciation of interior design.

"Sometimes things are propelled by ignorance," Holzman says about how *Nest* began, conceived on a whim in 1996, when he was working on his first and only book of interiors. The book was derailed, but the experience of editing and laying out pages gave him an appetite for print and inspired the idea to create a "smart shelter magazine" that did not accept the genre's conventions. With capital from the sale of his apartment, Holzman sought out the costly consultation of magazine publishing experts who told him that if he wanted to succeed he had to define his readers' demographic. Although it was a reasonable request, Holzman admits, "I believed that the reader was anyone that wanted to read it. The consultants, of course, countered that 'It doesn't work that way in the real world' and insisted on knowing whether the reader is this age, has that kind of economic background, and so on. I didn't think it had to work that way at all." The consultants also looked at the preliminary layouts, which they pronounced a disaster. "They didn't think I should be designing my own magazine," recalls Holzman, who said, "Fuck it, I'll do it myself." So he kept the money he would have spent on advice and put out a magazine "just to see if it flies."

He did get assistance from friends and hired staff, and, to help with the prototype issue, he hired a Baltimore designer who introduced a clean neo-Modernist typographical grounding. But Holzman was not keen on that approach and promptly injected an aesthetic that was much more cluttered and ornamental. He even insisted that the upper-right-hand corner (but *not* the lower) of the first issue be curved, like a catalog or notebook, which, although it made no logical sense, gave the pages their idiosyncratic character. Although he had been told his design was too anarchic, when he showed the prototype to people at Eastern News distributors, they were taken by the effort, and pushed copies into certain key markets, such as Barnes & Noble. Although the first issue hit the newsstands without any promotion or fanfare, it generated interest.

The cover photograph of the prototype was a black and white photograph of a bedroom completely papered on the walls and ceiling with rows and rows of fashion magazine covers featuring the former Charlie's Angel Farrah Fawcett—illustrating the issue's story devoted to the residence of a fanatical Fawcett fan. The cluttered image also included a full-color inset of Fawcett on a TV screen at the bottom of the image (printed with a fifth-color glossy varnish)—it was like nothing else around. The editorial of that issue declared that "*Nest* wants to be read by anyone who wakes up in the morning or in the afternoon with a healthy curiosity about how others express themselves where they live. We hope to show you things you've not seen before—perhaps not even imagined, as well as shed our own light on some familiar places. And, reader, be advised: Our houses have private parts. *Nest* is no waist-up publication." To Holzman's surprise, over the eleven months between the first and second issues, the entire 25,000 print run sold out, and so did an additional 10,000 more. *Nest* also began to get subscribers. Now the challenge was to keep the momentum going.

Holzman's exuberant design style masks a very reserved, if not downright shy personality. His chancy leap into magazine publishing not withstanding, he insists that he lacked confidence to take charge. The example he gives is the naming of the magazine. Although *Nest* is a perfect moniker, it was then and still is not his favorite choice. "The title is not what I would use if I were starting over," he says with dead-pan sincerity. "When I agreed on the word 'nest,' I had not learned to make decisions myself. In fact, I used to be afraid to let my advisors and staff know that I was the chief. So I kind of feel that I was pressured by them into accepting the word. Sure it works, but every time I say it, I stumble. I'm a little embarrassed to say on the phone, '*Nest* magazine.' People used to say 'Next?' 'Nast?' Okay, now, they get it."

Nonetheless, those simple four letters, N-E-S-T, embody the magazine's essence. And under this rubric, in just nine issues, Holzman has successfully created a publishing hybrid, a kind of off-kilter *National Geographic* of shelter magazines. *Nest* has attracted a good number of loyal "crossover" readers like myself. And while its current 75,000 circulation may not attract *Fortune* 500 takeover bids just yet, it is larger than many other niche magazines. The reason has to do with magazine's unadulterated honesty and uncompromising focus. There is not a story or page that panders to an imposed commercial trend or fashion, not a word or picture that manipulates the reader to consume something that he or she does not need. The stories report on phenom-ena created by people in an attempt to command their environments. While *Nest* focuses on objects, things, and spaces, it is really about the weird, nonconformist, and creative individuals who conceived them. Sure, the magazine propagates taste—Holzman's taste—but he is very quick to assert that while he designs every feature and chooses each photograph, the magazine has numerous voices: "I think that a lot of magazines, especially the shelter magazines, often possess a singular taste," he says. "Our range is broader."

The magazine has become laced with some well-known artists and photographers who, impressed with past issues, have approached Holzman to do work, including conceptual photographer Nan Goldin, architect and theorist Rem Koolhaas, and Simpsons creator Matt Groening (who created a flip book for issue number 8). As for the writ-ing, Matthew Stadler, a fiction writer from Seattle, is *Nest*'s literary edi-tor. "I give him unbridled license. He's as obsessed with words as I am with lampshades," says Holzman. In turn, Stadler has lured celebrated authors like Maureen Howard, Naguib Mahfouz, and David Plante, who are free to express their personal fascinations with decoration and ornament. Holzman insists that it is important to let them address these concerns in their own ways as long as they stick, at least margin-ally, to his overarching mandate. "Our writers can write what they want," he says. "But if it veers too far from the decorative arts, however, I'll supplement the story with captions." He further emphasizes that since more "art photographers," as opposed to architecture and interior photographers, are contributing to the magazine, his only editorial criterion is that "they document the full space and not just send back details." For Mies van der Rohe, god was in the details—for Holzman, heaven is the total environment.

Holzman's nests are drawn from various locales and numerous conceptual realms—none are pedestrian. Among the most curious is a "nautical bachelor pad" designed by Roger Weeden, carved from the bridge of an ocean-going tugboat. Another is an urban apartment completely wrapped in silver foil. And still another is an entire home with wall coverings made from common lead pencils arranged in hypnotic patterns. Holzman does not see them as freak show oddities but as integral works of personal expression. "I tend to look at a sociological or anthropological story as a decorative story," Holzman explains, referring specifically to features he's done on, among other things, an igloo and a treehouse. "Yet, while I push a story that would be anthropological in another magazine toward the decorative arts, I will look more anthropologically at a Fifth Avenue apartment." In just this way, Holzman, a relentless contrarian, recently commissioned a writer to live in a homeless person's cardboard box. "When the text first came in, Arlene Miles, the author, was being rather sociological, but I really wanted the text to be about *occupying* this box. What is it like tactilely? The story is not really about homelessness because that would be awfully presumptuous; after all, I had a guard on her all night. So she's not experiencing what it's like to be homeless. She's experiencing what it's like to live in the box, which is a shelter."

Holzman also takes pains to seek out both undiscovered and rediscovered shelters. One such rediscovery focused on the remarkable haute-Modern "see-through" apartment of Yale University's former dean of architecture Paul Rudolph, located in a building on New York's plush Beekman Place. Everything in this open triplex was constructed out of glass and other transparent materials, even the bathroom. The layout adroitly approximated the experience of being encased in glass. One of *Nest*'s newer old discoveries was shown in "Southern Gothic"—Diane Cook's photographs of a house in Florida's Upper Keys designed by Ed Leedskalin and made entirely from coral rock.

With this major emphasis on contemporaneous esoteric shelters, Holzman tries not to lose track of his favorite period, eighteenth-century design. "I like to show the Great Houses, but in a different way," he says. "It's interesting to a young reader to understand that these places were in bad taste, sort of Donald Trump when they were first built. Chippendale was new money." So for a story on the ancestral home of a British noble, Holzman convinced the current heir to dress up like his ancestor and pose amid the artifacts. "This is a way that we present this kind of house in a way that *Architectural Digest* would not dare."

Holzman does not think of himself as a tastemaker, even though *Nest* certainly exposes its readers to alternative tastes. Holzman has only one real mission: to redress what he believes are the diminished standards in the practice and aesthetics of interior design today. "I think the contribution that designers have made to design in the last forty years has been eclecticism," he notes. "I would like to see it end. I really think we have to learn how to design again, and not just assemble objects that look back or are revivals. I'd like to find a designer who can create. I'd like to walk into that room that hits you in the chest, and not because there's a great painting on the wall. What I really want to do in this magazine is find a great young talent. And they're hard to find."

Cover of The Progressive *with painting by Brad Holland, 1999.*

THE REGRESSIVE PROGRESSIVE

A redesign is supposed to improve a magazine. Yet frequently it is little more than a cosmetic cover-up for real and imagined deficiencies. Which seems to be the case with the *Progressive,* one of America's oldest and savviest leftwing political and cultural periodicals, which underwent a (type)facelift that may have taken the wrinkles out but removed the graphic personality as well.

For the last two decades, the *Progressive,* art-directed by Pat Flynn, was an engaging journal with an inviting and functional, though not slavishly stylish, format. Given its production constraints—notably no inside color—the magazine was clean, clear, and readable: no tricks, just tasteful, contemporary typography. It was also a wellspring of conceptual editorial illustration by a stable of keenly acerbic young and old artists. Flynn was certainly an illustrator's art director, trading low fees for creative freedom in what one contributor called a "politically righteous" context.

Although Flynn's preference for typography did not change much over the past twenty years, it was a deliberately neutral frame that gave emphasis to illustration. Although from time to time I would speculate about why Flynn had not introduced new design components, I also realized that this consistency was a virtue in a medium where frequent shifts in graphic style signaled editorial insecurity in other periodicals. Like its cousin, the *Nation,* the *Progressive* stuck to a lively, conservative, though contemporary, look that underscored its role as news and commentary provider and self-appointed watchdog of mainstream media. In a somewhat less partisan way, Steven Brill's *Content* has intruded into this realm with a snazzy new design, but not at the expense of the *Progressive*'s stalwart subscriptions. And I believe that Flynn's sober design and sharp illustration choices can be credited with some of this retention of readership.

Nonetheless, a little over a year ago, Flynn and a new editor, Matthew Rothschild (the *Progressive*'s former managing editor), disagreed about the magazine's visual direction. Irreconcilable issues of taste, as well as problems with polemical artwork, drove a wedge between the two, causing Flynn to leave his position. Of course, things like this happen when a new chief editor takes over and wants demonstrative shifts—or what is euphemistically referred to as "creative realignment." Sadly, though, Flynn's work for the *Progressive* was not the typical "job." After twenty years, he was truly committed to its mission, as well as to his promise to nurture young political artists.

For a few issues after Flynn's departure, the magazine, ironically, looked the same. Even most of the artists were retained. But in May of 2000, a change occurred. It was not a radical change, to be sure, yet it was clearly different in that it eliminated all the typographical nuances that distinguished the *Progressive* from a desktop publication. Flynn had a flair for using typefaces, differentiating columns, formatting pull-quotes, and all the other minor components that, added together, determine a house style. Flynn balanced artfulness with function. The new format, on the other hand, is not only artless—it is bland to the zero-degree. From the generic new logo and cover typography to the monotonous columns of gray type in the interior, the redesign is decidedly out of touch with anything contemporary—indeed anything of visual interest.

Where Flynn varied the presentation of feature articles by enlarging, reducing, and overprinting headlines and pull-quotes, the current format treats every feature exactly the same, with Franklin Gothic headlines and bylines mindlessly stuck flush-left at the top of the page. Even the anchored columns (commentaries, critiques, and the editorial) follow the exact same scheme. The only emphatic shift is the "interview" feature, with its indented columns and extra white-space margins. Comparatively, it is a breath of (fresh?) air. Flynn's design was well paced. And although the magazine rarely used full-page type or art "openers," there was a sense of movement through frequent shifts

Cover of The Progressive *with collage by Steven Kroninger, 1987.*

in scale. Not so in the new improved design. "Progressive" is not an appropriate word. In fact, even the table of contents is dulled down to the point that it resembles other staid political journals. Sure, it's readable, but it's uninviting.

The new format was launched auspiciously and inauspiciously, without fanfare but with a new focus. While Flynn's best covers were routinely strong polemic illustrations by the likes of Brad Holland, Jonathon Rosen, Henrik Drescher, and Sue Coe, the first new cover broke from that tradition with a photograph of folk singer Ani DiFranco. In his editorial, Rothschild explains that this is not the usual fare for the *Progressive,* yet DiFranco has been an outspoken musician for the left and deserved its coverage. Fine. But the photograph is duller than dull. Given how outrageous DiFranco can be, one might have hoped for a more powerful, eye-catching image. The second issue of the new format returned to a cover illustration, yet it was uninspired and, oh yes, a cliché (a hand holding a hammer poised over a piggy bank!). Odd, since the artist, Eric Drooker, is often quite caustic with his imagery—the difference signals an editor's heavy hand at work.

For over two decades, the *Progressive* lived up to its name in terms of its art and writing. Arguably, Flynn's original format might have been revisited with an eye toward functional and cosmetic renovation that would have made the magazine even more viable. But sadly, the new format is not simply retrograde—it's gradeless. In shedding all its design conceits (like its typefaces with subtle character), the change has reduced the articles to veritable text documents, which is not what a redesign should do.

One of Flaunt's *two tandem front covers.*

TRUST FUND FASHION MAG FLAUNTS DESIGN

Stomp. Crush. Flush. Kill. All fashion magazines are expensive, ugly and imbecilic; *Flaunt* is merely the most so. Among all the indie trustafarian sub–Condé Nast coke-dusted fashion/dance club/lifestyle fag rags out there, *Flaunt* makes *Black Book* look like *Foreign Affairs.* There is literally no sign of intelligent life in its skimpy and moronic editorial content, but you expect that from this genre. What's worse is that it looks like such shit, from its profligately pointless die-cut covers to its monstrously inhumane fashion spreads; it is everywhere assaultive to the eyes, the year's clearest evidence of that old saw that high fashion is the gay man's revenge on women.

—*New York Press*

So, other than that, Mrs. Lincoln, how'd you like the play?

It's hard not to be taken aback by this level of vitriol from the *New York Press,* Manhattan's free weekly broadsheet. Can there really be nothing whatsoever in *Flaunt,* an admittedly lush and ambitious twenty-something culture, lifestyle, and fashion magazine for both sexes, worth its $5.95 cover price? Or perhaps the newsprint *Press* suffers from a case of paper envy?

I've been following *Flaunt* since its premiere in the spring of 1999. And despite our generational fashion differences—I don't wear seven shades of black or short, brushcut, moussed blond hair—I have been very impressed with the art direction, photo editing, and design. And even some of its nonfashion content has merit, too.

Although *Flaunt* is a full-color magazine with the panoply of upscale consumer ads, including those for Guess, Absolut (what magazine does not have Absolut ads?), Dolce & Gabbana, Bacardi, Dockers, Jean Paul Gaultier, and Lucky Strike, we're not talking about a top flight–circulation, Condé Nast "downtown mag." This is, however, one of a few independents that are attempting to make inroads in the youth cult demographic. And the evidence, given its fairly good distribution and display in news shops and hair salons, at least in New York, Los Angeles, San Francisco, and Seattle, suggests that it has a fighting chance for success.

Given its smart design, it is certainly worth more than a casual perusal. *Flaunt* rejects the layered, cluttered, and otherwise so-called post-Modern design clichés that have stigmatized the perennially hip style and fashion magazines, *Details* and *Paper*. And it's managed to avoid the hybrid-Modernist tropes initiated by *Wallpaper,* such as the factoid pages with overlapping Eames-like color boxes and overstylized column headlines. With the exception of the cover—whose "pointless" die-cuts have, in fact, given its first four issues a distinctive personality—*Flaunt* is decidedly restrained, as hip magazines go. Despite the magazine's name, Eric Roinestad and Jim Turner, the "creatives," as they are listed on the masthead, do not flaunt the type, or even play with anarchic typography. Only one sans serif display face family is used in varying weights—light, medium, and bold; similarly, the text type is a justified sans serif, with the occasional Times Roman thrown in when there is a literary or documentary feature. The back-of-the-book columns—"Sound & Vision," "Music," and "Art"—are headed by little logos featuring gray arrows in vertical lozenges with the titles printed over them. But these spare, tasteful devices are the closest things to graphic embellishment in the entire magazine. Otherwise, empty space, so rare in magazines these days—particularly fashion magazines—is used generously and intelligently to distinguish editorial from advertising and to frame the principal feature of *Flaunt,* its photography, which is the single most profound editorial element in the magazine.

The fashion and product photographs in *Flaunt* are well styled and impressively presented, usually as full pages or double-truck spreads. The studio shots are indeed staged, but they're far from "monstrously inhumane." Sometimes they're mildly ironic recastings of the banal photography found in the vintage fashion magazines, such as the underwear feature in June/July 1999, titled "Correspondence," show-ing guys in their skivvies standing beside suburban mailboxes, or the male sweater models who are crying in the August 1999 feature "Lost Boys." In this same issue, the magazine ran a series of humorous, though respectful, photos of elderly women modeling de la Renta and Ferré frocks in their rooms at their nursing homes. This feature is at once jarring and warm, and suggests that *Flaunt* is not locking in step with the traditional magazines that emphasize flawless beauty and per-petual youth.

Since fashion photography today is a game of who can outcon-ceptualize whom, the fairly restrained quality of *Flaunt* is refreshing by contrast—at least for the moment. Of course, that's not to imply that all the photo features depart from convention. The August 1999 issue con-tains one fairly trite set of images in an article called "The New Tan" (subtitle: "Youth fades, beauty fades, your tan needn't"). But, even here, there appears to be a wink and a nod at typical features that employ the typical Adonis- and goddess-like, sun-baked, male and female torsos. In a feature in the October 1999 issue, titled "Viktor & Rolf: Haute Couture Winter 1999/2000," photographer Sarah Moon contributes a portfolio of eerie Muybridge-inspired sepiatone fashion photographs, as gorgeous and memorable as anything I've seen of late.

The magazine is not without somewhat serious content, either. In the August 1999 issue "Hour Town" is a travel feature on a short-term hotel, called Mermaids, in Cabo, Mexico, the workplace of showgirls of "a very high quality." The images are presented in a jour-nalistic manner, not designed to titillate but to inform. And a few pages later, in "Another Country," vintage photographs of early twentieth-century Tibet are featured throughout a few handsome pages that might have been pulled out of the *National Geographic*.

Unlike the established fashion and lifestyle books that cater exclusively to either males or females, *Flaunt* is decidedly for men and women, boys and girls. With the exception of the photos of the grand dames in the nursing home, which are entirely respectful, the men and women share the same characteristics, sometimes cardboard, other times animated. *Flaunt* runs its fair share of young celebrities, and these photos have not pushed the envelope very far. At worst, *Flaunt*'s images are like those annoying Gap commercials, in which bored slackers stand around singing in celebration of leather. But *Flaunt* is best when the photographs are parodies, such as Paris 16EME by Louis Décamps, showing all male models showing off black clothes while wearing cheap women's wigs. Okay—so far, Avedon they're not—but the times, they have a-changed, and an alternative approach is welcome.

So, let's get back to the cover. It isn't easy designing a magazine cover in this market. Publication designers routinely bemoan the fact that publishers and marketing experts demand that layers of cover lines announce every last asset of the magazine, which often obliterates the mandatory celebrity cover photos. So it is lauditory that *Flaunt* has assiduously avoided falling into the usual traps. Sure, every issue has a celebrity on the cover, but they've managed to avoid the common stereotypes. In fact, there are two covers for each issue—the special-effect one on top and a photographic one underneath. The use of die-cuts is not at all pointless: As teasers, they work much more effectively than the conventional half-sheet printed with cover lines, as the *New Yorker* puts on its newsstand editions. Because like the brown paper wrappers on *Playboy* and *Penthouse,* these curious special effects entice the reader to play a cover game. In fact, I bought the first issue, with a die-cut of leaves (or bamboo) covering the starlet Leelee Sobieski's face (actually, the same cover was printed in two versions with two different actors' faces—a male and female), because I wanted to see who was partially hidden. The die-cut is a minor pleasure, to be sure, but since that premiere issue, I have plunked down my cash in order to play the game. Moreover, *Flaunt* has not overdone the conceit. For the October 1999 issue, an Egon Schiele–like portrait of David Bowie adorns the front. On second glance the face (which is photographed inside) is per-forated so as to become a mask. It is a very nice touch.

Flaunt is not *Flair,* the brilliantly designed magazine edited by Fleur Cowles, which was published in the 1950s and which raised the standard of magazine-as-object with its many die-cuts and slipsheet special effects. But *Flaunt* does follow in that tradition while defining a contemporary aesthetic. Frankly, I'm not concerned whether it's financed by a trust fund, a MacArthur Foundation grant, or venture capitalists. For what it purports to be, for the audience it is trying to reach, and for this older magazine aficionado, *Flaunt* has evolved nice-ly into a magazine worth savoring—even saving.

The back of a basic Pokémon card showing a Pokéball.

POKÉMON: A DIALOGUE

From Godzilla to transistor radios to Honda motorcycles and cars, the Japanese have influenced American pop culture every bit as much as, and probably more so, than we have influenced theirs. And now with Pokémon, the Nipponization of America has reached an all-new pinnacle. Pokémon—which means "pocket monster" in Japanese, of which there are 151 characters that children are challenged to collect and trade until they have them all—originally began as a Nintendo computer game and TV cartoon show in Japan and quickly grew into a billion-dollar industry of toys, clothing, accessories, posters, and a feature motion picture. Of all the products, the Pokémon trading cards are the most sought-after treasures. Hundreds of cards in a variety of expensive (average $7) packs and theme boxes (average $25) have flooded the market over the past year. And every time kids think they've collected them all, a new series emerges. Older cards instantaneously increase in value upwards of $50 or more per card. The market for Pokémon cards is so enormous that counterfeit versions, which are expensive to produce given the graphic details and holographic printing on a large number of them, are flooding the market. The profit margin is so high for counterfeiters that Nintendo issues Internet warnings and maintains a hotline to report the sellers of the contraband.

Pokémon is comprised of fined-tuned, computer-generated illustrations and graphic icons that indicate the power of each monster and the strategies used in defeating and capturing the various characters. Kids collect the cards both to play the game and simply to savor them as objects. Here is one card game that has captured at least part of its audience through innovative design. Recently, my son—who buys, sells, and trades (he sold over $500 worth while at summer camp) Pokémon cards—and I discussed what makes them so appealing.

STEVE: *So why do kids like these things so much?*
NICK: They're cool because they are mutant-type people and animals.

STEVE: *What appeals to you about Pokémon cards?*
NICK: Say you open a pack and there's this card that you really want. It's exciting just to see it.

STEVE: *My favorite card is Electrode because it looks Bauhaus-influenced. What's yours?*
NICK: Yeah, right, dad. My favorite is Evilgoldbat. Because he has a really cool background. He's stuck in a tunnel with spider webs. And my favorite color [holographic green] is used for the background.

STEVE: *I like these cards because the type is well set. What do you think makes these so popular?*
NICK: I think it's the holographics. But they make a lot of merchandise that can pull kids in.

STEVE: *I see that there are Japanese and American cards. The Japanese are all in Japanese characters—which looks very hip. What other differences are there between the two?*
NICK: In every Japanese pack you get a holographic card. In the American packs you have a fifty-fifty chance of getting one. So, the Japanese ones are not as rare. I like the backgrounds of the Japanese cards better—they have little shiny stars and circles, and the Americans only have stars in the background.

STEVE: *Do you like the Japanese letters as much as I do?*
NICK: It frustrates me because I never know how characters are supposed to move. Most kids that I know don't play, they just collect. But I play.

STEVE: *Are these the prettiest cards that you've ever collected? They're the best designed I've ever seen.*
NICK: Yeah. They're all shiny and a lot of other cards aren't as shiny. Some cards are shiny on the outside and are not on the inside. The rarest card is shiny all over, and it's called Ancient Mew.

The front of a basic Pokémon card with Nidoran, one of 151 cute monsters.

Typical show card displays, 1930. They might not be sophisticated but they did sell the goods.

Show-card Lettering and Display is today an everyday business necessity and has fully established itself as a definite branch of the commercial art industry.
—James Eisenberg, instructor at the Edward Bok
Vocational High School, Philadelphia, 1945.

In the early twentieth century most commercial artists learned about type and lettering through a graphic arts genre known as show-card writing. This ubiquitous craft and common profession has gotten short shrift in most design history books, in part because Modernism (and the rise of sophisticated graphic design throughout the late twentieth century) was a reaction to it as crass, commercial, and void of artistic merit. And indeed there is some truth to this assertion. Nonetheless, show-card writing was an important, if indispensable, facet of mass visual communications for much of the twentieth century. Schools were devoted to it, books were written about it, and livelihoods were made from it. Moreover, it is not totally obsolete today. While graphic designers have become more involved in designing signs and displays, contemporary fabricators emerge from a long lineage of show-card makers, a movement that, in turn, represents an outgrowth of the nineteenth-century sign craft.

No one ever bothered to write a definitive (or even an anecdotal) history of the show-card (which was also called the sho-card). There was little need to record its milestones because show-card writers were not interested in history per se; they just wanted to earn viable livings working with their hands in a pleasant field. As the commercial art correspondence schools promised, students could "make $50 a week doing lettering" for stores, merchants, and businesses. All they needed was the know-how and tools. And so, for a small tuition fee these schools provided layout templates, typefaces, pens, brushes, and tricks galore—like how to dry paint quickly with the business end of a cigar butt.

Nonetheless there is a history, at least a practical evolutionary one, to be cobbled together. James Eisenberg, who taught the craft to his Philadelphia high school class, reported in *Commercial Art of Show-Card Lettering* that "Show-cards were formerly executed by the sign painter, who employed the same lettering technique as that used on other forms of sign work. The show-card was first pinned up vertically on a wall or easel and then tediously lettered by the sign painter, who used a rest or mahlstick to steady and guide the hand." In those days, he added, special show-card brushes and free-flowing show-card colors were nonexistent. To paint a show-card, the sign painter used slow-working oil colors or laboriously mixed his own colors from various pastes and powders. As the pace of industry and commerce quickened, the need for more elaborate show-cards and posters became proportionately greater. It soon became necessary to work with more speed and efficiency. To meet the demand, various artists began to specialize in specific genres and with certain media. Soon, new working methods, tools, and materials were introduced.

The innovations in show-card lettering were hardly as earth-shattering as, say, the New Typography, but they were important for the practitioners. Moreover, they established stylistic trends of their respective times. But better functionality was the most important historical development, as Eisenberg noted: "Instead of being placed upright, the show-card was laid flat on a specially prepared work table or bench. The mahlstick was dispensed with and the operator learned to work in freehand style directly over the card." To facilitate his work, specially prepared red sable brushes and show-card colors were manufactured. "All these things contributed to the development of the craft as a specialized branch of the advertising arts." Incidentally, a few of the later correspondence school brochures emphasized the past as a selling point: "The modern show-card artist," stated one brochure proudly, "works in clean dignified surroundings. The work is fascinating, providing an endless variety of experiences."

A show-card letterer might not have known how to distinguish the nuances between one cut of Bauer Bodoni and another foundry's variation, but he was usually well versed in the best kinds of novelty brush letters that would grab the greatest attention. He also knew what quirky lettering combinations would liven up a store window or display case. The show-card letterer was not interested in getting work into AIGA competitions designed for the upper echelons of fine printing and type design, but he knew how to make the most effective word pictures from type with "illustrative features," such as speed lines, nervous squiggles, icicles, and lightening bolts. He was also expert in the ABCs of card dynamics (e.g., where exactly to put those icicles for dynamic effect). The work extended to every facet of graphic arts—show-card makers were letterers, decorators, cartoonists, and authors. (A good slogan made all the difference on a show-card.) As Eisenberg stated in his book: "Attractively designed electric signs, window display cards, price tickets, paper streamers, store window backgrounds, theatre posters, decorative panels and titles, all these and many more, constitute the work of the show-card letterer."

Show-card work was usually of "a sedentary nature, requiring little or no physical exertion," hyped another correspondence school brochure. Although show-card writers did get their share of strained necks, pinched nerves, and bad backs, the fact was that they did their job in either a sitting or standing position in front of a waist-high adjustable bench or drawing table. Better than digging ditches, to be sure. "Since most of the work is executed on paper or cardboard surfaces with water colors, there are no harmful or injurious paint odors to contend with. This, in itself, is conducive to the health and well-being of the artist."

With the growth of a widespread commercial culture during the late nineteenth century, show-card advertising became a fast and economical means of announcing wares and selling products. In the early twentieth century, with the advent of vaudeville and motion picture theaters, chain stores, smaller shops, and thousands of other business enterprises, show-cards and displays rapidly became a big business. Frank H. Atkinson was one of the early exponents, and he developed standards for the fledgling field, taking methods developed by sign painters in the Victorian era and modernizing them in the early 1920s. In one of his many books on show-card writing and sign painting, *Sho-Cards,* he wrote: "There are no 'experiments' in the book; the practical and technical matter reflects the methods in vogue with the foremost 'talent' of the present day." He admonished the users of his books to be creative, but also acceptable.

Show-card writing was never intended to be a hotbed of avant-gardism. But it was simply an effective way of selling the goods, from "viands to violins, varnishes to vacations; to reach that much sought-after person, the man in the street." As one proponent of show-cards wrote: "The abstractionist with a dogmatic, nay—professorial—viewpoint, should beware of becoming too hidebound in his opinions, too bigoted. Such an idealist laying down rigid rules—thus and so must it be—makes himself ridiculous." Yet he advised that show-cards should not be matter of fact, either: "We are in the business to make money; ignore such counsel; go your own way, and keep to your own letter style. If your lettering should look so like type, all bespurred to death, all feeling crushed out of it, why not go to the printer and have our cards stamped out in lead."

Scores of books, booklets, and guides were produced for wannabe show-card letterers, providing them with countless pages of fetching options. "Ideas," by H. C. Martin, is typical of the genre. It offers profuse visual examples, with a text that is a huckster-like selling pitch for show-card lettering itself. "Display advertising is one of the greatest commercial forces of today. The display card is in itself a sales-man, who talks to every customer before he comes in to the store."

Despite the standardized forms, it is interesting to note that show-cards were not usually a ready-made or kept-in-stock product, but, wrote Martin, "must be made as required by the artist workman. In his brushes and paint lie unlimited possibilities. It remains for him only to mix gray matter with them and to give them concrete form. No two jobs are identical, types of letter legion. Now, to make the black card a 'picture' so to speak, expressing that imagination, that artistic craftsmanship, that capacity for visualizing the message in lettering into some sort of lettering design."

Despite its everyday use and anonymous craftsmanship, the show-card required great skill, and for some it demanded real imagina-tion. Martin insisted that "Lettering should be as individual as handwrit-ing; should be alive and vital and personal. The cardman should exercise greater care and strive more for the 'flavor' of this style of letter. Keep ver-satile. Don't get alphabet crazy, but be able to switch styles at will."

Show-card lettering will not be included in a graphic design history canon any time soon. It is like that embarrassing second cousin who is best kept from the family reunion. Yet it was (and to an extent still is) an aspect of design practice as consequential to commercial cul-ture as the more sophisticated genres, movements, and schools cele-brated today. What's more, it really took talent to do it well.

Hand-painted show cards were troves of novelty lettering.

Chinese pin-ups sold everything from coffee to candy.

THE CALENDAR GIRLS OF COLONIAL HONG KONG

In 1997, at the end of its ninety-nine–year lease, the United Kingdom returned Hong Kong to the People's Republic of China. At the same time, a warehouse owned by the venerable Asiatic Lithographic Printing Press Ltd. was reopened after decades, revealing a huge cache of mint Art Deco advertising posters and calendars from the 1920s to the 1940s. These graphic artifacts, produced prior to World War II, which are currently sold in antique flea markets around New York, San Francisco, and Paris, represent a period when colonial Hong Kong was the nexus of Eastern and Western commercial trade. They are also the lost treasure of a veritable dynasty of commercial printers, the Kwan family.

Artist Kwan Chuk Lam (also known as Lamqua) settled in Hong Kong in 1845, where he established the "Handsome Face Painter" shop that produced advertisements for the China trade. These were mostly portraits of a generic quality, created in the romantic style of his teacher, the English mannerist painter George Chinnery, and used to promote a wide range of imports and exports. The flourishing business was handed down to Kwan Chuk Lam's descendants, the most notable being Kwan Wai Nung, who during the 1920s was hailed as the "King of Calendar Art," for his distinctive portraits, mostly of beautiful women, that combined traditional Chinese brush painting with European art Moderne stylizing. He learned his craft from Western sources as well as the "Mustard Seed Garden Manual," an eighteenth-century Chinese guide that taught artists drawing and composition. Kwan Wai Nung was also the art director of the *South China Morning Post,* although he left in 1915 to found the Asiatic Lithographic Printing Press Ltd., which introduced five-color chromolithography to China.

Prolific is not a descriptive enough word to characterize Kwan Wai Nung's immense output. Over a twenty-year period, by his own hand or under his direction, he produced thousands of individual images. Each, however, conformed to a similar formula. Every model was elegantly dressed, purposefully posed, and colorfully painted in a romantically realistic manner. The models' demure yet sultry eyes rarely looked directly at the viewer. And Kwan preferred three dominant motifs: the single woman (known as "calendar girls"), two women suggestively together, and a woman and child. Men were barely present. Unlike most Western posters, the products being advertised were not incorporated into the main image; rather, blank spaces were left above and below for the typography and package reproductions. Most lettering was exclusively Chinese, except brand designations for the Western imports.

Kwan Wai Nung catered to a wide range of clients from a San Francisco medicine firm to the Hong Kong government's first anti-smoking poster. He also produced images for use by cigarette, liquor, cosmetic, confection, and even insecticide companies. It was not uncommon to find his images, which had been either bought or stolen, used on packages or promotions for very different products created by other printing establishments. In fact, Kwan's sons and nephews established a number of competing companies (and used many of the King's original designs), including the Mercantile Printing Company, Tin Chun Lithographic Press, and the Paramount Advertising Company. During the 1930s Kwan Wai Nung passed on his honorific as King to Cheung Yat Luen, a poster artist who continued painting calendar girls until the 1950s. These images continued to be used for a decade afterward, until they were replaced by photographic pinups.

An advertisement for insect spray.

An advertisement for cigarettes.

An advertisement for Scotch.

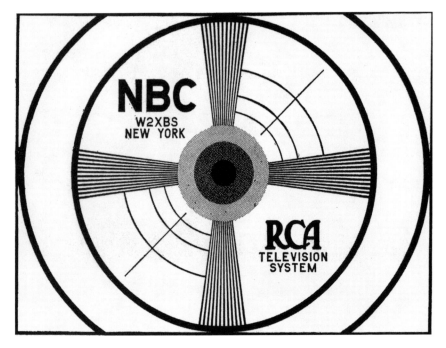

The first TV test pattern for NBC's W2XBS experimental station from the late 1920s.

THAT PESKY TELEVISION TEST PATTERN

What came first, television or the television test pattern? By all accounts, the once ubiquitous, static bull's-eye that appeared on kinescopes and cathode ray tubes from the 1940s through the 1970s, before stations began airing their scheduled programs (or when malfunctions occurred), may not have preceded the actual invention of television, which surprisingly began during the 1880s. But it was, nonetheless, the first real transmission that was seen on TV. Although the earliest dimensional image to appear on the screen in the mid-1930s on NBC's experimental station, W2XBS, was a rubberized model of Felix the Cat (the only object that would not melt under intensely hot studio lights), the test pattern was the most consistently broadcast image since the early 1920s.

The origin of the pattern is a story of form following function. Aesthetics were irrelevant to the primary purpose, and the technical draftsmen who anonymously designed it could never have predicted that, decades later, it would become a nostalgic icon. The intent was to enable engineers, who in the so-called "pre-television" days were the only persons to actually receive broadcasts, to calibrate the extremely small, very crude black-and-white scans that became the TV picture. While the circular target may seem odd, given the rectangular shape of even the earliest screens, the initial test patterns in fact conformed to the circular shape of an oscilloscope that showed engineers the electrical equivalent of an image in the form of a wave. But there was an even more deliberate rationale.

In the 1920s, test patterns (or test charts, as they were referred to then) were more or less varied, but in the late 1930s, when a few hundred receivers became commercially available, a standard was embraced by broadcasters. The chart was designed both to check transmitter performance from the studio to the antenna and to allow the audience to determine the degree of performance of their individual receivers. In addition to the advantage of being a static signpost of sorts, the chart revealed geometrical defects, horizontal and vertical degrees of picture resolution, and a range of shading gradations.

The archetypical chart used by NBC/RCA, which in the 1930s had merged to form the first television "network," consisted of an outer circle that had a diameter equal to four-thirds the diameter of the inner circle; the former touched the sides of the screen and was cut off on top and bottom, while the latter touched the top and bottom of the screen and remained well within the side boundaries of the television. This conformed to the standard aspect ratio of 4:3. If the picture was too narrow (less than the aspect ratio), the circles took on an elliptical shape, with the major axis of the ellipses in the vertical direction; the converse was true if the picture was not high enough. The chart was, therefore, a diagnostic device to determine whether the transmitter scanning was too wide or narrow, too great or too little. The large circles had another important use. The scanning of the beams at transmitter and receiver had to move at a perfectly uniform rate or else the image would be expanded or condensed. If the circles were egg-shaped, then the scanning was not uniform. The perceived defects could then be fixed by precision controls on the transmitter. Presumably, home receivers required only a one-time setting upon installation, but invariably dials would shift so that the test chart would aid the viewer in making the necessary adjustments.

The interior of the pattern was divided into sections. The innermost, shaded circles, consisted of three concentric circular areas of differing density: The central area was black; the next bore an intermediate gray tone; and the outer was white. These were used to measure and set the contrast controls either at the transmitter or receiver. If the contrast control was set too high, the two inner areas turned to black, eliminating any degree of shading. Conversely, if the contrast was low, the picture became very flat or gray.

The bars that shot out from the bull's-eye in four directions, called "definition wedges," consisted of vertical and horizontal black and white lines, arranged to increase in width as they moved out from the center. The horizontal lines were used to measure vertical resolution, and the vertical lines measured the horizontal; the measurements were based on scan lines (a maximum then of 350 lines) of the screen. Like registration marks, the wedges highlighted faulty resolution and electrical focus that could be fixed at the point of origin. If the home users had read the TV manual, they would know how to use the test chart, which in the early days of television appeared more frequently than the live programming. But by the 1950s the test pattern was shown only in the early morning or very late at night, and most users randomly fiddled with the knobs and antenna, ignoring its functional benefits.

By the early 1950s, every TV station in America was using a version of the same basic test chart, until twenty-four-hour broadcasting made it obsolete in the 1970s.

JULIAN ALLEN'S PICTORIAL LEGACY

A visual artist's legacy can be measured by the number of familiar mental pictures conjured up by his work. The illustration field is stocked with so many generic images tied to forgettable texts that it is a major feat to emerge from a long career with even a handful of pictures that are distinct from the mass and that transcend their original function. It is indeed extraordinary to have produced dozens that both stand the test of time and define the time in which they were produced. Julian Allen, an editorial illustrator, visual journalist, and representational realist who died of cancer in 1998 at the age of fifty-five, had a gift for making mysteriously compelling pictorial narratives often within the confines of a single image (although he created two comic strips, as well).

Allen had a unique style but was not a modish stylist. He was caught between the desire to tell important stories and the need to create exemplary art. He understood that the camera had made total verisimilitude in illustration unnecessary, so he developed a method whereby he recreated and then commented on the world as he saw it. Allen proved that realism was not dusty, musty, and obsolete—nor rigidly objective—but was rather a means to make personal statements through a universal language. His most memorable illustrations are not mere solutions to typical editorial problems, but those in which he invested himself as witness. Here are ten pictures out of dozens that for me continue, years after they were first published, to have this resonance.

THE NIXON BLUES (1972)

Unlike the Clinton/Lewinsky scandal, where mental pictures served no useful purpose, during Watergate the world hungered for images of a besieged President Richard Nixon and his White House henchmen carrying out their illegal acts. At the height of the congressional hearings, when a stunned America learned that Nixon had taped all Watergate-related conversations, and the president's resignation or impeachment was on the horizon, Allen brought the event vividly to life through a series of illustrations. Commissioned by Clay Felker, editor, and Milton Glaser, design director, of *New York* magazine, Allen's job was to recreate the key events in a scandal replete with remarkable highlights. He made concrete Watergate's most private and secret moments and gave the readers of *New York* a voyeuristic opportunity to see what was only suggested through testimony. But not all his illustrations depicted sensational events; this cover art showing Nixon playing the piano was based on reports coming from the White House of how an increasingly despondent president whiled away his sorrow with drink and music. This may not be Allen's crowning achievement as an artist, but along with his other Watergate depictions, it is one of his most important contributions to the history of that period.

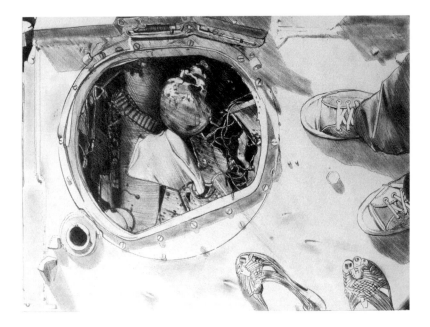

THE SEVEN DAYS WAR (1973)

Strict news blackouts imposed during the Israeli/Arab Yom Kippur War prevented press photographers from getting film out of the war zone. So, *New York* magazine editor Clay Felker dispatched Nora Ephron to report and Allen to visually record Israeli operations in the Sinai. The war had been contained, so the danger to journalists was lessened, and Allen enthusiastically jumped at the opportunity to continue the tradition of the great nineteenth- and twentieth-century war artists. A few days into the assignment, the vehicle in which he was traveling through a desert battlefield hit a land mine, inflicting severe leg wounds. He was treated at a field hospital shared by wounded Israeli soldiers and Egyptian prisoners, and there he began drawing pencil sketches of his fellow patients that were later published along with an article he wrote for *New York* magazine. These simple, real-life moments were testaments to the horrors of violent conflict and the resilience of the human spirit.

THE RAID ON ENTEBBE (1976)

When Israeli commandos liberated the passengers of an El Al airliner held hostage by Red Brigade and Palestinian terrorists at the Entebbe, Uganda, airport, probably the first thing the world longed to see was live footage of the event. This was in the 1970s, before CNN broadcast every major international happening live, and repeated it constantly throughout the day. It was also a few years before two made-for-television movies dramatized the episode. Again, Clay Felker, understanding the voyeuristic urges of his readers and the journalistic value of re-creation, assigned Allen to render in one double-page painting a critical moment—the literal split second when Israeli forces stormed the airline terminal where the passengers were held. Since there was no photographic record, Allen returned to Israel to interview surviving passengers and commandos in order to piece the event together from their unique vantage points. Accuracy was essential and the result was a vividly detailed, ersatz eyewitness account that not only illustrated but illuminated the story.

THE DEATH OF TODD CLARK (1984)

Allen was not solely a war artist, but his ability to capture the grit and horror of war was unmatched—in fact, untried—by other editorial illustrators. Although he was unable to gain access to Beirut during its deadly civil war, he was commissioned to illustrate the death of a Canadian journalist, Todd Clark, who was kidnapped and murdered by a militia faction. Allen once said about recreating events, "There's a strong emotional element in a lot of my work. It doesn't just stop at the re-creation of a scene. Very often there is a definite mood with which I try to provoke reactions." Indeed, the cold blue that bathes the killing room in which Clark's bloody, motionless body lies face down on a pillow, a bottle of mineral water beside the bed on the floor, and a bloody pillowcase casually thrown over a chair, is as horrific as Allen's most action-based pictures. The haunting stillness of the image is what makes its so unforgettably sad.

IRANGATE (1986)

President Ronald Reagan bartered guns for money that paid for the Contra insurgency against the legitimately elected Sandinista government in Nicaragua. In doing so he broke laws against doing business with a rogue nation, Iran, and interfering in the internal affairs of a sovereign nation, Nicaragua. Congressional investigations into Irangate produced much testimony during the Iran/Contra hearings and elevated to prominence one American hero/antihero, Marine Colonel Oliver North. For some people he was the good soldier who stood up to a democratic inquisition; for others he was the embodiment of foolishly blind patriotism. During the hearings his stalwart good looks made him the darling of conservatives, but for opponents he was a picture of deception. Allen was asked to recreate the hearings, but he chose instead to focus on North as a figurehead, and caught the man's contradictions in one painting. This is not a caricature because Allen understood that no amount of exaggeration could depict North better than his actual features.

RONALD REAGAN (1988)

Allen enjoyed painting Ronald Reagan. What was not to enjoy? The president's features were made for caricature, but Allen rarely, if ever, exaggerated him because he felt it wasn't necessary. Reagan's face spoke volumes. As with Watergate, it is hard to single out a single Reagan painting, but perhaps the most memorable is a scene done for *Newsweek* that Allen recreated from news reports, an image that captures the president in his hospital bed following tests for what was reported as a minor heart malfunction. Here Reagan confers with two of his top aides about the Iran/Contra hearings. The president slid easily, unscathed through the investigation, owing to his convenient memory lapses, which Allen suggests had a basis in truth. Humor and humanity are exuded in this picture of the world's most powerful figure, candidly depicted in a vulnerable situation.

THE PROFUMO SCANDAL (1963)

Allen was an illustrator who could command attention, not simply fill in an empty space, because he embodied the voyeur in all of us, and he had the talent to open a window onto what we all wanted to see. Wherever there was a chink in the human armor, he was there to record it. Allen would probably have been happy working on a tabloid newspaper—as fascinated as he was with scandal of all kinds, especially those involving government officials. Had he lived, he would have had a field day with Bill Clinton's indulgences. Allen created an entire series of "Scandal" paintings for a book that he hoped to get published but was just slightly ahead of his time (scandal is now the lifeblood of TV news). One of the most compelling of these illustrated exposés is a recreation of the doozie of all British scandals, the Profumo Affair, in which the government's high-ranking war minister was discovered keeping a call girl, Mandy Rice Davies, who was believed to have serviced Russian callers as well. Allen chose and froze his key scenes carefully, and his painting reveals the critical episode and the first time Profumo met his paramour-to-be, who ultimately caused his downfall.

FATAL COUPLE (1990)

During the late 1970s and early 1980s, Allen was obsessed with Punk culture and music. He was fascinated with Johnny Rotten, who was called "the only real punk" and painted him in at least three different tableaux. However, Allen nurtured an even deeper interest in Rotten's Sex Pistols band mate, Sid Vicious, whom he had witnessed at a New York dance club slash another partygoer with a drink glass. Vicious lived up to his name and image. In contrast, Allen was a coolheaded, mild-mannered guy, but he was drawn to Punk's underbelly for reasons that he only vaguely alluded to. Based on the Sid Vicious episode, he began an unpublished book called *Famous Brawls of New York*. Yet what captured his imagination even more than the brawling was the famous suicide pact, which was later portrayed on the silver screen, between Sid and girlfriend Nancy Spungen at the Chelsea Hotel in New York. Allen's painting, titled "Fatal Couple," showing a strung-out Sid and Nancy in the lobby of the hotel, subtly captures their nihilistic abandon, a fitting icon of that period in cultural history.

GERTRUDE STEIN AND FRIENDS (1968)

Allen came to the attention of Milton Glaser, who then brought Allen to the United States from London, because of his incredible paintings of improbable situations done in the late 1960s for the *London Sunday Times* magazine. This illustration for an article about the famous Stein family is typical of images in which Allen amassed a gaggle of celebs, who may or may not have ever been together in real life, into one convincing tableau. In this instance, Gertrude Stein and Alice B. Toklas (in the car) look on as the literary luminaries of the 1930s (Hemingway, Fitzgerald, Joyce, etc.) sit and stand around them. Allen meticulously rendered each figure with flawless verisimilitude from numerous photographs, and the fun, the game so to speak, was the identification.

THE LAST BRUNCH (1995)

Lest anyone think that Allen drew only from real life, this painting conceptually depicting the art scene in New York City proves otherwise. It is an example of the artist's unique ability to create an icon (based on the religious and cultural senses) through wit, humor, and imagination. In Allen's later years, he was increasingly called upon to comment on more mainstream cultural situations. This assignment from *Vanity Fair* employed his signature talent for amassing celebrities together in a single improbable image. The masters of art's glitterati are all assembled here, from SoHo art dealers Ivan Karp (as Christ) and Mary Boone (under table, left), to the artists Andy Warhol and Keith Haring (on ladder) in a recreation of the Last Brunch. Allen loved to parody, and with his skill at rendering, he could do something like this without straining the idea one iota.

Not a bad legacy for an illustrator.

PEOPLE

SECTION III

Boris Artzybasheff was a master of metamorphosis.

BORIS ARTZYBASHEFF'S CLEAR COMPLEXITY

The theme of design clarity suggests that attention be paid to the usual suspects, among them George Tscherny, Ivan Chermayeff, Rudy DeHarak, and Massimo Vignelli, who adhere to the tenets of clear, clean, rational Modernism. Yet clarity is not the provenance of Modernists alone, nor is it characterized solely by minimalist layouts with Helvetica (or Bodoni) type. Clarity is the art of conveying unfettered information *and* unclouded interpretation through whatever means captures attention and imparts lucidity. So, let's be perfectly clear: Design clarity comes in a variety of forms (and styles), and some of them may, on the surface, be unclear.

Are we clear about this?

The work of Boris Artzybasheff (1899–1965), a Russian-born, American painter and illustrator, is neither Modernist nor anti-Modernist. In fact, his book and advertising art, and especially his *Time* magazine covers (from 1941 to 1965), are Baroquely detailed and realistically rendered because these motifs constitute his preferred visual language. Most of his art is so rich in graphic detail that it seems like a multilayered cake of information. Therefore, when I was once asked to write a "Historical Critique" about someone who exemplifies clarity, Artzybasheff did not immediately spring to mind. His oeuvre, which I had wanted to write about for many years, fits into other potential thematic categories, such as fantasy and complexity. After considering (and rejecting) the obvious choices, however, I realized that in order for

Artzybasheff's brand of complexity to be appreciated, it had to be certifiably comprehensible. His penchant for allusion and metaphor not withstanding, Artzybasheff leaves nothing in the shadows, no questions go unanswered, and no mysteries are left unsolved. Indeed, clarity bolsters his bizarre and macabre interpretations of reality, giving him needed credibility as a graphic commentator in the national media.

Nonetheless, I am usually asked to write "Historical Critiques" about graphic designers (or designers who illustrate as part of an overall design process). Narrative illustrators per se are eschewed, because critique is concerned with the marriage of all design media into one discipline. From what little I already knew about the tall, slim, pince-nez–wearing Artzybasheff—who was born in Kharkov, Ukraine, Russia, and who briefly studied law but decided he wanted to become an artist "ever since [he] stopped wanting to be a fireman"—I presumed that he was more of a visual storyteller and caricaturist than a graphic designer. And while I believe that the keenest illustrators have design acumen, I was concerned that my subject might not exactly fit into this particular forum. Until, that is, I came across the following statement in a 1945 edition of *Current Biography:*

> "I hate art for art's sake!" says Boris Artzybasheff, whose drawings have won almost unanimous critical praise; but he hates almost equally being pigeonholed as an illustrator, although he has decorated half a hundred books, has painted many covers for popular magazines, illustrated many advertisements, and is one of the four leading designers of book jackets. The explanation is that he looks on himself as a designer, "as every true artist is," whose field is "any object which is beautiful and useful," and resents having "either the beauty or the meaning stressed at the expense or the other."

Eureka! He was a designer. And beauty *and* functionality were indeed the most critical elements of Artzybasheff's work—which in addition to book and editorial illustrations included designing women's dresses, stage sets, a nightclub interior, a mural, and a cathedral altar. In fact, he built up a reputation for "making complex relationships clear," states *Current Biography,* through "extremely useful" statistical charts and graphs for *Fortune* magazine in the late 1930s and then during World War II for the geographer at the Department of State. He developed an atlas used by the U.S. Army Training Command, which gave military strategists invaluable information about European terrain. His precisionist chart-making skills came in good stead when, simultaneously, he created visual satires for *Life* and *Time* magazines, which were jam-packed with farcical details. In these pictures Artzybasheff transformed war machines into men and animals that vividly personified the horror of the enemy's weaponry. Such was the emotional impact of his comic pictures that several American Army and Navy units asked him to draw insignias, which had to be clear enough to be recognized on the battlefield.

Artzybasheff, whose first job after immigrating to the United States in the mid-1920s was doing lettering, ornamental borders, "and other hack work for $15 a week" at an engraving shop in New York, maintained that "idea content" was paramount above all other graphic considerations. Style was a vehicle, not an end in itself. But his work exudes unmistakable style born of technical mastery and macabre vision. His "favorite gambit," as a *New York Times* critic referred to his obsession with anthropomorphism back in 1954, is "the reliable move of giving eyes and ears and hands and demonic expressions to rampant machinery." Artzybasheff sarcastically explained in his 1954 monograph, "As I See," that "being slightly myopic, all I have to do is to take off my glasses and the world around me looks that way." Whatever his true reasons, he had an uncanny ability to render the minutest detail with such exactitude that the viewer was forced to read a picture as though it were a page of hieroglyphics. And while these glyphs required some translation, they were never so dense, arcane, or absurd as to hinder comprehension.

Artzybasheff's work was often labeled as surreal, yet he vehemently objected to this category because he contended that his "burlesque or grotesque" style was introduced long before Salvador Dali's. And, more importantly, unlike Dali, Artzybasheff communicated unambiguous messages through the mass media rather than artistically contrived renditions of convoluted dreams. While at times his images were Disneyesque—such as his 1956 *Time* cover titled "Russia's Khruschev," which is a little too comically facile and formulaic—his best work, like the 1960 *Time* cover for "Rush Hour in Space," has just the right balance of truth, fantasy, and prescience. Each spaceship in the latter cover was an individual comic statement, which when joined together in the overall design became something of a manifesto about the problems of the space race. Yet while he desired that viewers decipher and interpret his pictures, Artzybasheff nonetheless declared that he was annoyed when being interpreted by so-called amateur psychologists. Said he: "I get irritated with those damn Freudians. They try to see something in everything. I think there is something wrong with their minds!"

This sounds a bit disingenuous. Artzybasheff was, after all, a master of visual tomfoolery who demanded a certain degree of audience interpretation. In fact, when commissioned by *Time* magazine in June 1941, after a stint at drawing caricatures (or "impressionizing," as he called it) for the *New York World,* he proposed that they allow him to draw what he called "expressive backgrounds," or additional symbolic and metaphoric props. Because *Time* had a tradition of straightforward portraits, Artzybasheff explained that he had to fight the editors until they relented. Which they did, and from then on all covers included backgrounds. But for Artzybasheff the backdrops were markedly important because they afforded the opportunity to inject personal commentary into otherwise neutral portraiture. This worked best when he was dealing with villains, like Joseph Stalin, whom he skewered on numerous occasions. But he had sly fun with less obvious pariahs as well, such as the 1960 cover of the R. J. Reynolds CEO Bowman Gray, who, by contemporary standards back then—when cancer was just emerging as an issue—was being surreptitiously attacked when positioned against a backdrop of lit cigarettes. Some of these backdrops were indeed quite clever, such as the 1964 futuristic landscape behind R. Buckminster Fuller's geodesic-domed head. Others were silly or mundane. But Artzybasheff's most significant and signature images for *Time*—and he selected the ones that he wanted to do—were illustrations about machines, which Otto Fuerbringer, the managing editor of *Time* during Artzybasheff's tenure, said reflected the trepidations of the machine age: "[He] held his own true mirror up to the twentieth century. In depicting the machine he had no peer. He humanized it, showed it as a monster, and laughed at it." Artzybasheff was clear about his relationship to them: "I am thrilled by machinery's force, precision, and willingness to work at any task, no matter how arduous or monotonous it may be. I like machines."

None of his work would be credible if Artzybasheff had allowed an iota of obfuscation. He instinctively knew how far to push the imagery while remaining realistic. Remember, he was not a typical realist. He prospered in mass media during a period when Norman Rockwell's many imitators ruled editorial and advertising media, perpetuating clearly banal realistic sentimentality. Artzybasheff was a precursor of the alternative form of "conceptual illustration" that blossomed in the mid-1950s with Robert Weaver, Tom Allen, and Robert Andrew Parker, and later exploded with the likes of David Levine, Ed Sorel, Robert Grossman, Barbara Nessim, Brad Holland, and Marshall Arisman throughout the 1960s and on to the present. Clarity was a part to Artzybasheff's success, but his ability to hold the audience's attention through intricate, visually provocative inventions—and not confuse them in the bargain, as lesser conceptual artists might do—was key. In summing up his work, a writer in *Life* magazine said, "The measure of his ability to put his point across in paint is that the more closely the paintings are examined, the more clever their details become."

Alvin Lustig in the doorway of the studio he designed, 1950. Behind him is a curtain he designed, too.

THE INTERIOR LUSTIG

I used to fantasize about my grade-school teachers getting undressed in front of the class. It was my preadolescent way of defrocking people in authority. Now, whenever I find a vintage piece of graphic design that piques my interest, I imagine the designer (fully clothed) in the throes of making it. Although creating art and design is not exactly undressing, it does reveal an intimate side of oneself. The act of creating is mysterious, and while I have no desire to debunk or demystify the creative process, as one who writes about graphic design history, I feel the need to know how the past masters performed their feats. It is also illuminating to see *where* they performed them. Since I have been unable to watch firsthand many of these important designers working in situ, I have found an alternative source of inspiration: old photographs. Much can be learned about designers through analyzing the photographs of their respective workspaces. Although studios are often designed as showrooms to impress clients, they are also private sanctuaries wherein designers dress and undress, as it were, or create and recreate. Indeed a workspace embodies the work spirit.

Alvin Lustig (1915–1955), one of the prototypical American Modernist graphic designers, designed a number of workspaces for himself and others that speak volumes both about the man and the postwar design epoch that he represented. Although best known for his experimental typography, photomontage, book jackets, magazine covers, and opening titles for the cartoon *Mr. Magoo,* as a former student of Frank Lloyd Wright, he was passionate about architecture and interior design. He designed the signage for Northland, one of the Midwest's first mega-shopping malls, the interior and exterior of the chic Sheela's shoe store in Los Angeles, and the rooms at the Beverly-Carlton Hotel in Beverly Hills. In addition he designed offices and apartments and planned the interiors for his three studios in L.A. and New York. These were not ad hoc or predigested schemes. In each space, he designed most of the tables, chairs, drapes, lighting fixtures, and wall coverings, which underscored his aesthetic preferences and ethical concerns (i.e., that good design was a benefit to society). And while these rooms were routinely photographed without any people present to highlight Lustig's formalism, it is clear that they were designed with people in mind.

Actually, one of the most revealing photographs (from 1947) shows a dapper thirty-two-year-old Lustig leaning against the narrow doorway to his Los Angeles office under a simple wooden sign with his name carved out in letter-spaced Bodoni. He is wearing a natty sport coat, white shirt, and short dark tie, typical of the era. Behind him, immediately upon entering the space, is a textile made into a curtain, which he designed and titled "Incantation." It is a field of abstract linear glyphs, influenced by Franz Kline and Paul Klee (which was mass produced by Laverne Originals, the manufacturer of some of his furniture). Both casual in posture and formal in demeanor, Lustig plays the role of the impresario in front of a stage where Modernism is performed. Used as a publicity photo at the time, it became something of an emblem of the Modern movement, because this glimpse into his workspace reveals something other than the typically dreary "art service" studio of the late 1940s. Instead, it is a hothouse where form and function are sublimely wed. This photograph further suggests that Lustig, a proponent of postwar "Late Modernism," was poised to alter the way that advertising, publishing, and industry communicated to the public, and this office was both a monument to and the nerve center of that new approach.

Lustig firmly believed that the workspace must echo the designer's total sensibility. His 1947 Los Angeles office expressed his complete immersion into Modern art. His private workroom is an array of harmonious modern forms. The desk, with its simple lines and cantilevered drawers, is inspired by contemporary architecture. The chairs are drawn from a modern mold. The floors are grid paintings reminiscent of Mondrian, with alternately colored intersecting lines that echo the linear quality of the back wall, which was comprised of parallel lines interrupted by a dark panel marked with numerical measurements. On the opposite white wall, an enlargement of one of Lustig's glyphs contrasts with the small African and pre-Columbian sculptures and Mexican straw baskets that punctuate the otherwise pure geometric ethos of the room. Incidentally, Lustig's desk is characteristically free of any artist's materials, save for a pen and pad of paper. This was not an effect done for the photographer. He was indeed fastidious.

Although he eschewed nonessentials, Lustig was not a devout minimalist. His 1943 Los Angeles office, an apartment that included a kitchen and two small rooms, was replete with the objects that defined his aesthetic, including the pre-Columbian artifact that reappears in all his spaces and a reproduction of a Rousseau painting. Still, nothing was ephemeral or without purpose. The floor-to-ceiling drapes opposite a brick fireplace gave the illusion of more area than there really was. A dark floor with lighter throw rugs gave the impression of higher ceilings. The overall effect was of a "living" room, rather than a working room. But for Lustig the two were mutually inclusive.

In 1944 Lustig was hired to develop new projects and design *Staff,* the in-house publication for *Look* magazine. He moved back to New York on the condition that he would also design his own office. At this time he was experimenting with the idea of a fluid environment. Unlike more traditional offices in the same Madison Avenue building characterized by blocky wood desks, high-back upholstered chairs, and imposing hardwood bookcases, Lustig designed the furniture to virtually float on air (well, at least on thin legs). The photographs taken by Maya Deren reveal a loose environment framed by linear masses and free of conventional sedentary dividers and other encumbrances. Lustig further toyed with contrasts. Glass tables and vases contrasted with light and dark wood surfaces; open shelves contrasted and alternated with closed cabinets; dark wood panels on which lights were hung from the ceiling contrasted with the light painted walls, which further varied in hue from wall to wall. Even a painting that hung in the main work area was a blend of contrasting realistic and abstract forms. Everything about the office encouraged, if not also symbolized, the creative process.

Lustig knew that an office was not a pristine, unfettered environment. Unlike a book jacket or magazine cover, he did not have the last word on how it would inevitably function, nor could he control the

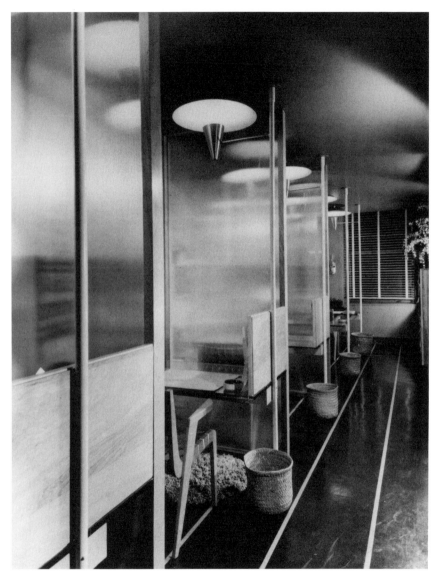

Offices of Reporter Publications in the Empire State Building designed by Alvin Lustig.

level of wear and tear on his design. He could only hope that the quality of the design contributed to a vital workplace. In 1945 Lustig fine-tuned his "open plan" through the design of offices for Reporter Publications in New York. He believed the open setting encouraged creative interaction. Reporter Publications—owned by Bill Segal, who published *American Fabrics* magazine—had a cramped space in the Chrysler Building. The problem for Lustig, according to *Architectural Forum* (May 1946) was "fitting an over-sized staff into undersized work space," only forty-by-forty feet for twenty-two employees. Lustig knew that he had to use every inch of space, and to do this without making the staff claustrophobic, he "dissolved solidity wherever possible while still retaining some sense of privacy," stated the magazine. Doors were completely omitted, and work areas were defined only by intersecting and curling screen walls. His most novel idea involved a lighting system of direct and indirect illumination, coming from stanchions with mushroomlike lamps that bounced light off reflecting disks to the desks below, which Lustig designed himself. Glass walls and glass-top desks further provided a sense of transparency and fluidity. Throughout the space small personal touches, such as soft area rugs and straw wastebaskets made the difference between sterility and intimacy.

Lustig achieved graphic impact on small book covers; likewise, he keenly maximized the limitations of small 3-D spaces. In fact, there is no better example than an office that he designed for himself back in 1952 in a grungy walk-up building on Manhattan's East 58th Street. Elaine Lustig Cohen, who worked for her husband and briefly ran the Lustig studio after his death in 1955, recalls that "It was absolutely hideous. In the first hour we ripped it apart and cleaned it up." Like his other spaces, none of the furniture, not even the flat files, sat boulder-like on the floor. Everything was elevated by small legs or open shelves. In addition to structural walls, Lustig devised a wooden blind (actually more like a slatted fence), which hung from the ceiling both to separate the reception from the work areas and to allow for transparency. A beaded curtain replaced the door on the storeroom. While he used certain existing chairs (e.g., he was a fan of Eames) and lamps, he designed custom sculptural lighting fixtures that were akin to the abstract linear designs he used on some of his book jackets. The main feature, however, was his own office, which included floor-to-ceiling drapes (to smooth out the edges of the room) and his legendary marble desk, which was always empty save for a pad, pencil, triangle, and scissors.

The interior of Alvin Lustig's studio in New York City.

Lustig did not consider himself an interior designer per se. "If you ask him what lamps to buy for your living room," explains Elaine Lustig Cohen, "he would say, 'I can't tell you what lamp to buy, but I'll redo the living room for you.' That was the deal with all his commissions. He was considered this genius. Clients let him do what he wanted." Whether or not he designed 3-D spaces in the same way that he designed covers and magazines is ultimately irrelevant. He fancied himself a total "designer." Everything he did had the same relevance, if not permanence. But if there was a professional hierarchy, it seemed to be that the workplace came first, and the art and design derived from this aesthetically inspiring environment.

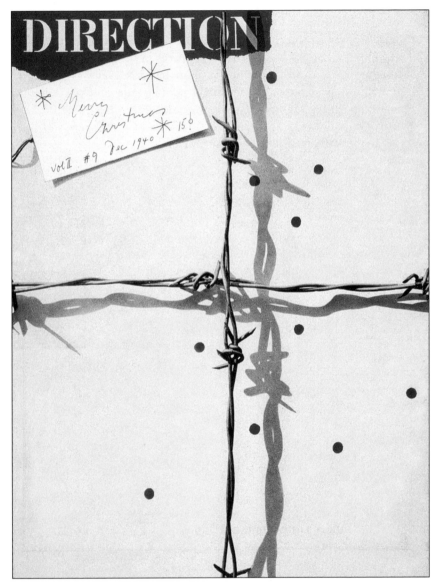

Cover of Direction *magazine designed by Paul Rand, 1940—Christmas on the eve of World War II.*

RANDISM

To call Paul Rand shy is to challenge the perception of the man as outspoken and authoritative. Yet shy was indeed one of his most perplexing traits. For much of his career, Rand refused to speak in front of audiences that exceeded three people. Other designers routinely stood before assembled multitudes, flipping through endless trays of personal slides, but Rand suffered from severe stage fright. The few times that he took to the podium the results were not satisfying, especially for him. However, in his mid-seventies, he made a curious reversal. Spurred by the need to publicize his book, *Paul Rand: A Designer's Art,* he agreed to do public speaking with the help of interlocutors, like myself, who peppered him with questions. He found his comfort level and self-confidence, and to his surprise, he also garnered large audiences who were disarmed by the candor, insight, and anecdote of what I call Randism.

Design as practiced by Rand, although rooted in European Modernism, was decidedly Randism. Unlike other contemporary American exponents of Cubism, Dada, Contructivism, DeStijl, and the Bauhaus, who mimicked these methods, Rand incorporated a Modern essence, or spirit, into his work. He was American, not German, Russian, French, or Dutch. His distinctive elocution made it quite clear that he was a Brooklyn-American—indeed a Jewish-Brooklyn-American. He was not born into the culture that gave birth to Futurism or *die Neue Typographie.* He was not schooled in the

European ways. He practiced drawing in the back of his father's small grocery store and was influenced by comic strips, advertisements, and the *Saturday Evening Post*. Emerging from a hermetic early childhood, he found enlightenment at Macy's department store, where in the bookshop he found two European graphic design magazines, England's *Commercial Art* and Germany's *Gebrauchgraphik*. In these pages he learned about contemporary commercial design and its kinship to the arts and was introduced to the Bauhaus notion that good design was an integral part of everyday life.

Once he decided to become an artist-designer, he could have fallen into conventional American methods of practice. In fact, his teachers at Pratt did not offer much guidance other than rote methods of lettering and composition. So Rand absorbed the lessons of Modernism in his own way, at his own pace, often by trial, error, and luck.

"I was apprenticed to George Switzer [a progressive industrial designer in New York], who was influenced by French and German typographers," Rand said about his earliest exposure to avant-garde design. "Among others I was directly influenced by Piet Zwart, the Dutchman; El Lissitzky, the Russian; [Laszlo] Moholy-Nagy, the Hungarian; Jan Tschichold, the Czech; and [Guillaume] Apollinaire, the Pole; not to mention the Chinese and Persians." In Rand's early work his inspirations were obvious—that is, to anyone in America who knew of these relatively unknown European masters. But before long, he found his voice, synthesizing European notions of typography and composition with a uniquely individual, Brooklyn way of conceptualizing.

As a young man, Rand was as nervous about the correctness of his words as he was convinced about the rightness of his design. A desire to be fluent in language caused him to read and reread critics and philosophers like John Dewey, Alfred North Whitehead, and Roger Fry, among others. He matched his intuitive methods to their reasoned insights, and by quoting them in his later writing on themes such as beauty, aesthetics, function, simplicity, and play, he found a means to articulate his own philosophical underpinnings. Ultimately, he used their ideas as armatures on which he built Randism.

So what made Rand different from other leading adherents of American Modernism? Alvin Lustig and Lester Beall, among them, frequently wrote and lectured on art and craft. But Rand was the first of the young American Moderns to publish a book *cum* manifesto,

Thoughts on Design (1946). It was the first serious "monograph" to lay down a theory about producing mass-market advertising. In perceptive declarations that eschewed pedantry, he wed Modern dicta (as borrowed from earlier books by Tschichold and Moholy-Nagy) to his own pragmatic methods, as in this rationale about why good design was a virtue in a world where mediocrity was accepted:

> Even if it is true that the average man seems most comfortable with the commonplace and familiar, it is equally true that catering to bad taste, which we so readily attribute to the average reader, merely perpetuates that mediocrity and denies the reader one of the most easily accessible means for aesthetic development and eventual enjoyment.

He also explained how to walk the tightrope of art and function:

> "Ideally, beauty and utility are mutually generative," he wrote. "In the past, rarely was beauty an end in itself." Rand introduced theory to a profession whose writing was heretofore predominantly how-to. Nevertheless, he rarely invoked academic jargon.

During the last decade of his life, when he started appearing in public, audiences did not know what to expect. Would he talk over their heads or drone on with show-and-tell monologues? His books and articles offered few clues, as they were tightly structured according to his determination not to allow himself the luxury of informality; he had arduously written and rewritten every sentence to achieve correct parsing, leaving his texts reasoned, logical, and terse. Yet in a public forum he was unable to edit himself, nor did he want to. His candor was infectious—evident, for example, at his penultimate lecture at Cooper Union in October 1996, when he received an ovation after answering a question about passion: "I just like things that are playful; I like things that are happy; I like things that will make the client smile."

Was this the orthodox Modernist who spoke religiously about the rightness of form? Yes. But Rand and Randism had a variety of inflections.

Rand said, "I hate words that are abused, like 'creativity,'" and he eschewed all fashionable slogans. Sure, he had pet phrases like, "for the birds," which was reserved for expressing mild contempt for bad design. But most of the time, he was strident about issues that he felt undercut good design. This critique of trendiness is just one example: "It's something that's superimposed on a problem. It has to do with being part of the scene, or doing what is the latest thing to do." Randism was not a smokescreen; it was a way of propagating the faith—his faith. Moreover, it was a way of educating those who knew little or nothing of design.

At times Randism was used as a tool to sell his ideas. Presentations to clients are often occasions when designers make hocus-pocus. Conversely, Rand believed, "A presentation is the musical accompaniment of design. A presentation that lacks an idea cannot hide behind glamorous photos, pizzazz, or ballyhoo." Anyone reading the presentation booklets that he wrote and produced for NeXT, English First, Ford, and a dozen others (reprinted in his three monographs) knows that each is a primer in logo design and visual communication. He meticulously walks the reader through his intellectual and aesthetic process, discussing the false starts and failed tries, until finally revealing the final product as though it were the only logical solution to the problem. "I never make a presentation personally," he explained in *Artograph* (1988). "I usually send it in the mail . . . because if it's going to be rejected I don't want to be there. But more importantly, I think that the thing has to stand on its own merits. I've seen skillful presentations made by people doing terrible work. . . . People spend money making presentations with three-dimensional things and lights and theatrical effects, dancing girls and music."

Rand was arrogant, but Randism was forged from truths in which he fervently believed. And he left behind a catalog of tenets about clients, style, and aesthetics that continue to have resonance, including these:

- What the designer and his client have in common is a license to practice without a license.
- A style is the consequence of recurrent habits, restraints, or rules invented or inherited, written or overheard, intuitive or preconceived.

• Simplicity is never a goal: It is a byproduct of a good idea and modest expectations.

Paul Rand's life was consumed by work. Randism was the sum total of his accomplishments—the words, deeds, and artifacts that comprise his legacy. But Randism is not a style or method; it does not exist without him. In fact, it is best summed up in his own words in the preface to *Paul Rand: A Designer's Art:*

> My interest has always been in restating the validity of those ideas, which, by and large, have guided artists since the time of Polyclitus. I believe that it is only in the application of those timeless principles that one can even begin to achieve a semblance of quality in one's work. It is the continuing relevance of these ideals that I mean to emphasize, especially to those who have grown up in a world of punk and graffiti.

Cover of Catalog Design *designed by Ladislav Sutnar.*

SUTNAR & LÖNDERG-HOLM: THE GILBERT AND SULLIVAN OF DESIGN

Gilbert and Sullivan, Rodgers and Hammerstein, Abbott and Costello, Sonny and Cher, Batman and Robin—the list of famous teams goes on and on. Likewise, teamwork is a way of life for graphic designers, who have a long roll call of well-known collaborators to prove it. Of all dynamic design duos past and present, one of the most significant is unlikely to be remembered today: Compared to Ladislav Sutnar and Knud Lönberg-Holm, few collaborations in communication have proved to be more historically significant. From the early 1940s to 1960, this writer-designer team radically altered the way business information was streamlined, designed, and packaged. Indeed, their work prefigures the kind of design Richard Saul Wurman has called "information architecture."

While Sutnar's accomplishments as a graphic and informational designer have been fairly well documented in design histories, his collaboration with architect and author Lönberg-Holm (or K. Holm, as he was also known) has received considerably less ink. One reason for this is the tradition of creating heroes of graphic design, in which design historians focus on individuals, as if true creativity can only be a solitary endeavor. Another reason is a curious tendency among historians to segregate the visual from the verbal, and the graphic from the strategic, as if these disciplines do not go hand in hand. Meanwhile, the question of creative integrity cannot be based on the illusion of sole authorship. While some designers certainly make formal and aesthetic decisions that contribute to a distinct voice for their projects, and while many have some influence in developing and directing content, unless they are solely responsible for all strategic, creative, and productive activities (a rare enough circumstance), then others must be recognized for playing both major and minor roles in the final work.

Lönberg-Holm and Sutnar worked as two halves of one mind when it came to designing information. "They were better together than apart; one plus one equaled 100," asserts Radislav Sutnar, Sutnar's son. If a collaborative team is part yin and part yang, a whole inconceivable without its constituent parts, Sutnar and Löndberg-Holm provide a perfect exemplar. But what's more important than the viability of their relationship is the fact that the informational objects they produced changed the way business addressed its public. They also changed the way the consumer accessed information at a time, like now, when data of all kinds was increasing by leaps and bounds.

The backdrop was fairly mundane. Beginning in the late 1930s, Lönberg-Holm was the director of research for Sweet's Catalog Service, a division of F. W. Dodge Corporation in New York. Then, as now, Sweet's was a clearinghouse for trade and industry catalogs, selling common and arcane building, plumbing, electrical, and other construction supplies to architects, contractors, and craftsmen. Sweet's omnibus was actually a binder, housing a variegated (and often motley) assortment of catalogs designed by different companies without any unifying visual or organizational principle. Sweet's service, assembling the catalogs in one volume, did make it easier for users to find what they needed; yet K. Holm's deeper mission was to synthesize these diverse parts into an accessible whole that would save users time and ease their confusion. However, while he possessed a genius for detail and a gift for organization, he knew that he was not a graphic designer.

Born in Denmark and trained as an architect, Lönberg-Holm spent his formative years in Europe, where he became an exponent of Constructivism and Productivism. In 1924 he was invited by the University of Michigan to teach an elementary architecture and design course. Once there, he proved to be an influential propagandist for the Modernist avant-garde. Between 1927 and 1929 he served on the editorial board of *The Architectural Record,* the voice of the Modern sensibility then rising in America. Lönberg-Holm was responsible for the magazine's "Technical News and Research Section," which drew not just from the usual architectural literature, but also, uniquely, from the tradition of scientific discourse. From the latter he borrowed the idea of using graphic charts and diagrams to effectively clarify complex issues in such subjects as building types and environmental control technology.

Out of his Modernist convictions, Holm became a member of the Congress for International Modern Architecture (CIMA), whose other members included Walter Gropius, Serge Chermayeff, Marcel Breuer, and Le Corbusier. Over the years, his Modernist, Urbanist philosophy grew to embrace all design activity, particularly information management, as potential forces for the betterment of human life. It was at a CIMA meeting in the late 1930s that Holm was introduced to Sutnar, whose reputation as a Constructivist designer he was already aware of.

Born in Pilsen, Czechoslovakia, in 1897, Sutnar became a dedicated Modernist while studying at the Prague School of Decorative Arts. In 1923 he was made a professor of design at Prague's State School of Graphic Arts. A decade later, he had become the school's director. Then, in his middle thirties, he was practicing exhibition design according to the tenets of Purism, and was a progressive designer of textiles, products, glassware, porcelain, and educational toys. From 1929 to 1930, he was also an art editor with Prague's largest publishing house, Druzetevni Prace, where he created photomontage covers (which look as though they might have been designed in 1999) for magazines like the socialist arts journal *Zijeme* (We Live) and *V'ytvarné snahy* (Fine Arts Endeavors); as well as book jackets for novels and essays by Upton Sinclair and George Bernard Shaw. Although somewhat overshadowed in Western Europe by his contemporaries, including Russian Constructivist El Lissitsky and Bauhaus master Laszlo Moholy-Nagy, Sutnar was nonetheless well known in Prague—a 1934 exhibit, "Ladislav Sutnar and the New Typography" earned major notices at the time.

Much of Sutnar's early design was concerned with communicating information, although the work couldn't be considered as "information architecture" per se. For books and magazines he developed strict, though mutable, typographic grids, framing sans serif Modern typefaces with white space in a way that prefigured the precise, architectonic compositions of postwar Swiss design. He practiced "new typography" as a means of presenting ideas through elementary forms;

although, without sacrificing its dynamism, Sutnar tended to humanize its sharper edges. An acolyte and friend, designer Noel Martin, says that "Sutnar always talked about function, but he created his own kind of ornamentation through geometry and repetition. Repeating symbols and forms helped him express an industrial sensibility." His interior designs for exhibitions (including the floor plan for Czechoslovakia's 1939 New York World's Fair pavilion, the project that brought him to the United States), were based on the same principles of dynamic flow found in his print design: He directed visitors, visually, through three-dimensional information in real time just as he directed the eye through pages of text.

Just after the fair opened, Hitler's armies marched into Czechoslovakia and dismembered the country. The pavilion closed immediately, and Sutnar, who was to have assisted in bringing the exhibits back home, decided to remain in New York—leaving his wife and two sons in Prague. (He was unable to send for them until the war ended, six years later.) He took up residence in the heart of the jazz district on 52nd Street, accepted freelance assignments, and soon met Holm, his future collaborator.

Lönberg-Holm had been hired by Chauncey L. Williams, vice president of the F. W. Dodge Corporation, to bring unity and identity to Sweet's catalog product. Holm redefined the problem, identifying a need for clarity and accessibility, and proposed to answer it by using navigational design aids and reductive language—which sounds very much like today's approach to Internet way-finding. He wrote countless memoranda detailing a sophisticated process of standardization. In order to give these ideas concrete form, he realized that he needed a graphic designer with similar convictions, so he convinced Williams to hire Sutnar as design director for research. Throughout this relationship, Sutnar continued working in his own design firm, with other partners, for other clients (including the Bell Telephone Company, for whom he designed the prototype of the area code). But for four hours each day, from about 11:00 A.M. to 2:00 P.M., he worked in Sweet's offices on West 40th Street—entering and exiting through a service elevator, for some reason.

Meeting daily, Sutnar and Lönberg-Holm thrashed out ways to simplify customers' access to thousands of supplies, from screws to roofing, in the Sweet's compilation. First among many tasks was to rewrite the universally awful catalog copy, which they did painstakingly. Next, after agreeing that every user comprehends information differently, they devised mechanisms—what Sutnar called "active design elements"—to offer multiple entry-points for each kind of user. An index was conceived to cross-reference each object in three ways: by company name, by trade or brand name, and by the name of the object (e.g., "windows"). K. Holm further observed that while objects routinely change, (e.g. "windows," "sliders," "portholes"), activities remain constant (e.g., "glazing"), and urged that this classification also be included as an organizing element. Holm agreed.

"Sutnar and Lönberg-Holm shared the same logic," says Radislav Sutnar. Both were philosophical Constructivists with practical leanings. Their habitual search for perfect form led them to deconstruct every potential form so as to reframe and synthesize the ideas underneath the forms. It was an article of faith that there could be no confusion. So in determining the best format, they moved from word (K. Holm) to image (Sutnar), merging the verbal and visual ideas into a seamless whole. At times they intensely debated the meaning of a single word (perhaps because neither was a native speaker of English), or the placement of a single picture. Each so revered precision that though arguments inevitably flared—once Sutnar stopped speaking to Lönberg-Holm for a month over a point of language—they would ultimately reach consensus.

Sutnar's first task at Sweet's was to redefine its corporate identity. He did this by changing the company's logo from a Victorian-style nameplate (typical of many venerable American corporations) to a sans serif S within a bold circle (typical of European Modernism). He also redesigned the binders themselves, in the course of which he introduced the tabbed divider page. While these departures demonstrated a change in attitude and approach, the most concrete and definitive explanation of their mission was given in three books, which today are still considered (by historians, at least) holy grails of information design. Holm and Sutnar conceived of and wrote *Catalog Design* in 1944 to introduce various systematic departures in contemporary catalog design. *Designing Information,* published in 1947, addressed a broader range of information in various media; and *Catalog Design Progress,* in 1950, concerned itself with making product selection simpler and the flow of information through various media faster. Each was designed as a manual to initiate the uninitiated into the belief that "good" graphic design is a panacea for jumbled thinking. *Catalog*

Design was a style guide *cum* manifesto written to encourage the catalog designers whose work Sweet's collected to follow more rigorous standards of organization, while allowing them to make their designs distinctive. From our vantage point, the ideas seem fairly simple, but at a time when most trade and industrial catalogs were a potpourri of miscellaneous pictures, crammed between lengthy descriptions and item numbers, the notion that text and image could be framed by white space, or that a catalog could benefit from grid layouts, was tantamount to revolution.

In a 1947 memorandum to Sweet's management concerning their next project, *Designing Information,* Lönberg-Holm foretold the essentiality of the designer's role in our current information age: "[T]he simplification of any information implies simplification of the visual task through clarity and precision—a functional goal of information design." Although Sutnar and Lönberg-Holm didn't coin the term "information design," *Designing Information* codified the tenets of clarity and accessibility like no book before it. "The treatment of the subject came about through our realization of the need to clarify design in everyday terms, and to demonstrate that design has practical values that go far beyond mere decoration," K. Holm said. Thus, in their hands, "the basic elements of design-size, blank space, color, line, etc. [became] tools for selectivity, simplifying the visual task" of the user.

Designing Information (which was planned as a huge volume but published in an abridged form) set out to define design as a tool for achieving the "faster flow of information" through principles of flow and unity. Sutnar and Lönberg-Holm took great pains to demonstrate the process of visualizing information by including scores of charts and graphs that addressed the needs of customers, employees, stockholders, and the general public. They believed that giving efficient form to information required more than just pictorial illustration ("Ease of seeing means more than easy to look at," wrote K. Holm). Their crystalline charts became the foundation on which comprehension could be built. In fact, in one simple chart the whole of *Designing Information* is efficiently summarized: "Transmitting: speed, accessibility; Seeing: visual selectivity, visual continuity; Comprehending: visual extension, universality."

This synthesis was the basis of their last collaborative book, *Catalog Design Progress,* a spiral-bound volume with a horizontal format that, incidentally, became the design standard for industrial design

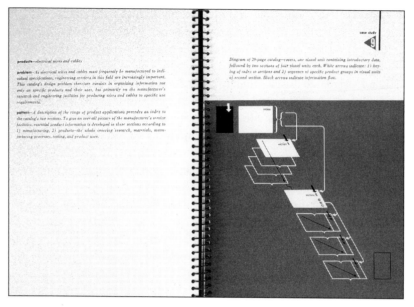

Spread form Catalog Design.

manuals (and arguably a model for later corporate graphic standards manuals). In it, Holm and Sutnar developed and refined the ideas they had presented in their previous books, showing how complex information could first be organized, and then, more importantly, retrieved. They addressed specific ways in which levels of information could be organized for easy scanning and gave designers suggestions for maximizing visual interest through symbols, typographic nuances, changes in scale, and so on. Perhaps Sutnar's most significant innovation in the design of the book itself was his use of full-spread designs. Indeed, he was one of the earliest designers to treat spreads as integrated units. Even a casual review of Sutnar's designs for everything from catalogs to brochures during his American period (with the logical exception of covers) shows that he used across-the-spread designs regularly. Using all the space at his disposal, he was able to inject excitement into even the most routine material without impinging upon comprehension: His signature navigational devices guided users firmly from one level of information to the next.

At the same time, Sutnar was not an invisible designer. While his basic structures were decidedly rational, the choices he made in juxtaposition, scale, and color were rooted in sophisticated principles of abstract design, bringing sensitive composition, visual charm, and emotional drama to his workaday subjects. He developed a distinctive vocabulary, or style, notable for arrows, fever lines, black bullets, and other repeated devices. He used all of the above to direct the reader through hierarchies of information, and indeed promoted these devices in *Catalog Design Progress* as the correct forms for guiding readers (which contributed to a kind of Sutnar-biased conformity among later designers). Nevertheless, the fact that Sutnar injected his aesthetic preferences doesn't diminish the effectiveness of his and his partner's ideas. It only goes to show that a strong, though not overpowering, design personality can be useful in information design.

Although their landmark work was published in 1950, the pair continued to develop and expand their ideas for another ten years. Sutnar designed many of the trade catalogs that appeared in the Sweet's binder, both as Sweet's staff designer and as a freelance consultant to

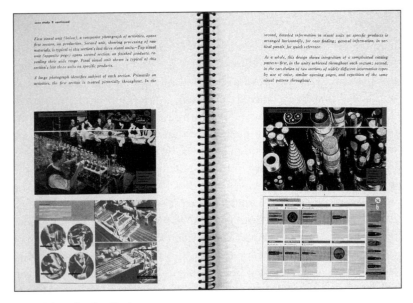

Spread form Catalog Design.

Sweet's contributors. In 1960 Chauncey Williams, Holm's original director, retired. With his departure, Sweet's golden age, like many before it, abruptly ended. Sutnar concentrated on his private practice; Lönberg-Holm, in consideration of his services, was kept on staff for a year or two more. Once the important work ended, the memory of this collaboration faded.[1]

Truly functional graphic design is often ignored as a result of its defining transparency, while stylish decorative mannerisms are honored in the popular taste. Though Sutnar and Lönberg-Holm introduced the theoretical constructs that define functional design for information management, the topic was barely addressed by American commercial artists until Corporate Modernism took over from its avant-garde Modernist progenitors.

Sutnar's contribution to the enlightenment of information design is remembered by the world of design because he left a rich visual legacy. His collaborator, if treated at all, is dismissed as a philosopher responsible for the invisible structure of the work, rather than as a vital contributor to its actual construction. In design histories, Löndberg-Holm's name, though it appears prominently on their books, has become an appendage to the name of Sutnar: He is mentioned, if at all, as the silent partner. It would not only be more accurate, but more honest, to acknowledge them together. Like Gilbert and Sullivan, Rogers and Hammerstein, and Lennon and McCartney, they made their most beautiful music together.

---

[1]This essay was written with the collaboration of Paul Makousky.

ment or diversion; amusement; sport; frolic.

PLAYBOY n.

(plā'boï). **1.** A sporty fellow bent upon pleasure seeking; a man-about-town; a lover of life; a *bon vivant.* **2.** The magazine edited for the edification and entertainment of urban men; i.e., in the June issue: "You Can Make a Million Today" by J. Paul Getty; a psychological portrait of Reno by Herbert Gold; five pages of color photography on the Grand Prix in Monaco with description by Charles Beaumont; cartoonist Shel Silverstein visits Hawaii.—**played out** (plād out), *pp.* Performed to the end; also, exhausted; used up.—**player** (plā'ẽr), *n.* One who plays; an actor; a musician.—**playful** (plā'fool; -f'l), *adj.* Full of play; sportive; also, humorous.—**playmate** (plā'māt'), *n.* A companion in play.—**Playmate** (Plā'māt'), *n.* A popular pictorial feature in PLAYBOY magazine depicting beautiful girl in pin-up pose; shortening of "Playmate of the Month"; i.e., Austrian beauty Heidi Becker in June issue; hence, without cap., any very attractive female companion to a playboy.—**playock** (plā'ŭk), *n.* [Prob. dim. of *play, n.*] Plaything. *Scot.*—**playoff** (plā'ŏf'), *n. Sports.* A final contest or series of contests to determine the

JUNE PLAYMATE

Cover of Playboy *designed by Art Paul.*

THE ART [PAUL] OF PLAYBOY

For the generations weaned on feminism and political correctness, *Playboy* magazine is a throwback to the Stone Age. But when it premiered in 1953, it was a breakthrough in an ossified culture. *Playboy*, in turn, enabled men to experience the sexual side of life unfettered by stultifying postwar mores and preemptive censorship that made nudity unsavory and sex taboo. Even *Esquire*, the first men's "lifestyle" magazine, which began in 1938 and published sultry pinup drawings by Petty and Vargas, had lost its bite after World War II. Which is why Hugh Hefner, who had briefly worked in the promotion department of *Esquire*, decided to invent a publication that would radically change the form and content of magazines, and in the bargain would incite something of a cultural revolution—the Playboy revolution.

Playboy was based on Hefner's belief that men had the right to be, or fantasize about being, libidinous rogues who listened to cool jazz, drank dry martinis, drove imported sports cars, maintained hip bachelor pads, and felt good about themselves. Through the magazine, he contrived a culture that encouraged hedonistic and narcissistic behavior on the one hand and social and political awareness on the other. But Hef, as he was known, did not accomplish this alone. In fact, his message would not have been so broadly accepted (with a high of over seven million in paid circulation) if not for *Playboy*'s innovative graphic approach. Therefore, the magazine's format, typography, and illustration must not be underestimated in the calculus of success, because with so much riding on *Playboy*'s premiere (Hefner invested his last dime and used his furniture as collateral to raise the initial $8,000), if it looked the least bit tawdry—like some nudist magazine—the project would be doomed.

Moreover, if Hefner had not enticed former Chicago Bauhaus (Institute of Design) student Art Paul to become the magazine's founding art director, it is possible that *Playboy* could have languished in a netherworld between pulp and porn. At the time that Hef was introduced to Paul, an illustrator and designer with a small office under the elevated subway on Chicago's Van Buren Street, the magazine was titled *Stag Party* (after a 1930s book of ribald cartoons titled *Stag at Eve*), and the initial dummy (designed by cartoonist R. Miller) looked like a movie star–screen magazine with cheesecake photos and puerile cartoons (a few of them drawn by Hef himself). It was not, however, what Hefner wanted.

"I was looking for a magazine that was as innovative in its illustration and design as it was in its concept," recalls Hefner, who studied art at the University of Illinois. He adds:

> We came out of a period where magazine illustration was inspired by Norman Rockwell and variations on realism and I was much more influenced by abstract art of the early 1950s and by Picasso. I was looking for something that combined less realistic and more innovative art with magazine illustration. The notion of breaking down the walls between what hung in museums and what appeared in the pages of magazine was very unique at that time and it was what Arthur was all about.

Art Paul was born in Chicago in 1925 and studied with Moholy-Nagy at the Institute of Design from 1946 to 1950. He was initially reluctant to join the fledgling magazine because he had a child on the way and needed security that he did not believe was possible with anything as speculative as this. But Hefner seduced him with promises. "He kept offering me stock and things of that nature," Paul recalls. "But the way he spoke and his enthusiasm was more convincing; he reminded me of the great dedicated publishers." The stock was a nice gesture, but the assurance of freedom to take chances in designing the magazine was decidedly more tempting. Paul agreed to do the first issue on a freelance basis, and ultimately signed on for the next thirty years (and yes, he was glad to have taken the stock).

The original inspiration for the magazine, says Hefner, came from the *New Yorker* of the 1920s and *Esquire* the 1930s. "I was very much influenced by the Roaring Twenties, Jazz Age, F. Scott Fitzgerald. I thought that it was a party that I had missed." Since Hefner was raised in a typically midwestern Methodist home with very puritan parents, "I believe that my life and the magazine were a response to that, and a direct reaction to the fact that after World War II, I expected the period to be a reprise of the Roaring Twenties. But it wasn't. It was a very politically and socially repressive time. Even the skirtlengths went down instead of up, which I saw as a sign. So the magazine was an attempt to recapture the fantasy of my adolescence."

Paul bought into Hefner's concept, but he was put off by the "Stag" title and suggested that the name be changed, which Hefner did only weeks before going to press, and only after *Stag,* a hunting magazine, threatened legal action for infringement. "We made up a list of names that suggested the bachelor life," Hefner explains. "Playboy was in disuse at that point and reflected back on an earlier era, particularly back on the twenties—I liked that connection." So with this detail out of the way, Paul proceeded to develop a format that reconciled nude photography with the sophisticated fiction and nonfiction that became hallmarks of the *Playboy* formula. For Hefner, *Playboy* was a mission to influence the mores, morals, and lifestyle of men; for Paul it was a laboratory that turned into a model of contemporary magazine design and illustration.

The deadline for the first issue was excruciatingly tight because he needed to get it on the newsstands before creditors came banging at his door. So, for the first issue Paul cobbled together what he now calls "a scrapbook" of things to come. "I took on the challenge in broad strokes," Paul explains. "I said to myself, 'This is a men's magazine; I want it to look masculine. I want it to be as strong as I can make it.' But I had tremendous limitations with the printing—the printers were doing us a favor by fitting us in. I was very limited in the number of typefaces and ended up using Stymie." Nonetheless, the slab-serif Egyptian was a perfect fit, being quirky yet bold. It worked well as a logo, not too overpowering, yet not froufrou. For the interior of the magazine, Paul employed white space to counterbalance the limited color availability of the first few issues.

The cover of the premier issue was the most critical decision that Hefner or Paul had to make. Only two colors were available, which could have been a real handicap. But conceptually, nothing could be more seductive than the photograph of Marilyn Monroe (a press photo of her in a parade waving to the crowd which Paul sillouetted) next to the headline:

First Time in any magazine
FULL COLOR
the famous
MARILYN MONROE
NUDE

Hefner obtained the centerfold photograph from the John Baumgart calendar company, who supplied various nude photographs, including one of Marilyn Monroe before she became a sex goddess. Hef bought the original transparency, color separations, and the publication rights for a couple of hundred dollars. As for the absence of multiple colors on the cover, Paul explains that it was a problem that turned into an asset:

> I was trying to figure out how in the world I could get a magazine that was in no way publicized to be seen [by readers] on the newsstands. So I looked at magazines in a way I never had looked before. I found out how ours would be displayed, and I saw the other magazines it would have to compete with. Most used big heads and a lot of color and type. I felt that ours would have to be simple and so using the black-and-white photo with a little red on the logo was a plus, because it stood out no matter where it was displayed.[1]

Paul initially wanted the logo or nameplate on the cover to be small and in a variable rather than a fixed position, which meant he could move it around as though it were a puzzle piece. Years later, however, it was locked in at the top. Today, Paul says that "some of the more innovative covers happened in the early years" when he could freely use the logo as a conceptual element—and when he had more conceptual license to manipulate the models. Much like Henry Wolf's

Esquire covers of the late fifties, Paul's *Playboy* covers were driven not by licentious half-nude women, but by witty ideas and visual puns, which included its trademark bunny. Paul based all his cover concepts around different ways to inject the bunny into the design. Covers became games that challenged the reader to find the trademark wherever it was hiding—tucked in a corner, placed on a tie clasp, or fashioned from the legs and torso of a cover model.

Hefner or Paul could not have predicted how world-famous the rabbit would become. Hefner wanted a mascot from the outset: "*Esquire* and the *New Yorker* both had male symbols [Esky and Eustice Tilly, respectively]. So the notion of having an animal as a male symbol was a nice variation on the theme. The notion of putting a rabbit in a tuxedo seemed kind of playful, sexy, and sophisticated." The initial version was a stag drawn by R. Miller, which for the first issue was quickly transformed by pasting on the head of a rabbit onto its body. "If you look at it, the rabbit has hoofs," says Hefner. Paul's then-wife made a nascent bunny out of fabric for a cover. By the third issue Paul's original drawing of the bunny in profile is what became the "empire's logo."

From the outset *Playboy* touched nerves. Despite the predictable moral outrage in certain quarters, a large number of men (and an untold number of adolescent boys) flocked to the sign of the bunny. Yet Paul argues that while sex was a significant part of the entire package, it was not a sex magazine per se. He saw *Playboy* more as a lifestyle magazine, or, as the subtitle said, "Entertainment for Men." Hefner wanted to present sex as a common occurrence, not a puritan's taboo. This was accomplished by Hefner's commissioning the photographs exclusively for the magazine rather than buying them through stock providers.

"By the later part of the first year, I began to do my own photographs," states Hefner, who oversaw all the early photo sessions. "The first centerfold was in the December 1954 issue, but it was early in the following year when we got what I was looking for, a natural setting that looked less like a calendar. Arthur played a role, but the concept was mine."

The important breakthrough came in shots of Janet Pilgrim, *Playboy*'s subscription manager, whom Hefner was dating at the time. In the picture, Hef is in the background in a tuxedo with his back turned, while Pilgrim prepares herself at the vanity, powdering her nose for a date. "I was trying to personalize it," says Hefner about the notion that nudity had to be connected to "art" or be considered obscene. "That's why the classic pinup art prior to that, including our Marilyn Monroe nude, was shot in abstract settings—they were considered art studies. So what I was trying to do to was make them real people and put them in a real setting so that the nudity had meant something more—it was a projection of sexuality. It was that nice girls like sex too, sex was okay."

Paul's contribution to the photography was to inject simple male-oriented objects, like a pipe or slippers, in order to underscore a human element—or to give the girls "a smell," as the painter Richard Lindner once said about *Playboy*'s photography. But Paul insists that he was less interested in nudes than in the other aspects of the magazine, where he made a more meaningful impact as an art director. This included feature page design and illustration.

Paul's first love was illustration, which he practiced in a minimalist and surrealist fashion. He says that as a child he savored "the pure magic of the 1920s and '30s [illustration], which idolized the familiar and romanticized the positive side of America." He admired both Norman Rockwell and Michelangelo but admits a preference for the former, reasoning that "fine artists like Michelangelo were in dusty art history books, but the commercial illustrators like Norman Rockwell were on the shiny new covers of the *Saturday Evening Post*." As Paul became more professionally attuned, he was increasingly perturbed by the distinctions made by critics between fine and applied art, which reduced illustration to uninspired formulas. "I felt that both the fine artist and commercial illustrator had their lasting qualities. I never liked the way schools refused to place the so-called high and low art under the same roof. It annoyed me to think that illustration art was considered a lesser form of expression because it was paid for by a publisher instead of the Church of Rome." When he became art director of *Playboy,* Paul had a plan to change the prevailing view.

"To implement a closer relationship between 'high' and 'low' arts," Paul noted in the catalog for "Playboy Illustration" (Alberta College of Art Gallery, 1976):

> I hoped to free myself from early concepts of the literal illustration and to commission pictures that needed no captions: I asked the commercial illustrators to create moods, not just situations, in their art and to work

with various materials to create these moods, often forsaking painting for a construction or a collage or a photo-art combination. I asked them to be more personal in their work.

Paul further commissioned "fine" artists to do what came naturally to them, to offer personal interpretations. The marriage of the commercial and noncommercial artists' work gave *Playboy* a uniquely progressive edge among most publications at the time. Hefner notes that "While we were doing and after we did this, Andy Warhol did almost the opposite of that: He took commercial art and turned it into fine art, and we took fine art and turned it into commercial art."

Playboy art was resolutely eclectic, ranging from minimalist to maximalist, and drawing from Surrealist, Pop Art, and post-Pop schools. The fine art alumni included such known painters and sculptors as Salvador Dali, Larry Rivers, George Segal, Tom Wesselman, Ed Paschke, James Rosenquist, Roger Brown, Alfred Leslie, and Karl Wirsum. And Paul frequently published (and boosted the careers of) many top commercial illustrators, including Paul Davis, Brad Holland, Cliff Condak, Robert Weaver, Don Ivan Punchatz, and Tomi Ungerer, to name a few of the artists from the over three thousand illustrations Paul had commissioned. Yet the art was not ad hoc; Paul provided tight layouts and parameters wherein the illustrator had to work. Within these confines, though, freedom was granted, and the art played a truly supplementary role that earned the respect of reader and writer alike. In the catalog, "Art of Playboy: From the First 25 Years" (Playboy, 1978), *Playboy* authors were invited to comment on the illustrations that accompanied their own articles. One such about Brad Holland's drawings for a humor piece by P. G. Wodehouse, was typical: "I find it rather difficult to pin down my feelings about those illustrations to my 'Domestic Servant' piece," wrote Wodehouse. "My initial reaction was a startled 'Oh, my Gawd!,' but gradually the sensation that I had been slapped between the eyes with a wet fish waned, and now I like them very much. I was brought up in the school of the *Stand* magazine and the old *Saturday Evening Post,* where illustrations illustrated, but I am not sure I don't like this modern impressionist stuff better."

Another innovative contribution was the manner in which he used illustration as "participatory graphics," which involved artwork in various forms and shapes printed as die-cuts, slipsheets, and other surprising inserts. One of the few magazines Paul emulated was Fleur Cowles's *Flair,* which employed ambitious die-cuts to enhance editorial content. Hefner concurs that *Flair* and also *Gentry,* a short-lived 1950s men's style magazine, were great influences. Emulating them, Paul wanted an illustration to do more than lie on a flat surface, so he employed cinematic narratives using foldouts and fold-overs either to give the illusion of motion, or shifting perspectives, or, like an advent calendar, to reveal hidden messages. "I didn't misjudge Hef in that area at all," Paul says about the promises made to him, "because when I came up with ideas like that, he was very willing to spend quite a bit of money on it." For Hefner the benefits were all his: "My relationship with Art was a postgraduate course for me in art and design."

To support these ambitious special effects, Paul developed a feature article format that, although based on a strict grid, allowed for numerous variations and surprises, including a wealth of contoured type treatments and other typo-image experiments. The 1990s were known for experimental tomfoolery, but during the 1960s and 1970s Paul was in the forefront with his experimental use of artwork and paper effects, which doubtless has had an influence on today's magazines.

Yet to separate Paul's design from the effects of *Playboy*'s overall message is to ignore an important part of the story. For many, the sign of the bunny continues to represent the objectification of women that perpetuated an unhealthy attitude and contributed to their exploitation until the 1960s, when the women's liberation movement began raising consciousness. Indeed, *Playboy* overtly encouraged sexist attitudes toward women for years to follow. Hefner does, however, argue that in addition to affixing cottontails and rabbit ears on fetching women, *Playboy* offered a more balanced cultural diet. *Playboy* published exemplary writing and in-depth interviews with cultural, social, and political figures; certain of the "Playboy Interviews" not only broke barriers, but they broke as news—for example, President Jimmy Carter's candid "lust in my heart" response to a question about whether he ever physically cheated on his wife, a confession that caused a furor at the time but showed that even Presidents had male fantasies.

Hefner titillated through *Playboy*'s photography (which often presented women in the same stylistic guise as cars and mixed drinks) and educated through articles that addressed societal issues and the *comedie humaine.* In the 1950s and 1960s *Playboy* was viewed as contraband for what in today's media environment would be described as no-core pornography. Which is why Paul believed that good art and design was one way to imbue the magazine with a certain kind of legitimacy, which had the dubious effect of sanctioning the sexism within. At the same time, he also pushed the limits of visual art. Paul's job was to integrate the editorial and pictorial in such a way that readers did not experience disruption from one realm of content to another, perhaps leading them to realize that *Playboy* was not concerned with sexploitation alone.

Speaking about his role in developing the *Playboy* stereotype of plastic women, Paul admits, "I didn't have any guilt feelings about it. But I thought it could be much better, and I either didn't know how to do it, or didn't have the people who knew how to do it." He did, however, take some photographs himself that were much more artful, which he describes as "designy nudes"—portions of bodies like one of a nude foot with a high heel at the end of it. "Ultimately, I wanted strong images," he says. "But I was also concerned about being sensual." In the final analysis, though, *Playboy* merely raised the level of the pinup a few notches.

During the thirty years of Paul's tenure, *Playboy* grew into a major entertainment corporation, with the magazine being only one piece of the empire. If he had not already taken the magazine as far as he could by that time, the ever-constricting corporate bottom line was infringing on his creative work and was the impetus for his decision to retire. "I wanted to leave the magazine two or three years before I did," he says, "because I got to the point where there was nothing more that I would be allowed to push." Playboy Enterprises was hiring a lot of new executives, notably Christie Hefner, Hefner's daughter, who earlier had worked for a couple of years as a summer intern in the art department, and who was now one of the cost-cutters. Hefner, who had left Chicago for Los Angeles, heard about Paul's plan to leave and asked him what he would want to stay on. Paul really wanted to paint (and subsequently had a few gallery shows of his work), but Hefner insisted on making accommodations. So Paul told him. "I couldn't stand *Playboy*'s TV ads, and to appease me he let me do ads." Paul found it "interesting" for a while. "But as far as the magazine was concerned, I was not that connected with it at all." Nonetheless, Hefner insists that today, "The editorial concept and design of the magazine, even though it has evolved since the 1970s, was and continues to be defined by Arthur Paul."

Paul, who now devotes himself to painting, is still something of a controversial figure. When he was asked to speak about his design at the AIGA Conference in Chicago in 1991, a few women designers protested on the grounds that *Playboy* created negative stereotypes and false notions of beauty. They claimed that Paul was complicit in his role as art director, an argument that continues to ignite debate. Yet such criticism must be measured. For in the 1950s and 1960s many of the most editorially progressive periodicals were including sexual material. Even *Playboy*'s imitators, such as *Rogue, Swank,* and *Cavalier,* gave opportunities to designers and illustrators (some of them women) that were not available in other media and helped establish their reputations. Paul's legacy is not just a sexploitative bunny, but a forum that demolished both artistic and cultural boundaries.

---

[1]Excerpted from an interview between the author and Art Paul, 1999.

"The Glutton," by Edward Sorel, 1977.

MASTERS OF A LESSER ART: DAVID LEVINE AND EDWARD SOREL

Caricature and cartoon are ephemeral arts, but the most accomplished practitioners are by no means ephemeral artists. Although relegated to a netherworld of so-called lesser art, the masters' reputations remain intact in the annals of cultural and social history: William Hogarth and James Gilray for satires of Britain's high (and low) society; Francesco Goya for bearing witness to the disasters of war; Honoré Daumier for lambasting the French petite bourgeoisie; Thomas Nast for combating America's corrupt oligarchy; George Grosz and John Heartfiled for skewering Nazi demigods; and Robert Osborn for assaulting the body politic. Influenced by their respective periods, each of these artists were both critics and chroniclers of their times and places.

Against the backdrop of this pantheon, only a few postwar contemporary artists have emerged as astute graphic critics of current culture, society, and politics. Like their forebears, these few have set new standards for critical cartooning that others have followed (or copied). David Levine and Edward Sorel are two-thirds of a notable troika (the other is Jules Feiffer) who have maintained venerable cartoon traditions through artistry and acerbity. They have also created some of the most indelible graphic icons of the past thirty years—images that symbolize crucial events in time or that have transcended the time when they were originally created, thereby representing broader truths.

To understand the intricacies of Watergate, the scandal that toppled Richard M. Nixon's presidency, one can read the voluminous histories of that era. But to capture the essence of the folly, look no further than Levine's caricature of Nixon as Captain Queeg, a parody of the skipper of the U.S.S. Caine, whose paranoid obsessions contributed to his personal downfall. Likewise, Sorel's drawing of Milhouse I, a reference to Shakespeare's villainous Richard III, portrays Nixon as the cunning micromanager bedeviled by his own craving for absolute power. In both instances Levine and Sorel do what cartoonists do best, borrow (or steal) recognizable symbols, which they twist and transform using scabrous wit and sophisticated humor, turning the commonplace into commentary. During the Vietnam War, the Watergate epoch, and the Reagan Tefloncy, Levine and Sorel created comic and satiric images for the entertainment and edification of a growing opposition, while sticking thorns in the sides of the powers that be. They influenced political attitudes every bit as much as the pundits and orators of the day.

No other postwar caricaturist made as many molehills into mountains as Levine since he started making caricatures back in 1958. Evidenced by a body of work that spans more than three decades, largely in the *New York Review of Books,* Levine retains a genius for pinpointing a benign physical feature and metamorphosing it into a fatal character flaw. In allowing his audience to see his subjects as they truly are, he goes through a kind of exorcism in which he uses his pen and ink to draw demons from their hiding places into the open. They may try to hide, but rarely is a politician skilled enough to crawl back into his skin after Levine isolates and exposes that inexorable physical trait. But his skill does not rest entirely on this proficiency alone. First and foremost, he is a cartoonist—an artist with ideas, a satirist with wit. For Levine, the distorted portrait must stimulate the intellect as it entertains the eye. At its most effective, it must employ such an inextricable marriage of sense and nonsense that it captures the essence of both the individual and the event or policy that the individual represents.

Levine employs convention to achieve his goals, though he eschews clichés. His signature large-head-on-small-body conceit is borrowed from nineteenth-century comic draftsmen. Yet his work is neither nostalgic nor timeworn. (Moreover, not all his caricatures conform to this precise formula.) Levine rejects convoluted metaphors in favor of universal symbols. One of his many caricatures of Lyndon Johnson, drawn during the Vietnam War, shows him crying crocodile tears, a timeworn reference that captured the president's penchant for melodrama. Similarly, for a *portrait charge* describing Johnson's hubris, Levine has him revealing an abdominal scar in the shape of Vietnam, a reference to a highly publicized front-page photograph of the president showing off a surgical wound. Little did Johnson know his exhibitionism would have such enduring contradictory results.

Levine is not known for flattering depictions, and for one of his cruelest, he used Ray Bradbury's "The Illustrated Man" metaphor as the basis for a picture showing former Secretary of State Henry Kissinger tattooed with images (guns, skulls, bombs, and bombers), suggesting his dubious diplomatic achievements. Originally commissioned for the *New York Times,* this eloquent visual concept was deemed too controversial to publish. Perhaps rightly so, because when it eventually appeared in the *Village Voice,* it became a memorable memento of Kissinger's legacy.

The recipe for an effective political cartoon includes four ingredients: remarkable subject, political savvy, scabrous wit, and skillful drafting. Sorel brought one additional ingredient to this mix— intense rage. Without it his Watergate cartoons would have been witty, even trenchant, but with it he savagely ridiculed the most protected public figures. The velocity of his angry pen stroke pierced the subjects' skins, exposing their physical and psychological flaws. From line to idea, rage against authority informed every aspect of his comic tableau. Sorel now claims that he was just following his instincts. "I was really no different from most people who are driven crazy by the stupidity and insanity that their governments do. I was not an activist. I was as self-centered and self-absorbed as any other middle-class person of the time," Sorel noted. And these expressions against sacred cows provided a vent for the public to let off their steam as well. Indeed people were grateful for any bit of anti-Nixon or antiwar sentiment. "It didn't matter how hackneyed or trite," he continued, "you were immediately raised to the level of working class hero."

In the early 1960s Levine and Sorel where hamstrung by conservative magazine editors and publishers, but as the decade (and all that it came to represent) developed, they benefited from a relaxation in the McCarthy-era suppression of political opposition. From the proliferation of left-leaning underground newspapers to the loosening up of liberal mainstream magazines, the late 1960s and early 1970s were a renaissance for political cartoons. This comparatively enlightened

"The Invisible Man" by David Levine, 1979.

media atmosphere intersected with the critical political and social events of the day, enabling Levine and Sorel to create graphic rallying points while continuing the tradition of graphic commentary that had been virtually dormant since World War II. They introduced a new style based on the revival of historical forms. "I parodied the old [British] masters—Rowlandson, Gilray, and Cruikshank—because they knew composition so well," Sorel admitted. But neither artist mimicked the past. And although both favored the left, they rejected the didactic socialist cartoons of the 1930s, instead adopting a decidedly more personal vocabulary based on individual thinking. In fact, both artists (and particularly Sorel) have dabbled with the comic strip as an alternative means of expression.

Between 1975 and 1980, following the end of the Vietnam War and Nixon's demise, the flood of cartoon activism was reduced to a trickle, and most outlets for such work likewise dried up. Levine focused more on his literary caricature and painting. Sorel limited his political activities because, with kids in college, he had decided to take on more "commercial" work. But when Reagan entered the White House, once again Levine took aim at a caricaturial target; Sorel began doing comic strips for the *Nation.* Curiously, these strips often included himself as a featured player, either as the barometer of some political event or in as an autobiographical tale. "I find the cartoons about me endlessly fascinating," he admitted. "I can stare at them for hours and hours. I suppose because I'm egocentric. But also because it shows me my dark side, superficial side, and competitive side. I suppose this is really my revenge for only getting $150 a page. If they're going to pay me that little, they're going to have to listen to what my life is like."

For almost forty years, Levine and Sorel have drawn exceptional political cartoons, expanded their range, fine-tuned their skills, and progressed the art of graphic commentary. Although many of their subjects represent a particular moment, their drawings are permanent records of an age. Orthodox art historians routinely relegate cartooning as a lesser art compared to painting and sculpture. But they are mistaken. Levine and Sorel are major artists in a field that will not be marginalized.

An installation by Barbara Kruger, artist, designer, propagandist.

BARBARA KRUGER, GRAPHIC DESIGNER?

Barbara Kruger is not a commercial artist, but she is a graphic designer. Although she does not create signs, symbols, or messages that promote mass-market consumption or corporate identity, she exemplifies the continuum of activist designers who, since the nineteenth century, have used the tools of mass communications to subvert the myths perpetuated by the powerful. In the late 1970s Kruger was one of a group of artists who "intercepted," as she calls it, various popular media—from matchbooks to advertisements to movies—by which social and political stereotypes are propagated, redeploying them as offensive weapons against social inequity. Today, the art world celebrates Kruger as one of its own, and graphic designers rightly claim her, too. Given her medium and message—and as a woman who challenged an ostensibly male-dominated art establishment—her work resonates for its audacity in attacking assumptions of power as much as for transforming, through her choice of public address, the essence of art itself. That Kruger has brought graphic design into the museum proves that she has made inestimable progress in bridging the gap between art and design. By creating an art of word and image built on the vernacular of mass communication, Kruger's art seduces as well as informs.

In adopting her method, Kruger had to quash certain art historical taboos regarding the unholy union between fine and applied art. Commercial art, which includes graphic design, is signs and symbols, layouts and formats, typefaces and typographies, conveyed through styles and mannerisms as entertainment and information. The most utilitarian and pervasive of the popular visual arts, it serves many masters, not just the artist's muse, including marketing experts, account executives, product managers, clients, their secretaries, and spouses. As a service to commerce, graphic design is usually shunted off to the sidelines of serious cultural discourse. It is a job that an artist may have done to earn a living before becoming a real artist, but certainly not afterward. And although the 1960s Pop artists (a few of whom were previously employed as art directors, graphic designers, or illustrators) monumentalized commercial art, they positioned themselves above the fray as commentators on and critics of consumer culture, reducing graphic design, particularly advertising and package design, to the raw material of artistic exploration, if not also the object of parody and satire.

The canard that graphic design is a distant and unwelcome cousin of art is not, however, entirely valid. In truth, graphic design has a consequential legacy throughout art history. In just one era, the early twentieth-century Modern movements, Russian Constructivism, Italian Futurism, Dutch DeStijl, and German Dada were in large part characterized by the anarchic type and layout of manifestos in various esoteric and commercial media. Graphic designers were artists who led rather than followed existing ideas of rightness. The designers of freeform Futurist typography in poetry and publicity, for example, gave voice to the ideals of a movement concerned with disrupting the status quo. Likewise, with Constructivist graphic design, the unconventional arrangements of metal type-case material combined with photographic collage and montage used for propaganda posters and manifestos, further underscored the role of art as a mechanism of the Bolshevik revolution, just as Dada was a wellspring of nonconformist typography in the service of leftwing German polemics. Radical ideas perpetuated at this time ultimately influenced the New Typography, which was an unorthodox *commercial* design aesthetic, with political underpinnings, that sought to replace archaic standards as well as bourgeois values with utopian simplicity.

Inevitably, though, progressive ideas became stylistic mannerisms within mainstream practice. And once the cutting edge was dulled, these design styles became perfectly acceptable for mass publicity and packaging, much the same way that in recent years outrageous typographic contortions that challenged convention, and originated in alternative media, have swiftly become visual codes that marketers use in targeting youth demographics. This natural feeding cycle is perhaps one reason why the postwar art world has marginalized the artifacts of commercial art and eschewed its practice.

There have indeed been blips where design plays a prominent role, notably with Fluxus, a collective of individual artists who produced reams of typographical printed matter. But it was not until the late 1970s that art was unquestionably awakened from its formalist somnambulism by art world renegades like Kruger, who used the language of commercial art—words and pictures in disciplined compositions—not only to address heretofore taboo subjects, like critiques of gender, racial, cultural, and economic stereotypes promoted by mass media, but co-opted the quotidian forms through which products are sold—ads, postcards, shopping bags, posters, billboards, bus shelters, and film. Kruger embraced graphic design as a component (not merely a tool) of her art. And thanks in large part to her accomplishment, the definition of what art is has changed during the past twenty years to include virtually any imaginable medium. With increased commingling of the verbal and visual, the once prohibited language of commercial art is quite permissible. And with the emergence of the street as a gallery and the billboard as a frame, the appropriation of graphic design and advertising methods has become as common as paint and watercolor.

In addition to communicating ideas to a broad audience, Kruger's assimilation of commercial art has had a residual impact on the graphic design profession itself. Since graphic design is fungible and since, like sponges, graphic designers soak up influences wherever they can, art that utilizes commercial art, even as critique, has motivated contemporary graphic designers to push the limits of their own field further away from convention. Designers have always looked to art for inspiration, but they have rarely found so many common formal characteristics. This sharing of specific visual forms suggests that, at least superficially, the once formidable boundaries between art and graphic design have temporarily blurred.

Perhaps because Kruger so completely ignored such boundaries in her mission to make art that transcends the insularity of the art world, she has arguably contributed more to current graphic design and advertising vernacular than many of the leading trend-setting designers have. Kruger's art (which is her message) and her bold, minimalist typography (which is her style) have become something of a standard for those graphic designers who reject the late 1980s' and early 1990s' trend toward excessive, decorative layering that obliterates content. She has also stimulated designers to use their skill to produce messages of social relevance.

Kruger's method was influenced by reductive Modernist graphic design—the kind that began somewhat idealistically but that dominated corporate identity during the postwar years—as well as by the so-called Big Idea, or Creative Revolution, advertising style of the 1960s, known for clever slogans and ironic single images. She certainly acquired her signature red bands of Futura Bold type from these sources, which she learned about as art director for *Mademoiselle* (when she was twenty-two years old in 1968) and as a freelance book jacket designer. Yet her graphic approach decidedly bucked the trend of complexity common in post-Modern graphic design, which claimed to be rooted in academic linguistic theory but that devolved into tony style.

Kruger did not merely adapt conventional advertising techniques in order to parody mass media; she tapped into a universal graphic expression that gave the public ready access to her ideas. As a frame for assertive commentary that questioned power structures and gender relationships, Kruger's graphic style—which is best characterized as a rational "system" that unifies her messages—was more mesmerizing than the self-consciously edgy commercial styles and fashions of the day. And yet graphic designers did not immediately warm to Kruger's art. In fact, it wasn't even known to most professionals until the late 1980s, when after a few highly visible exhibits, this curious hybrid art form (at least from a designer's point of view) began to surface on their radar. The few commercial artists who encountered her work—notably the 1989 march on Washington poster "Your Body is a Battleground" and the 1990 shopping bag with the now classic slogan "I Shop, Therefore I Am," as well as billboards, posters, and postcards—were surprised to see graphic design (*their* métier) in prestigious galleries and museums. Forget for a moment, if that is really possible, that Kruger's content, her form—the black, white, and red that are perhaps the most eye-catching of all color combinations (e.g., the early *Life* magazine and the Nazi emblem)—was so graphically powerful it unhinged the complacency of graphic designers. Add to this the message, and Kruger became a force to be reckoned with.

Nevertheless, for some it was difficult to reconcile such an overt use of graphic design as art. Sure, the Guerrilla Girls produced anonymously styled advertisements criticizing gender inequality in American art museums. But these were ads by artists, not integral pieces of art. Kruger's work, conversely, was perplexing because she propagated ideas in the same manner as mass product promotions, but the ideas were anything but. Among designers, the parochial attitude was to criticize a "downtown artist" for usurping their methods, while the more enlightened welcomed the graphically powerful work as subversion of the status quo. Presumably, conservative patrons of art were nonplused that such overt advertising was anointed as art. But what Kruger accomplished in melding art and graphic design—indeed art *as* graphic design—made art more populist, enabling a wide audience to consume social and cultural dynamics that in other art might be more inaccessible. Which is not to say that Kruger's work is transparent. Again, it is anything but. Her pictures and words are almost like teaser advertisements—in fact, she arguably influenced the current trend in teasers—that hint at a message and stimulate attention by prompting curiosity. The parts that she leaves out—the ideas tucked in between the picture and the words—demand viewer participation and interpretation.

"Creative advertising" (current jargon for imaginative as distinguished from hack work) does not give the audience everything on a silver platter, but rather conditions the viewer to "expect the unexpected" in order to capture brand loyalty. Just think of Absolut Vodka; the campaign began a decade ago as an abstract notion using art and over time has built upon an identity based on curious juxtapositions of product and image. Kruger's work is based on consistency and surprise too, but for a different purpose. Her audience has come to expect the black and white "stock" images and Futura type that give the work its rational order and graphic identity. But the surprise comes through in her countless variations on the basic form, from installations with huge type exegeses on floor, walls, and ceiling, to wrapping a New York City bus with quotations about power and liberation.

Once, gallery and museum artists balked at making art on commission for commercial advertising or editorial clients. Sure, a few might do the occasional book jacket or magazine cover (before Absolut came along), but often it was a reproduction of an existing painting or drawing. As Kruger's popularity grew within the graphic design field, editorial art directors began calling her to "illustrate," or rather complement, texts that matched her concerns. Completing the proverbial circle from when she was a magazine art director, Kruger's work has appeared on the covers of *Esquire, Newsweek, Ms,* and the *New York Times Book Review,* revealing the adaptability of her method—a possibly dubious virtue. Since she has achieved high visibility, various designers now brazenly mimic the Kruger style. And yet she is rarely perturbed, because when her style is stripped of its meaning and used only for its graphic surface, it validates her critique of the entire system. But when it is used to promote issues that she believes in, such as the case of a 1998 advertising campaign for women's free choice that appeared on the sides of New York City buses, Kruger doesn't mind at all. (Incidentally, regarding the pro-choice campaign—which has won a few advertising industry awards—she was approached to do the campaign herself, which she could not do; then her permission was requested to use her style, which she gave.) Kruger asserts that she does not retain exclusivity to Futura Extra Bold or any of the design conceits that she borrowed from the vernacular.

Popular style in graphic design has a short lifespan. The more that designers copy a trend—whether it's layered Grunge type or French curves or black matte—the sooner it becomes cliché. So with such unfettered access to her style by graphic designers, does Kruger risk becoming ineffectual? Only time will offer the definitive answer. Nonetheless, this is where the similarities to graphic design—or any art of the moment—cease. Although Kruger employs the language of mass communication, and has developed a visual personality as unified as any corporate identity, her graphic design is but a framework for organizing ideas into decipherable units. As an artist, however, she continues to expand her means of communicating by broadening the scope of her media and adding new forms, including satiric sculpture and documentary video. There are changes from year to year and installation to installation whereby all elements evolve. But more importantly, her art is a vision motivated by a history of social involvement. As an individual, her mission is constant. The commitment to her art and the society it serves insulates Kruger from the vicissitudes of fashion.

Contrary to the assertion of this essay, Kruger rejects the terms design and advertising in defining her work, stating, "I'm someone who works with pictures and words, and people can take that to mean anything they like." However, by using graphic design vocabularies, Kruger has not only influenced graphic designers, but is a key figure in the field. At a time when many designers are looking for ways to balance their work for commerce with social responsibility, Kruger is a role model who proves that graphic design is an influential medium for good and ill. And since the medium propels the message, the designer is a conduit through which myth and reality are passed on to the public. Through her own interventions, by using the techniques of mass media to critique mass media, she proves that the public can indeed be conditioned by design to expect the unexpected in public media—the truth.

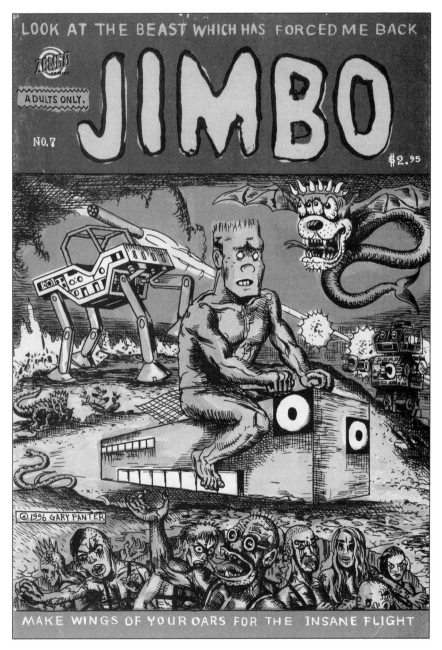

Cover of Gary Panter's Jimbo No. 7., *1997.*

GARY PANTER: ON THE MARGINS LOOKING OUT

Avid readers of alternative comics know Gary Panter's ratty line, eccentric yarns, and quirky characters. Jimbo, his post-underground commix hero of the late 1970s, helped define the Los Angeles Punk aesthetic and is today an icon among aficionados. Yet most savvy designers do not follow arcane comics or know its masters, including Panter—which makes the bestowal upon him of last year's Chrysler Award for Design Excellence incredibly audacious. Panter is an outsider, and yet, as the prestigious award implies, he has made a significant contribution to contemporary visual *and* design culture—indeed even more resonant than the Chrysler jury knew. "The judges had to be educated after seeing Panter's work for the first time," explains Peter Girardi, a former Chrysler Award recipient and member of the selection committee. "I kept urging them to look at the work and not think about it in terms of comics or funny illustrations. And once they looked longer than ten minutes, they went beyond formal shock and settled into learning a new language."

"Formal shock" is an apt description, because Panter's work does not fit into conventional graphic, industrial, product, or any other design genres. Although he has made plenty of commercial art (including an award-winning *Time* magazine cover portrait of The Who), on most days he is a renegade, storytelling image-monger who transmits ideas through many means, from print to puppets. His venues change too, from wall to page to stage to screen. The "new language" is a peculiar fusion of pop iconography, private demon, and primal fantasy expressed with frenetically scratchy marks, madly impudent brush-strokes, artlessly distorted figures, and comically construed letterforms. Panter is also a master of disguise—one style today and another tomorrow, yet all his own.

Panter has strong ties to the Zeitgeist (or more accurately, it is tied to him), yet he functions on his own terms and in his own space, a veritable junk-heap of a loft in the industrial section of Williamsburg, Brooklyn. Here, amid the debris, he paints huge iconic canvases, sculpts creepy hand-puppets, creates weird light shows, and produces absurd shadow plays in a dark makeshift studio rented by the Manhattan-based multimedia design firm Funny Garbage as an ersatz research and development annex. In this laboratory of imagination, Panter revels in his esoteric inspirations, from Japanese film monsters and Mexican magazine ads, to Dante, Boccaccio, Joyce, and Dick (Philip K., that is).

"He certainly stays in touch with his inner nitwit and inner child, but he's clearly a thoughtful artist," says Art Spiegelman, author of *Maus: A Survivor's Tale* and publisher of some of Panter's strips. Spiegelman's now-defunct *Raw* magazine was engaged in finding the razor-thin line between applied and pure art, and, as Spiegelman affirms, "Gary fulfills that perfectly." Panter's comics must indeed be read as surrealistic literature.

HERMETIC WORLDS

At age fifty, the artist resides in a hermetic world that is not, however, entirely cut off from the rest of civilization but situated on the margins where his roots dig deep. Born into a devout fundamentalist Christian family from Brownsville, Texas, Panter's father, who ran a five-and-dime, drew skillful copies of Dick Tracy, Popeye, and Daisy Mae types, which encouraged young Gary to believe that he could make graven images, too. Low and behold, he had a talent for drawing but also acquired an insatiable appetite for profane popular culture. Later, with the help of some progressive teachers at East Texas State University, where he studied art, he became a bona fide misfit—an artist in search of place. "On the landscape of my childhood, comics stand out," Panter recalls, "because they easily show views into other worlds, and [I was] most often transported somewhere somehow."

The adversative dynamic of Panter's genetic material and acquired passion have fused to produce a mad artist. Yet he remains unburdened by the sins of clashing cultures, because art carries his emotional baggage. Panter's art is about moral and aesthetic contradictions. His drawing can be at once wretchedly grotesque and unfathomably charming; he delights in the underbelly and revels in the prosaic. The marriage of these opposites is incredibly resonant and genuinely exquisite. His pictures sometimes look as though they were rendered with a fork, but each line has an expressive purpose. "To really appreciate Gary you have to have an epiphany where all of a sudden you 'get' why he is so brilliant—it's all about his drawing. All his sketches, to me, are better than any final products," asserts Helene Silverman, his wife and former *Metropolis* art director. "It is the rare artist that makes other artists want to draw," adds Spiegelman. "Panter has a devouringly compelling line, and is willing to try anything."

Panter's work is also an eloquent dissertation on celebrity, pornography, mass consumables, vernacular kitsch, and other pop-cult minutiae. "Popular culture will always contain important messages for the collective organism made *by* the collective organism, regardless of the intentions of its creators," he says about these mass-market monuments. And over the past two decades, pop references have become hip to quote as part of an ironic mass cultural critique. Panter, however, does not engage "in the lame kind of highbrow/lowbrow arguments which are just condescension anyway," inserts Peter Girardi. "He can really appreciate all forms of pop and does not make any kind of hierarchical judgments. It's all in the mix." How he processes and analyzes twentieth-century phenomena is found in the convergence of Godzilla and other sci-fi creatures with old toys, Twiggy, Raquel Welch, Jim Morrison, Frank Zappa, Mama Cass, Elvis, Bruce Lee, Monster trucks, Yul Brynner in "Westworld," "Famous Monsters of Filmland," and bad candy packaging. Most recently, these comprise a retelling of Dante's *Purgatorio,* a three-year-in-the-making comic opus that Panter just completed.

While it is tempting to compare him to Jeff Koons or Mark Kostabi, among other post-Modern samplers, Panter does not harvest pop culture's detritus for cynical purposes. He is too damn sincere to put everyone on, and not deluded enough to be innocent. In fact, "what sometimes seems like innocence is really wisdom," says Leonard Koren, the former editor of *Wet* magazine, one of Panter's earlier venues. Panter does not exploit the vernacular; he addresses its societal influence in narrative sequences that critically celebrate the twentieth century's love and hate of consumer culture. "He is the poet of post-Modern maleness, this weird hidden energy that society denies whether it be in violence or sexuality," adds John Carlin, a principal of Funny Garbage.

PEE WEE'S LABORATORY

Asked to sum up his impact, Panter modestly replies, "My stuff has been influential in that it looks easy to do, and that's encouraging to viewers." But while Panter's imagination has inspired cognoscenti for over thirty years, it has also, when reduced to its purest concept, been entertainment on a mass scale. This is most evident in the scenery and props that he designed for *Pee Wee's Playhouse,* the innovative Saturday morning TV series that ran from 1986 through 1991. In the early 1980s Paul Rubens (a.k.a., Pee Wee Herman) recalls that when he saw Panter's artwork for Punk bands, "I thought it was exactly what I wanted and approached Gary to do a poster for my stage show . . . but he said, 'What about the rest of the show?'" And Rubens, who was often accused of micromanaging his productions, gave Panter total license: "Gary was my answer. If I know the right people I will delegate."

Among the array of ingenious objects (created with Wayne White and Ric Heitzman), Rubens notes that the playhouse exterior, a dystopic Hansel and Gretel cottage precariously balanced on a sliver of imagination atop a faux mountain peak, is probably his favorite of all Panter's creations. Then comes the enveloping anthropomorphic chair and the bitingly acerbic front door that bids snooty welcome to Pee Wee's pals. "There is nothing that I don't love, in fact love isn't the word, I am obsessed with it all," extols Rubens.

Pee Wee's is the archetypal post-Modern children's theater, replete with affectionately sarcastic winks and nods to the American mythos. It was the perfect vehicle for Panter's obsessions with (and reappraisal of) those myths. "As a child I was very serious about my notions of what I would do if I ever got the chance to tell the people who made stuff for kids what I thought they should make," Panter says. "The stuff that reached me in a small town out on the prairie acti-

vated very useful, fun, parts of my brain that may not have been acti-
vated otherwise. I've always wanted to make stuff like that." But on the
downside, Panter admits, "Pee Wee did spawn endless ugly new-
wavey cereal and fruit roll-up–type commercials. Groovy little kids in
big sunglasses with little quivering pink and lime green boomerangs all
over everything."

Pee Wee's Playhouse proved, however, that Panter's playful
madness could appeal to a wide audience. Perhaps Panter is the "trick-
ster" found in primitive cultures whose existence releases the tensions
of everyday life. His current commercial work for kids (and older people), *Pink Donkey and the Fly,* an animated cartoon series for the
Cartoonetwork.com produced by Funny Garbage and directed by Ric
Heitzman, is the artist at his most maturely childish. "To make characters that make sense and seem to come to life is a real pleasure," he
beams. Yet while reduced to the bare conceptual essentials, *Pink Donkey*
is an example of Panter's paradoxical meandering. As Spiegelman notes,
it is no coincidence that the protagonist looks like "a cross between
something Hannah Barbera might do and the horse in Picasso's
"Guernica." Panter knows exactly what he's doing. "As an underground cartoonist, transgression is my business—and yea, verily I have
transgressed, mightily," he says. "I would not want the clock turned
back to before 'Ren and Stimpy,' but personally I would like to make
something as wide-eyed and amazing as old *Mighty Mouse* cartoons."

Panter mediates rocky cultural terrain by catering exclusively
to his obsessions. In the early 1970s, when he emerged as a comic strip
artist, "The alternative cartoonists were following the large highway
that R. Crumb was paving," explains Spiegelman. "Panter moved
through the surreal end-period of that time without any relation to
drugs as catalyst. He created an interior landscape that touched down
on reality." And he also forged a "more is more" approach, the coun-
terpoint to the benign less is more of, say, Charles Schulz's cartoons.
"Panter was revealing a new kind of visual density, like Cy Twombly
with a whiff of art school entering the cartoon planet," concludes
Spiegelman.

When Panter started out, "the punk idea was that you could
do it yourself—turn your back on the tried and true existing venues for
art, music, and publishing and create something new," says comic artist
Charles Burns. "That's what Gary did. He wrote and drew books and
Xeroxed them up for his friends and few paying customers. He did

record album covers and illustrations for Ralph records (a small record company owned by The Resident) in exchange for studio recording time so that he could put out records of his own twangy, clunky songs." "Gary is a powerhouse of visual ideas," injects Matt Groening, *The Simpsons'* creator, who met Panter in the 1970s. Panter had just started drawing "Jimbo" comic strips for *Slash,* the Los Angles Punk magazine, and the work was getting noticed. "He had so much ability to do whatever he wanted to do and pull it off. He made things crazier and uglier than anyone else." Panter's early graphics defined the California Punk ethos, the alternative 'zine scene, and although he never achieved the notoriety of Keith Haring or Kenny Scharf, the post-Pop painting world is also in his debt. "He was a source for a lot of this trend," says Spiegelman.

TRANSCULTURAL ENIGMA

Comics are the purest expression of Panter's art. And Jimbo is his most alter-ego–like, unifying entity that has agelessly endured for almost thirty years. A transcultural enigma clad in a tartan loincloth with buzz-cut hair, Jimbo emerged fully formed in a cartoon story of 1974 called "Bowtie Madness," and Panter says he resembles "Joe Palooka, Alley Oop, Dennis the Menace, my brother Tommy, and my friend Jay Cotton." He also claims that Jimbo was an unplanned birth: "He just popped out. [But] I knew that I would be drawing him for a long time as soon as I first drew him."

Groening contends that, out of the whole Punk scene, "Jimbo was the best looking, most competent, and reached a level of virtuosity in its crazed ratty line. Jimbo is also funny and insightful," and adds that "none of Gary's stuff is mean even though he does such ghastly imagery."

Jimbo will never be as popular as Homer or Bart Simpson, but his character has incredible emotional and philosophical depth, and his story is a contiguous odyssey with a past, present, and future. Like most ongoing comic book characters, readers can dip into Jimbo's life at any point along the continuum. "In my personal comics, I play around all the time with experimental anti-narrative games," says Panter. Nonetheless, it is advantageous to follow Jimbo's exploits from the beginning to appreciate the full range of expressive development. *Cola*

"Burning Gall," a detail from a comic strip by Gary Panter, 1996.

Madness, a "lost" 1984 graphic novel recently published by Funny Garbage Books that Panter had created for a Japanese audience, fills a few holes in Jimbo's (and the artist's) life. Here Jimbo is the fulcrum of a compact, though intricate, plot that underscores Panter's central theme: "We live in a culture that borrows significantly from the past, but we combine and inhabit these familiar signposts in a unique and ultimately disturbing way," writes John Carlin in the book's afterword. "Panter seems to be saying that we continue to live with the symbols and rituals of traditional belief systems but have lost their sense of spiritual purpose." And that, enigmatically speaking, says Carlin, "is the madness that is *Cola.*" The genius that is *Cola* is that, out of absurd drawing and disjointed dialogue, Panter has conjured a dream that effectively critiques reality.

ARTIST'S PURGATORY

Jimbo is also the protagonist in Panter's most ambitiously transcendent comic strip, a reinterpretation of Dante's *Purgatorio,* titled *Jimbo in Purgatory.* Panter drew a single panel each night (after putting his young daughter, Olive, to bed) for three years in order to complete the twelve panels on each of the thirty-three *New York Times*–sized pages. Every page is devoted to a chapter or canto illuminated with a staggering array of characters and scenes, precisely built upon a stoic grid and hypnotically framed by intricate decorative ornament. Panter possesses what Spiegelman calls "the painstaking patience of a monk on belladonna." The aim is to satisfy an almost maniacal intellectual curiosity to find the resonance between classic literature and how different authors' obsessions through different books over centuries were influenced by Dante (i.e., Boccaccio's *Decameron* influenced Geoffrey Chaucer's *Canterbury Tales,* which influenced James Joyce's *The Dubliners,* and so on). "These works are independent pieces of art, but a lot of the reward for studying them is the way in which they . . . dissect and salvage and mutate to build upon each other," says Panter.

Panter spent several years studiously comparing Dante and Boccaccio to find everything they had in common and then found countless additional literary and pop references to Dante, which he diligently injects into the dialogue balloons of the reinterpreted cantos.

"Its influences derive from the pop culture of earlier centuries as well as that of recent decades," Panter explains. In the original, Dante is lead by the Roman poet Virgil on a journey of the soul from chaos and ignorance to enlightenment, using the imagery of the Catholic religion. As a stand-in for Dante, Jimbo (who in an earlier comic strip was imprisoned for resisting arrest) is guided in every panel by Valise, a parole-robot, who is a small ambulatory valise that resembles a miniature Corbusier house.

Jimbo traverses a vast infotainment-testing center built in the shape of Dante's Mount Purgatory. Within its borders every man or robot stands in for a character of the *Divine Comedy*. In Panter's drama all the participants must respond to one another with a literary fragment that demonstrates knowledge of a particular passage and ability to quote other works alluding to the theme, specifically of that location in the original poem. With dizzying lunacy, the logic of the work folds in on itself with the introduction of contemporary cultural figures, just as Dante had included personalities of his own time. In the end, since the whole of purgatory is a testing center, all the characters are striving for what Panter calls "University of Focky Bocky degrees in literature," leading to the presumption that this may be Panter's own quest for a doctorate of pop culture.

Panter offers that through comics he tries "to connect with a smarter part of me for part of the time." As for how this work will be judged, he says, "Secretly, most artists are hoping that some alien art historian, 50,000 years from now, will come across some remaining fragment of their life's work and go 'Wow!'" But since he is powerless to control the future, he continues to pursue images and ideas that reveal personal truths for the moment. "Usually my brain chemistry is such that I stare at the wall with occasional guilty lists flitting through, but I'm waiting patiently for something else: blasts or strings of mental images. But they don't come until you're thinking about nothing, when the mechanism of memory is often switched off. So one has to learn to look when the looking-around mechanism is disengaged. I certainly don't find all my notions usable or even desirable, but it's good to be able to have a look at them. Then to be critical of them." To ensure that the results will be uniquely his own, he remains ensconced in his drafty hermetic world that, as the Chrysler Award judges learned, has made a curious impact on this world.

Sequences from two promotional movies for Herman Miller Inc. (left) and Jostens, a year book company (right).

NUMBER SEVENTEEN: QUICK-CUT CULTURE

Incarcerated on a sinister resort island in the classic TV show *The Prisoner,* the protagonist known only as Number 6 routinely wailed against being a number—"I am a person," he said in anguish. But no one will hear this complaint from Emily Oberman and Bonnie Siegler, two willing inmates of Manhattan island whose multidisciplinary design partnership is known as Number Seventeen.

Oberman (age thirty-eight) and Siegler (age thirty-seven) graphically design videos that have established contemporary auras for MTV, VH1, Herman Miller, *Saturday Night Live,* and Condé Nast. They also design magazines, advertisements, and logos for these and other media companies. The eight-year-old firm might lack a signature graphic style, yet it possesses a distinctive attitude in part rooted in its principals' shared film and pop references. And while a consistent Number Seventeen imprimatur will not be found on their various work, their cultural sampling and witty sarcasm is unmistakable.

The number seventeen is itself a flippant reference, something akin to a "MacGuffin," the term Alfred Hitchcock used to describe the relatively arbitrary props on which his movie plots turned. Similarly, seventeen is not the duo's office address or the number of designers in their employ. It is rather more arcane. As if by divine intervention, the numeral hauntingly surfaced many years ago when Oberman and Siegler were vacationing together in Spain and found seventeen everywhere they went. It was on their airport rental car space, their Barcelona hotel room, their Gaudi museum bag check ticket, as well as in fourteen other occurrences (seventeen in all). So, it was providential that they chose this numerological hyperbole as their enigmatic moniker.

Given the metaphysics of their lives, it is tempting to overemphasize (though not overstate) Oberman and Siegler's phenomenal chemistry. They give synchronicity new meaning. When Siegler met Oberman on the first day of their first design job in 1985 at Marcus Ratliff Incorporated in New York, they instantly bonded. Over fifteen years later, they finish each other's thoughts and sentences, share the same infectious laugh, use the same dry cleaner, and work in unfettered harmony. Moreover, they were born in the same year (six months apart), were raised only miles from one another in the New York suburbs, and they look alike, if one squints. Many partnerships certainly rise—yet usually fall because of creative tensions, but not here. Number Seventeen has succeeded because, while Oberman and Siegler are distinct individuals with their own egos, they agree to be parts of a single, two-digit entity.

It took eight years and a few jobs before becoming Number Seventeen, during which time each garnered enviable experience in film and video and became visual storytellers in their own rights. Oberman was at M&Co, where she collaborated with Tibor Kalman on, among other things, the type-in-motion lyrics for the Talking Heads' "Nothing But Flowers" music video and solely designed the poetically typographical logo for Friends of the Earth. She also worked on the screen typography for the Suburu automobile commercials, directed by Kalman, which helped launch a trend in kinetic letterforms used on TV spots. Siegler worked at VH1 for four years and was its design director for two. She was responsible for the highly visible "Everything Will Be Okay as Long as I Don't Turn Into My Parents" outdoor advertising and video campaigns, which had a profound influence on the music channel because of its ironic candor and twenty-something voice. Its fast-motion editing style was also a novel way to address an audience that was raised on TV. These and other experiences made the pair realize that a niche for graphic video design was waiting to be filled. When they quit their jobs within a few months of each other, they jumped headlong into making what they call "very very very small films" and have been doing it ever since.

Oberman and Siegler are serious about their work but refuse to take themselves too seriously. For example, when asked to share their design philosophy, a question that often invites hollow rhetoric, they were characteristically glib in their response: "Girl Power, Show Me the Money, Try a Little Tenderness, Life is Like a Box of Chocolates, Stay on the Sunny Side, Let a Smile Be Your Umbrella, Pork Is the Other White Meat, Stop and Smell the Roses, Just Do It, There's No Place Like Home, and Better Living Through Chemistry."[1] Yet when asked if they pursue a contemporaneous visual style, they were more sober: "Clients sometimes want trends but we can't deliver that. We are more attracted to the bigger landscape, ideas that endure. We like work (whether it is our own or others) where you can't immediately tell when it was made. That doesn't mean we don't appreciate things that are current; it just means we choose to make work that hopefully will seem as fresh in ten or twenty years as it does today. It goes back to the drive to make an emotional connection with the audience as opposed to a stylistic one. Emotions will always outlast trends."

This is doubtlessly sincere, but not the total picture. When pressed on how they plan to avoid the usual pitfall of graphic design—superficiality—and rise above the ephemeral, they argue: "What's wrong with the ephemeral?" Pop is indeed ephemeral, and the duo admit that "Everything from Bob Dylan to Britney Spears, from Tater Tots to Captain Crunch, from Pong to Zelda, from Fred Friendly to Fred Flintstone, from *Mad* magazine to the *New Yorker,* from Kmart to Miu Miu" influence their work. And it shows.

Number Seventeen is a representative of the visual Zeitgeist, but not a slave to transitory fashion. A case in point is their adaptation of Paul Rand's classic lowercase logo for ABC (the American Broadcasting Company). When commissioned to create an identity for ABC Daytime programming, they seamlessly added the word "day" in the same emblematic typeface as Rand's original and placed it in a yellow circle juxtaposed to the ABC logo as if it had always existed in this form. But when it came to animating it for on-air broadcast, they morphed the static mark into Busby Berkeley–inspired choreography, wherein multiple ABC logos kaleidoscopically dance around the word "day" to a 1930s musical score, intercut with actual Berkeley clips. Some designers would have taken the opportunity to reject tradition altogether, but this spot, designed by Oberman, Siegler, and studio member Matthew Jacobson, was a reverent homage to the Rand icon while sublimely reinterpreting a landmark of early cinema in an inventive and mature manner.

The term *mature* is, however, an admittedly ambiguous tribute. It is like saying something is interesting or handsome or fine. But without maturity, which is the ability to self-edit what is superfluous, Number Seventeen's signature playfulness could very well be anarchic and ineffectual. The fact that Oberman and Siegler have become mature storytellers in a medium where ideas must be conveyed quickly—between ten and sixty seconds—underscores a mastery of aesthetic form and a confidence in concept. Maturity means that they will not settle for an easy look at the expense of meaning. "Everything is storytelling," Siegler underscores, "and what we are always trying to do is communicate an idea . . . be it an abstract solution or a narrative one . . . and always inherent in the idea is an emotional component that will hopefully work on a more subconscious level."

An instance where an aesthetically alluring visual design is built upon a complex narrative foundation, often triggering the desired subconscious response, is the opening credit sequence for the weekly, late-night, TV comedy series *Saturday Night Live*. It is not overstated, yet it builds upon a profound visual theory. "Although we didn't know it at the time," Siegler explains, "we applied something my husband calls Animator's Logic to the piece. When you are creating abstract animation, it is human nature to have a back story for every frame and even give them anthropomorphic characteristics. Our SNL opener goes a little like this: A bunch of blue lines are looking for something, so they run across the screen, then some of their friends join them from the other side, then they all go off and a blue line is hanging out alone for a moment and starts to feel lonely until a whole bunch of his friends join him and then they all dance together. You have to watch the piece to see what happens in the end." All this is accomplished in around sixty seconds and demands that every frame must be precisely timed. There is no room to falter, no time to lollygag. But being children of the television generation, Oberman and Siegler instinctively understand the art of quick-cut economy.

Oberman and Siegler's speediest film, and possibly their best, is a kinetic timeline told in word-in-picture that spans the beginning of recorded time to the year 3000 in only six minutes. Created for Josten's, a company that makes yearbooks and class rings for high schools throughout the United States, the film is implanted with scores of subjective visual icons from Earth's dawn through, surprisingly, the next millennium. It flashes forward in a witty quick-cut montage of unexpected real and faux historical imagery and is bound together by an acutely clever narration that goes like this: "Nineteen-year-old Joan of Arc is burned at the stake but doesn't make the headlines because print doesn't begin until Guttenberg invents the printing press. Later people burn books instead of people." Not an iota of sappy or prosaic nostalgia is evident. Although commissioned to promote "memories," the timeline effectively stimulates recognition of past, present, and future by weaving in the familiar with the probable and the speculative. "We were actually bartering with events in history," Oberman recalls, as in "We'll give up the Salem Witch Trials if we can keep Gandhi." The work loosely parodies a vintage educational film genre, but this formative reference does not overpower the idea. Number Seventeen's intelligence shines through the seamless marriage of the film's component parts, from graphics, type, photographs, and music, to the hilarious narration, cowritten by Oberman, Siegler, Glenn O'Brien, and Scott Burns. This entirely self-contained entity transcends its commercial function—which, incidentally, is a result, not a goal.

Oberman and Siegler do not intentionally make standalone work. "We are commercial artists," Siegler insists, "and there is a great challenge in doing work that we can stand behind while solving the communication needs of someone else." A case in point is a video for Herman Miller, the contract furniture company, which was used at a trade fair to introduce a new line of integrated, contract office furniture. It was never intended as a hard-sell commercial, but like the timeline it had to plant a seed in the audience's cerebrum. The video, with its Jazz-patter narration, written by Glenn O'Brien, and its uptempo syncopated score, is a dance of abstract and figurative forms, some in kaleidoscopic motion, smoothly paced and totally integrated in a visual rhythm that represents the interlocking shapes of the workstations hypnotically joining together. It recalls the abstract experimental films of the 1950s and early 1960s while at the same time quotes 1970s television sitcom opening sequences. "We are fans of and influenced by both narrative and experimental film," Oberman explains. "But we are also influenced by the Jumbotron in Times Square, public access television, and home movies." Oberman also studied filmmaking in college, and Siegler married an experimental filmmaker, so the influences are hard to avoid.

Number Seventeen excels in the soft-sell environment, where it can make allusions through stream-of-consciousness and montage. While routinely adhering to tight storyboards, their most effective videos involve impressionistic image editing that provides story fragments, forcing the viewer to fill in the empty gaps in between. But they are also sharp when creating iconic moments in the form of interstitials. One such was for a Red Hot Organization's MTV special titled "No Alternative," which used the visual language of MTV to imply that "Safe Sex is Hot Sex." Only five relatively static shots were used in a rebus-like puzzle—a safe and a banana equals a candle and a volcano. It was simple, pointed, and hip. Another iconographic piece was an animated MTV Productions logo used to brand its films. For this Number Seventeen looked back twenty years earlier at how MTV introduced itself to the world of television. "We took the [mascot] astronaut and had him leave the moon to explore new frontiers, just like the film business," Siegler notes. "We did this job around the time that the Beavis and Butthead movie came out. So although we presented five different ideas, we think they chose the one they did partially because we named the idea 'Uranus,' which everyone got a kick out of saying." Number Seventeen certainly knows how to read its clients. Likewise, for *Saturday Night Live*'s SNL Studios logo, they were first hired to design a static mark, but, "because it was for a movie studio, we designed even the static version to have a kind of motion to it." When it was time to animate it, Oberman and Siegler knew instantly that it should be "an abstraction of a drunken cab ride through New York City on a rainy night," a reference to one of the many SNL TV show openers during its over-twenty-year run.

Oberman and Siegler refer to themselves as graphic designers, not as filmmakers, perhaps believing that making "very very very small films" does not entitle them to that lofty job description. But as designers, they contribute invaluably to other directors' films and videos through graphics and typography. For a Group Health antismoking commercial, directed by photographer and illustrator Matt Mahurin, they designed the type and created and edited the type animation "to enhance the meaning behind Matt's footage." Their most playful typographic concoctions, however, are parody commercials for *Saturday Night Live,* directed by Jim Signorelli, including Crystal Gravy ("Lighter, Cleaner, More Transparent"), a send-up of Crystal Pepsi, and Cookie Dough, a send-up of trendy sports drinks like Gatorade and Powerade. Number Seventeen's type parodies are acerbic riffs on a genre at a time when more and more TV commercials are using type to circumvent the increasing popularity of remote "mute" button.

When asked what commissions they take or refuse, Siegler instantly replies, "It's all about the Benjamins, baby [translation: hundred dollar bills]." But their work belies this glibness. They don't accept commissions where they cannot make a meaningful contribution, and they have their bêtes noir. But more importantly, they do what they do because each partner simply loves translating pop into ideas, into moving pictures. And this is, after all, the ideal métier . . .

---

[1]Interview with the author, 2000.

Cover of Dear Diary, *a children's book by Sara Fanelli, 2000.*

SARA FANELLI'S WILD THINGS

I was introduced to the work of thirty-one-year-old, Florence-born, London-based Sara Fanelli a few years ago, when her 1998 children's book, *A Dog's Life,* came across my desk. At the time I was art-directing the biannual Children's Book supplement of the *New York Times Book Review,* and the number of new children's books flying over the transom exceeded my ability to carefully peruse each one. However, I was grabbed by Fanelli's book cover, with a flaming red background and tartan–Mondrian-like grid affixed with randomly placed, childlike sketches of curiously colored canines. Since most of the picture books published that year were tightly rendered, *l'art brut* quality of Fanelli's illustration, akin to the approaches of Maira Kalman and Henrik Drescher, was enough to initially captivate. Yet what kept me engaged was not the artfully crude surfaces, but the personality of the drawn and collaged characters. Unlike Kalman's popular canine hero Max, Fanelli's dogs are not individual protagonists; rather, together they quirkily represent the diversity of an entire species, all breeds of dogs from everywhere. Still, each of the pooches has a unique, witty, visual persona, and I especially warmed to a tiny doodle of a pup roasting bones on a spit over an open fire. But it is one thing for an artist to scribble a childish likeness and another to make idiosyncratic attributes come alive so that the creature resonates beyond the drawing. Fanelli does this with aplomb.

In addition to the drawings and collages, *A Dog's Life* is a virtual pet, not in the computer sense, but as a book-as-object. The inside front and back covers are fitted with foldout pieces of an imaginary dog's face, ears, legs, and tail, with a paper bone woven into the binding as a bookmark. When the front and back covers are splayed, the book is transformed into a mutt. What's more, Fanelli's eccentric lettering, randomly alternating from hand scrawls to scripts to jumbled typefaces that change from page to page, is design play at its most silly. That the book eschews a continuous narrative, a dominant central figure, and a beginning, middle, and end, might be a drawback for some. But since every page is such a visual surprise, and Fanelli fills these pages with such a plethora of unanticipated sight gags (a French *chien* shaped like a baguette), a conventional story line would be superfluous.

I wondered, however, whether or not Fanelli was capable of developing a character-driven plot. As much as I enjoyed the kibble of the dog book, it is easy to make a scrapbook of related images. Making a compelling story and winning characters, on the other hand, demands more proficiency.

And then I came upon another Fanelli book, *Wolf!,* actually published in 1997, a year before *A Dog's Life,* that included these two attributes. *Wolf!* is a fully realized story about a wolf, called Wolf, who "decided to go for a walk into the city to make some new friends," reads the narrative, and encountered a book-load of misunderstandings and misadventures when he was wrongly presumed to be ferocious.

I could tell what was in store from the look of the main character rendered in frenetic pencil scrawls (resembling Ed Koren's scratchy *New Yorker* cartoon creatures), with small cut-paper teeth, claws, ears, and eyebrows pasted on. Wolf also wears two different-colored shoes that change hue throughout the course of book. His scary reputation and untidy appearance belie his inner innocence. His encounters with children and adults end badly when they realize that he is a wolf. Sure, it's an old story with a familiar moral (i.e., appearances are deceiving), but Fanelli's enchantingly contrived main and supporting characters give this book dimension beyond the obvious. Her scenes are rendered as cut-paper collages and she creates dynamic visual tension through the contrast of dark and light and cluttered and minimal settings in alternating spreads. Fanelli is precocious with form and has no qualms about using any element, scraps of yellowing newspaper, vintage wallpaper, and old ledger sheets, to push her ideas across. Mischievously, she combines this minutiae with drawings and paintings in pen, pencil, watercolor, and gouache to create pictures that are uninhibited and seemingly naïve.

But, despite her admission to me that "I didn't do any art training in Italy where I come from," she is not untutored. After all, she left Florence because she wanted to be an illustrator. She attended Camberwell College of Arts in London and, having earned a B.A. in graphic design, advanced to the graduate program and earned an M.A. at the Royal College of Art. As a student, she also won the prestigious MacMillian prize in 1991 for her first children's book, *Button,* which originated as a school thesis project and was published in 1993. Furthermore, she hails from an art-savvy family. Her father teaches the history of architecture and has written essays on graphics as well, and her mother researches the history of textiles.

Fanelli is diminutive, with precisely molded features. She speaks English with a lilting Italian accent, enunciating her words (and thoughts) with perfection, which sharply contrasts with the anarchic-looking alter egos that fill her pages. Yet as brutish as they are, none of them, especially Wolf, are menacing—which is not to imply that they are prosaic. The word spiritual may be an apt description, but not in the religious sense. There is just a kind human spirit that imbues her repertoire of animals, minerals, and vegetables. While Fanelli admits that her art is personal expression, she doesn't seem to be exorcising the psychological demons common to other *l'art brut*ists. Instead, through her art she experiences what in real life is impossible: "For me, the main thing with children's books is entering a world that takes you somewhere else," she explains, "or even if it doesn't take you somewhere, it gives you some thoughts you didn't have before."

Sometimes, Fanelli's images are intricate, other times simple. Sometimes they are pictorial, other times typographic. For instance, in *Wolf!* the beleaguered hero is sitting in a barber's chair contemplating whether or not to wear a mask to fool those who find him objectionable. "Maybe if he did wear a mask he could make some friends," reads a narrative that is cleverly typeset in jumbled words forming the shape of a light bulb. Fanelli uses letters and type as both graphic and storytelling components. But whatever the tool, the idea is paramount, and whatever the idea is, it must work on a number of levels. "I find it quite hard to accept an image that works only on one plane," she told me. "When I create an image, I feel it's almost too one-dimensional to have a picture that is only a gouache painting, so I bring in different layers and different worlds from old stationary and labels to suggest that there is more than one story being told."

Fanelli's 1994 *My Map Book* is her most clever overall concept. The maps comprising the book (and serving as the narrative) tell a story of discovery and are essential way-finders in a world rooted in her memory. The concept is built on her long-held fascination with the form: "I love maps, both the very old ones, like Biblical maps, and then medieval maps, and then maps for the London underground and so on," she explains. "This project started when in my sketchbooks I was drawing maps of the area where I lived in Italy. I was not living at home, so I was thinking back on memories of places, and I created maps of these places for myself."

She adds that this book is also an exercise in language; her challenge was to build a story from the verbal snippets of map coordinates. "By having a map quite simple but with quirky details, it suggested a narrative that wasn't explicit," she says. "So I decided to have quite simple maps (probably the ones in the sketchbooks are simpler than the ones I was doing). I chose to have a way of looking at things that was map-like, with elements of things that are not usually represented as maps, like the 'Map of the Heart.'"

Fanelli says that she does not do children's books to expressly satisfy particular demographic demands. And Eden Ross Lipson, children's book editor of the *New York Times Book Review,* agrees these are not entirely for children: "I'm intrigued by her work, but not sure how child-friendly it is. Not that that has much effect on what is being done these days." Nonetheless, *My Map Book* is clearly simpler in terms of texture and pattern than any of her other books. "It has more pastels, less deep colors," Fanelli explains.

> I tried to keep it quite young, which meant that I didn't want to put in too much detail. I try never to compromise because of the sake of having to reach a specific audience, but it became very much a personal book that I wanted small children to use. On every page there's a dotted area, and in theory the child could add a drawing of what is their favorite game or their favorite food, and so on. And in the foldout map on the back, the child is supposed to make their own map, too.

Still, this book, like Fanelli's others, is playful but not solely juvenile—rather, it's more like a personal diary.

All artists maintain sketchbooks or diaries. Few, however, get away with publishing such haphazard material as a book. Since Fanelli's finished art is sketchlike, it seems logical that her most recent book, *Dear Diary,* is a visual diary—in fact, a diary within a diary. The premise is simple, and the form has seen other incarnations, notably Nick Bantock's *Griffin & Sabine.* Fanelli's story is conveyed through a series of diary entries by the different characters (human, object, animal, and bug—Lucy, Chair, Spider, Firefly, Knife and Fork, and so on). Although the narrative is more episodic than contiguous, Lucy does float in and out and is featured in her own postscript section at the end, where many of the characters come together. "I love the structure of the book," Fanelli says proudly, "having the climax and anticlimax and pages that can be just for a moment resting on or enjoying a certain visual element of the story, and then carrying on again." I have seen children drawn into the book, but not necessarily because of the story. The form is the glue. Fanelli cut-and-pastes the contents of her flat files, filling *Dear Diary* with every scrap of found-object in her collection, and employs every technique that has ever caught her fancy. In fact, I focused as much on the bits and pieces because I recognized similar items from my own collections. This distraction could pose a problem, but Fanelli does not care. She wants readers to experience her books on many levels, and one of them is the pure pleasure derived from the artifacts that she uses.

Accordingly, Fanelli does not just confine herself to children's books. She is an editorial and advertising artist counting a 1999 British postage stamp among her most visible commissions, commissions that also include book covers, jackets, posters, and other media. She also smartly illustrated the 1998 *Folio Book of Short Novels* (*Turn of the Screw, The Call of the Wild, Death in Venice, Gigi,* etc.) with a suite of collages that bring these classics up-to-date. There is, however, very little difference in her method, whether for children or for an older audience. The idea is always paramount, the raw materials are taken from the same drawers, and the style is routinely brutish. I will not fault her for maintaining a recognizable style, but the repetition is sometimes monotonous because her one-off editorial illustrations lack the same tension achieved in her books.

Her children's books are complete entities, and therefore more compelling—which brings us to her 1998 *It's Dreamtime,* a book that was compared in a British design magazine review to Maurice Sendak's opus, *Where the Wild Things Are.* Fanelli's book reveals the dreams of the characters Zeno, a boy; Bubu, a dog; and Bird, a fowl, who find themselves together with the moon (a character) and a space creature, Martini; and Marty, its dog. The dream is told in two parts as ersatz reality and visionary fantasy—the former, a double-page tableau filled with Fanelli's visual stuff; the latter, a series of comic strip panels printed with large halftone dots to give the illusion of an illusion. This book is Fanelli's most cinematic, as it moves in and out of conscious and subconscious realms. The dream is a perfect métier for her surrealistic proclivities, making this is her most mature work.

Although the comparison to Sendak serves as a benchmark, it is like equating Tom Wolfe's *Bonfire of the Vanities* with Tolstoy's *War and Peace.* Sendak's *Where the Wild Things Are* forever altered the children's book genre. Fanelli's books have a place in that continuum. They have not changed the field, but they have measurably added to it. Her books are engaging because the artist's genuine quirks and passions capture our imagination, certainly mine. Fanelli has grown as an artist and storyteller, and on her own terms, this is certainly tribute enough.

INTROSPECTIVES

SECTION IV

An anti-Nazi decal sold in Italy, 2001.

SWASTIKA GUILT

When I was eight years old, a friend gave me a Nazi flag that his father had brought back from the war as a souvenir. Despite my parents' warnings not to upset my grandmother, whose family (I much later learned) had perished in Auschwitz, I would often streak through the apartment in her presence wearing the flag as a kind of Superman cape. At the time, I knew nothing about the Holocaust except that Jews were not beloved in Germany, but since religious taunting was not uncommon in my Manhattan public school, this fact was of little consequence to me. I was also addicted to watching movies on TV about World War II and, as a wannabe artist, drew more pictures of Nazis than of Americans because their uniforms were better. The German steel helmets, with those menacing, ear-covering brims, were a thousand times more threatening than the G. I. "pots" or Tommy "pans." And I was enthralled by the black SS uniform with the silver "Death's Head" badges on the hat and the red, black, and white swastika armband that made the entire costume so graphic.

As a designer I have long been fascinated by the unmitigated power of the swastika. Yet as a Jew I am embarrassed by my fascination. This paradox is one reason why I wrote the book *The Swastika: A Symbol Beyond Redemption?*—though working on it did not resolve my conflict. Indeed I have become even more obsessed with the symbol— more drawn to and repulsed by it. I have curious dreams about it. Yet, I am embarrassed to hold my own book in public, with its striking swastika jacket, lest anyone think that I support the symbol and what it stands for.

I still own that Nazi flag and have subsequently amassed a collection of over one hundred additional swastika artifacts, from buttons to banners of Nazi, neo-Nazi, and non-Nazi origin. Something of a fetish, you say? Yes, and frankly I feel guilty about it. So five years ago I decided that I had to find out why this symbol had such hypnotic force for me (and others), particularly in light of the horrors it represents. I began researching the origins of the swastika as a Nazi symbol, which led me to seek out even earlier historical roots dating back to antiquity (even prehistory), when it was ostensibly benign. I often wonder whether this inquiry was simply a justification of my fetishistic attraction or an honest scholarly investigation. It is probably both.

How Adolf Hitler created an aesthetic and ethos that millions of people willingly followed is, for me, a continual source of bewilderment. (I have often wondered, if the circumstances had been different, whether I would have followed it, too.) The swastika was his instrument, though not solely the mark of his political party. It was his personal emblem—the surrogate of the man and the ideology. Arguably, like any symbol it is only as good or bad as the ideas it represents. But as the icon of Nazism, the swastika was transformed from a neutral vessel into heinous criminality itself. A case can be made, and I try to make it, that the swastika is not the bottle in which an evil genie lived; it is the incarnation of that creature. In this sense my fascination with the swastika is an entry into a horrific world where I find myself trying to somehow make a connection with the victims and the victimizers.

I know this is vicarious. And I've often questioned my motives. Studying the swastika has been a means for me to ameliorate my guilt over being what I call a Third Reich voyeur. I often wonder how my grandmother would feel about my obsession and my book. She had emigrated from Galacia in the early teens. Her father had left her and a couple of siblings in New York while he returned to collect the rest of the family. The Great War prevented his own emigration, and after it was over, he remained in Poland with his ill wife and younger children. The only time my grandmother ever spoke about the Holocaust was when I was thirteen and she showed me a postcard, dated 1940, which she had received from her father a few years after the war. It had been posted from the Lodz ghetto (although apparently not mailed at that time) and was stamped with three official Nazi seals that included the swastika. The postcard had an acrid smell, as though it had been in a moldy bag for all that time; the words said that everything was fine. But the swastikas said otherwise. In 1946 my grandmother learned of their fate. I always remember that smell when I see a swastika.

She never spoke of the Holocaust again. But the postcard piqued my interest to the extent that I read whatever I could find (and in 1963 there was not a lot on the subject of the ghettos and death camps). I could not get the idea out of my mind that my own flesh and blood had been subjected to such cruelty. I often pictured myself in their situation, being continually in fear, constantly abused, and ultimately murdered. I developed a healthy hatred for Nazis. Yet I continued to be engrossed (perhaps even awestruck) by their regalia, especially the swastika.

I know some African Americans who collect "coon" ephemera, insulting, racist pictures of black people in grotesque caricature. They reason that it is a part of their collective history that must never be forgotten or obscured. I know Holocaust scholars who continue to collect the gruesome details of this history so that the world will never forget. And I accumulate and write about swastika material because I believe the form must forever be remembered as a kind of portal to evil. Because if I can be seduced by the swastika as a form—and I know the legacy—then just think how younger generations will be engaged as memory of Nazis fades (and other atrocities supersede it).

My book is a way for me to address two things: how Adolf Hitler came to adopt the symbol for the Nazis and what it meant before it was appropriated. I knew that it had other incarnations within other cultures; I had seen it on old greeting cards and architectural decorations. But even when I stumbled across benign applications, I felt as though it were a knife in my face. So I began to read many vintage histories of the swastika. I learned that it had a long heritage and that in the late nineteenth century a swastika cult emerged in Germany within a youth culture similar to the hippies. I found that it was adopted by German racialist and nationalist cults, which imbued it with anti-Semitic connotations, and this filtered its way into the Nazi liturgy. I also learned that it had roots in various other lands, where it was a sacred religious icon for Buddhists, Jains, Hindus, Native Americans, Africans, and many others, akin to the Cross, Star, and Cresent. When Hitler wrote in *Mein Kampf* about the mark's symbolism, however, he ignored all these earlier representations. In the mythology of Nazism, the swastika was immaculately conceived—it was Hitler's sole invention. Although this was false, Nazi myth triumphed over reality.

Prior to the rise of the Nazis and the eventual adoption of the swastika as the German national symbol, many peoples used the symbol for benign reasons. Once it became the focal point of this highly designed political and national movement, all other meanings were altered. The swastika has been forever tarnished beyond recognition. At least that is my premise. And I have been criticized for it.

Since my book was published in March 2000, I have received various letters from well-intentioned people accusing me of bias. A Native American wrote that the swastika is his people's symbol and that my assertion that it should never be revivified in Western culture is patronizing, presumptuous, and racist. He argues that the whites stole his land and now his icons. Another critic stated that no one remembers the logos of Attila the Hun or Genghis Khan—likewise, in a thousand years or less, who will remember the symbol of Hitler's twelve-year Reich? He feels that the ancient meaning of the swastika will ultimately triumph. Similarly, an Asian American wrote that in his culture the red swastika is his emblem of good fortune, and he described how his local greengrocer displays it inside the shop. Why, he asks, if the meaning is diametrically opposed to that accorded it by the Nazis, should I care whether or not it is used in this cultural context? Along these lines, a former student of mine, an African American practitioner of Buddhism, told me that the swastika had great significance for him as a guidepost of peace. He then proceeded to hang a large backwards iteration (the Nazis went from left to right, rather than from right to left, as in Buddhist iconography) over his workstation at school. Frankly, I was offended.

But should I be? This may sound weird. But it was like dangling a cigarette in front of someone who was trying to quit. At the same time, it was like waving a red flag at a bull. Here I am, obsessed with the swastika for deep-seated reasons, guilty that I have such feelings, while I also despise everything that the swastika embodies in Western culture. Respectful of his religious beliefs, I did not ask him to remove the swastika, but deep down I was angry with him for seeming to flaunt it, knowing what it means in my cultural context. In the end I told him how I felt—he sympathized but did not remove the sign.

My book has been called too polemical. I agree. After laying down the history, I attack neo-Nazi uses of the swastika and condemn work by ignorant graphic designers who incorporate it into their hip graphics. I also argue against those who want to reclaim, through art, the swastika in its benign form. It is too late for such righteous attempts. The atrocities committed under this magnificently designed form, the same form that continues to hypnotize and fascinate me, must never be forgotten. Because the swastika has such allure, and because memory is so fleeting, it functions as a mnemonic. While I agree that people of other cultures have a right to this symbol, nonetheless, I would be guilty of neglect if I did not take a stand against its use in this culture as anything other than an icon of evil.

Drawing by Felix Vallaton from L'Assiette au Beurre, *1902. This is how my back felt before having a microlamectomy.*

HOSPITAL BLUES

Like anyone facing surgery I was incredibly anxious about spending even twenty-four hours in a hospital. Not because I was certain that even *if* I came out of the general anesthetic, I would never walk or play the piano again, but because I hate—no, abhor—the look, sounds, and smell of hospitals. They're just so, well, *designed* to represent sickness. If you want wellness, go to Yankee stadium. No, better yet, stay home.

So I was pleasantly surprised when upon my arrival on a hazy, hot, and muggy weekday morning, New York's Cornell Hospital on York Avenue and the East River wasn't *ER, St. Elsewhere,* or the depressing St. Vincent's emergency room near my home (where I had gone after being rescued from a fire). It was something akin to a fancy hotel, from the courteous doorman at the front door to the smiling clerk at the registration desk to the boutique and garden cafe on the main (shining marble) first floor. The only problem: It *was* a hospital, not a hotel, and I was there not to visit an out-of-town business associate or hooker, but to be admitted for a disc operation that my surgeon called "a piece of cake" (for him!) but that for me was a full-course meal.

Knowing that I would be released pain-free, twenty-four hours later, was small consolation for having to be there at all. Nonetheless, I was put somewhat at ease when I entered the "Same Day Surgery" unit, a large, light-filled room with river views and fairly comfortable contract furniture chairs. Unlike other hospitals I've encountered, this was neither confining nor crowded—and it had a large-screen TV too. After less than five minutes, a pleasant nurse with an Island accent took me through two large doors into a more medical-looking, though decidedly modern, area where I was handed a sprightly designed gown, slippers (the ones with tread on the bottom) and pajamas and told to change in a spic and span dressing room. Next, I was escorted into one of four mini-waiting rooms—each with televisions and river views—where I commiserated with a fellow patient waiting for a quadruple bypass. The surroundings were so pleasant that we (and our wives) couldn't help but feel good about our futures.

That is, until a man wearing hospital greens came to walk me into the OR. What, no gurney? Since he had given my glasses to my wife, I blindly followed him through huge double doors into what I'd always imagined purgatory to be like and down a maze of long intersecting corridors that reminded me of Orson Welles's film *The Trial,* punctuated only by large closed doors. Curiously, there was no one in sight. Finally, we reached my operating suite (such a quaint term) and were greeted by a nurse who invited me to climb onto the operating table. The next thing I knew I was in recovery with my glasses on but no pajama bottoms.

The surgeon said the operation had been a success, which is the kind of response one gets from a waiter after asking if the fish is fresh today—what else is he going to say? So, after less than an hour in recovery, I was wheeled, on a gurney this time, up to my spacious—and I mean large—private room for the final leg of my surgical journey. Now this was some room, painted in a pleasant taupe, with red mahogany closet, drawers, and TV stand. The chairs were matching wood with purple cushions, and the view of Roosevelt Island out of the five-foot-high windows was superb. However, before I could say "Bathroom, please," a young man had me sign a rental agreement for the TV ($12.50 a day, no less). Problem was, I was too intensely nauseous from the anesthetic and morphine cocktails to enjoy the lush accommodations—or the Turner Movie Classics.

But wait, this is a hospital after all, so what was I expecting? In fact, I was expecting something much more depressing. Neverthless, six hours later, after the nausea had subsided, I found myself on the most uncomfortable motorized bed with its leatherette pillow and rubberized slipsheets and an annoying under-the-mattress nightlight. Every half hour, throughout my sleepless night (a nurse later told me she would have given me something to sleep), attendants arrived to fill my IV with antibiotics or take my temperature and blood pressure. And, believe me, although I was grateful for the attention—and also grateful that this hospital, at least my ward of it, was designed to be a little less hospital-like and more comforting—I was still in a place of sickness. Despite the mahogony and taupe, it made me feel sick just to be there. I was never so happy to get back to my own bed and TV, even though I can't get Turner Classic Movies.

The New York Times

Book Review

Section 7 Copyright © 1999 The New York Times

October 3, 1999

American Manhood Takes a Dive

In her new book, 'Stiffed,' Susan Faludi says today's consumer culture has left workingmen all dressed up, with nowhere to go but down.

Reviewed by Judith Shulevitz **8**

'Plainsong,' by Kent Haruf: a novel of things as they are on the high plains of America. *Reviewed by Verlyn Klinkenborg* **7**

Brent Staples on 'All Souls,' Michael Patrick MacDonald's memoir of the other Boston: poor, white and nasty. **13**

Cover of The New York Times Book Review *with an illustration by Ed Lam, 1999. I'd rather stay put than move to the new flagship skyscraper.*

THE TIMES THEY ARE A-MOVIN'

I miss the old *Times* building on West 43rd Street, even though it may be four years before Renzo Piano's architectural wonder, our new world headquarters, is built. I'm already nostalgic for the place where I have worked for the past twenty-eight years, where I thought I'd work for just as many more. Most of my colleagues eagerly antici-pate moving around the corner to 40th and Eighth, but not me. I prefer the small *Times* lobby, with its sweeping marble staircase, Deco-styled appointments, and curtained windows above the revolving door, to Piano's proposed commercial atrium—the so-called democratic space—that will doubtless be less intimate and remind me less of Loretta Young.

This old *Times* building is my second home. The prospect of a larger, more beautiful, more public building that will accommodate other tenants does not fill me with delight. I like things as they are: worn, venerable, and comfortable. To confirm these prejudices, I stopped by the new Condé Nast building across the street, which is clean, cold, and corporate. It may be fine for a megapublishing con-glomerate, but for not my hometown paper.

The *Times* is not a faceless enterprise, and our edifice is not a monument to corporate power. In the long-awaited 42nd Street Development tower-play, the existing *Times* building, which looks like a Loire Valley chateau, is, admittedly, an anachronism. But as Times Square becomes the electronic media park of the world—the site of

Viacom, ABC, MarketShare, Condé Nast, and Reuters—and with the World Wrestling Federation *themestaurant* on our corner, the building has become an anchor securing tradition and continuity. Moving into Piano's post-post-Modern skyscraper is like eliminating the Latin Condensed typeface from the *Times*'s front page. Latin, a nineteenth-century vestige, is the *Times*'s typographical signature; it has survived many shifts in graphic styles. Similarly, this building with its baroque ornamentation is a symbol of the *Times*'s continued excellence. Although the *Daily News* and the *New York Post* exchanged their historic old office buildings for bland new ones, neither paper has the *Times*'s legacy of eminence, and both probably benefited from the change of scenery (now, if only they'd change their editorial policies . . . but I digress). This old building is filled with so much pride, one can feel it in the communal spaces—lobby, elevators, and cafeteria. This is one building where the walls do talk; I can't imagine what the new building will say.

I am not a cranky opponent of change. I have occupied three offices since joining the *Times*. The first was in the enormous, incandescently lit art department, where waist-high mahogany partitions separated more than twenty long rows of narrow tables punctuated by rusty metal flat files. Void of such amenities as ergonomic chairs and tables, this space remained unchanged from the 1930s through the 1970s and was in desperate need of renewal. From there I happily moved into a renovated, semiprivate office that had been carved out of a mammoth old photo studio. Finally, I moved into a slightly larger, modern warren with a sliver of window facing north, where I have remained—and where my belongings have multiplied—for almost fifteen years. I was sanguine through the demolition of the hot metal composing room, elimination of the Museum of the Printed Word, renovation of the now-defunct Sunday department, and construction of the grand duplex newsroom. So I am certainly able to accept change without experiencing the existential nausea of longing.

Anyway, it is not change that makes me object to Piano's building; it is the anticipated loss of community. No matter how beautiful Piano's design, the old building, like the fabled TV bar Cheers, is a place where everyone knows your name (or at least your face). In the new quarters I predict there will be such a throng of transient faces that intimacy will be lost. I saw it at the Condé Nast headquarters and at office buildings throughout midtown Manhattan, where people drift without a sense of place and the joy that comes from belonging. This is exactly what the old *Times* building gives me—a sense of belonging—whether I'm aware of it or not.

Exchanging our small hotel-like lobby for an exclusive and separate bank of elevators in a shared entryway (or even a separate reception/waiting room, as in the Time Warner building) is not my only regret. Community is not shaped by one space alone. There are so many details in this building that collectively define the space. I will miss the staircases with tile brick walls designed so that the maintenance staff could easily wipe off the ink soot that once wafted up from the press and composing rooms. I will miss the modest twelfth-floor veranda, where on a warm day one can eat lunch or soak up the smog-filtered sun. I will miss the inaccessible balcony outside my own window; the entrance was long ago covered over for safety reasons, but I still imagine being out there. I will miss the recently renovated formal reception room on the fifteenth floor, which half a century ago was a magnificent photo studio with a high-pitched ceiling and skylight (there are still spirits in that room). I will miss the WQXR auditorium and sound booths, abandoned half a decade ago when the *Times*'s classical music station moved to new off-site quarters. I will miss the delivery room where the newspapers were transported on conveyor belts from the basements and were bundled and thrown into waiting trucks. I will miss all these remnants of things past because the old *Times* building is an archeological dig—a chronicle of newspaper history.

The Piano building will be a showpiece, not a home. Yet given the inevitable relocation, I must make one humble request. Rather than raze the old building, or as has been suggested, turn it into a hotel, consider the option of converting it into assisted-living quarters for old *Times*-persons, like me. For a while, at least, it would be one hell of a living museum.

This promotional booklet for Ex-Lax, the laxative company (c. 1920), looks like something one of my students might design.

SCHOOL TIE

Design is not rocket science, though I have a sense of what the pioneers of space travel must have felt like when, after decades of theorizing, they landed a man on the Moon. My moon is more down to earth; in fact, it's right in Manhattan, at the School of Visual Arts (SVA). In 1996, I conceived the M.F.A. Design program based on the theory that authorship and entrepreneurship were the field's next big thing. Graphic design would converge with other design and communications media, and designers would have to decide whether to continue pushing type around on a page or to use their design talents to conceive and create ideas and products. The aim of the program is to transform designers into authors, producers, editors, and entrepreneurs.

Since SVA was designed to train students to enter the marketplace and cultural arena, the M.F.A. program seemed the perfect extension of this objective. The program encourages designers to work and think for themselves while creating products of value for others. The proof comes at the end of two intense years capped by a year-in-the-making thesis, a fully realized "product" ready to be brought to market. The experience of creating and leading the program has been extraordinary and has had a profound effect on my life.

I was a college dropout. I quit NYU in 1970, halfway through my sophomore year, because I was working full-time for underground newspapers. Six months later, I enrolled in the School of Visual Arts to escape the Vietnam draft. Four months after that, I was expelled by

Marshall Arisman, chair of the undergraduate illustration department, for not attending classes (fortunately, I was never drafted). The following year, I was given a job teaching SVA students how to design the school newspaper; I left when I was hired as art director of the *New York Times* Op-Ed page. Two years later, the saga continued: I was rehired to teach illustration history in Arisman's new M.F.A. Illustration program, which I did until invited by SVA chairman Silas Rhodes to found the school's first design M.F.A. program.

It was an offer I couldn't refuse. How many times does someone give you carte blanche to start an educational program? Yet I knew absolutely nothing about serious pedagogy. The word, I thought, had something to do with children's feet.

But I did have experience putting together design conferences and editing books, so I used these as models. I asked myself how I would schedule an event or edit a book whose subject was the designer as author. First, I drew up a list of potential contributors. Some were already teaching at other schools; others had never taught before. From this roster, I was able to build a faculty with disparate expertise but with a common goal. On my recommendation, SVA hired Lita Talarico, who'd had experience as an administrator at Cooper Union and SUNY Purchase, to run the program on a daily basis (she later became cochair). We built a large physical space to approximate an actual design firm, recruited the Class of 2000, and began to build what we hoped would be an educational hothouse. The excitement was palpable, and so was the stress.

It's one thing to organize a two-day event and quite another to orchestrate two years in the lives of students and faculty. Yet as a total neophyte, I never imagined that I would become so emotionally wrapped up in the program and its participants. It is truly an extended family, replete with all the attendant psychological complexities of sons and daughters, mothers and fathers. Those who are veteran teachers can understand the bond to even the most detached student. It is a relationship that comes perilously close to blood ties.

The ties that bind: The first time I met Katherine McCoy at a design conference, the former cochair of the legendary Cranbrook Academy of Art design program was acting like a mother hen to her student brood. I watched as the students circulated throughout the event, invariably returning to Kathy's nest to talk about their experiences and get her guidance. She made certain that they went to the right lectures, asked the right questions, and met the right people. I have to admit I was relieved that in my own teaching, I kept my distance. I decided early on that I did not want to encourage dependent relationships. This was hard enough with family and friends.

Students have a propensity to drain the oxygen out of a teacher. Even the best students, the ones that are so far along that they should be teachers themselves, require an inordinate amount of attention. I have the utmost respect for academics, like Kathy McCoy, who have the requisite strength and dedication for this, along with the ability to somehow sublimate their egos to the students' needs. Of course, I never appreciated how difficult it could be for the chair of a department to distance himself from these pressures. I'd been routinely bored when department chair friends would go on about how exhausted or burned out they were after a single semester. I'd think to myself, "Come on, it's not like you're putting out a magazine every week and have to deal with capricious editors who can ruin your best work." But now I know better: I've learned that being involved with students who look to you as a mentor-father-mother, as well as at times as an obstructer-impediment-reactionary, can sometimes be far more difficult to deal with than the most exasperating client.

Students return to graduate school because they have a variety of unresolved and sometimes subconscious needs. They're particularly vulnerable at this stage in their lives, and improving their abilities is just one issue on their minds. I'm not saying that all grad students are mentally fragile, but since their emotional, not to mention financial, investment is considerable, they do feel they are entitled to a teacher religiously devoted to students. Some teachers avoid this entanglement; others willingly yield to it. Most, I realize, walk a center path. As a cochair, I am increasingly torn between two poles—a compulsive need to be omnipresent (if not omnipotent) and a determined desire to stay on the sidelines. One day, I will find the right balance.

But students can teach the teacher a lot, which adds pleasure to the angst. Indeed, one sobering realization for me is that many of them are better than I was when I was a student, and some have astoundingly more potential than I ever showed.

I find myself thinking of the students in the program in the same way I regard my own young son: as individuals who, with the proper guidance from me (and faculty), can far exceed my capabilities. It's dangerous to view them in that way, however, because they then become recipients of my psychological baggage, negative as well as positive. I want to instill in them the belief that they will create objects of distinction that we as a profession can respond to with praise. But achieving this means curtailing my desire to take them by the hand and tell them exactly what to do. This may be acceptable for undergraduates, but not for grad students. Knowing this, I still sometimes become angry with those students who have not developed their vision in a timely way consistent with my wishes. The lesson I keep learning is that each student has a unique way of working, and within the parameters set for finishing assignments, each must be allowed to function at his or her own pace.

A class has a dynamic forged by the students' combined chemistries. The demonstrative alphas make more noise than the subdued betas, but both groups consist of extremely talented and sometimes less accomplished students. If everything goes well, each student finds a role in the group that is beneficial to all, though sometimes the alignment of roles is not harmonious. Before starting this program, as a teacher, I could feel the energy or lack of it in a class, but since I was only one part of a larger team, I was not really affected. Now, as a cochair, I realize I have little control over how seventeen to twenty individuals, strangers to each other, will coalesce as a unit. But it is difficult not to try to intervene, and my cochair continually reminds me that the process is out of my hands.

Nonetheless, cheerleading is a large part of my self-defined job description. Through overt and covert means, I try to guide the classes into places I feel will be productive. Frankly, I should let nature take its course. The dynamic evolves at its own pace, anyway.

We have two groups of students—the first-year and the graduating class. Because our graduating class of 2000 was the trailblazer, I won't ever forget those students. That first year, they truly functioned in a fishbowl and had our undivided attention. By the following year, when the class of 2001 entered, there was a palpable change in atmosphere; as with a second baby coming into the house, the focus shifted from the firstborn. The Class of 2000 students were cognizant of the fact that their first year had been the only time there would be a single class in the program.

A graduate program is more intense than an undergraduate one. There is more at stake because for most students this is a last refuge before they enter the real, professional world. Therefore, we try to simulate that world as much as possible. While the first year of the program is a kind of conceptual boot camp in which students are forced to test the limits of their intelligence and ability through scores of projects, the second is a period of research, contemplation, and production, focusing on the product that will represent their marketplace goals.

In one sense, I find it easier to deal with the first-year students, because they are thin-skinned and open to suggestion. If they fail, they learn from their mistakes. In the second year, they harden to the fact that they must succeed within a finite period. But being second-year students does not automatically mean they are any more mature than when they began the curriculum. In the three years since starting the program, we've found that most students mature quickly, while some struggle mightily to spread their wings. I've learned that this is a perfectly natural process. The faculty gives the students as much support and guidance as possible, but, ultimately, personal and creative development is up to each individual.

We get formal feedback from students twice a term. But I regularly elicit informal comments. Though most of the students are totally committed to the idea of authorship, some are not prepared at first to actually try it. Being "free" to define and develop their own ideas scares them. This is the biggest hurdle they face. By term's end, however—and we've only had one graduating class and another on the way—they are completely devoted to their projects. I can't say everyone becomes an author, but everyone assumes an author's attitude.

The final thesis presentation, the last faculty critique before the students enter the marketplace with their fully developed ideas, is exhausting and cathartic. While any definition of success varies from student to student, we come into the crit room with high expectations. I personally have not seen the evolutionary permutations of their work, so I am surprised by everything. I can't say that all the students have met my expectations, but the majority exceeded them. By the end of the school year, when everyone, student and faculty member alike, is drained, this single event makes the whole process worth doing.

Founding a grad program is a lot like going to grad school. I learn from each step or misstep. When I began, I could not have anticipated how the students would function in this environment, and I gain knowledge from each succeeding class. While I have not shifted my fundamental concept, I've adapted courses and programs in order to be responsive to the students. I've also learned that I must not always respond to students when they complain about this or that. I usually aim to please them, but their wants, such as more high-end technical workshops or fewer courses, are often unrealistic, given the program's constraints and goals. I have enough confidence in the program to know that, while aspects of it can be tweaked, with elements added or eliminated, its basis is solid.

An academic career was never something I wanted or anticipated, and I admit that I still wince when I'm referred to as an educator. But this has been one of the most exhilarating experiences of my professional life. I can only hope that the program has the same resonance for the students.

As I write this, we have selected our fourth class. This process always excites me, and when the students enter the program next fall, I'll be even more excited. There is something truly awesome to me about this revolving set of people I encounter—individuals I am actually helping to mold. It makes me appreciate real teachers all the more.

MEMOIRS
SECTION V

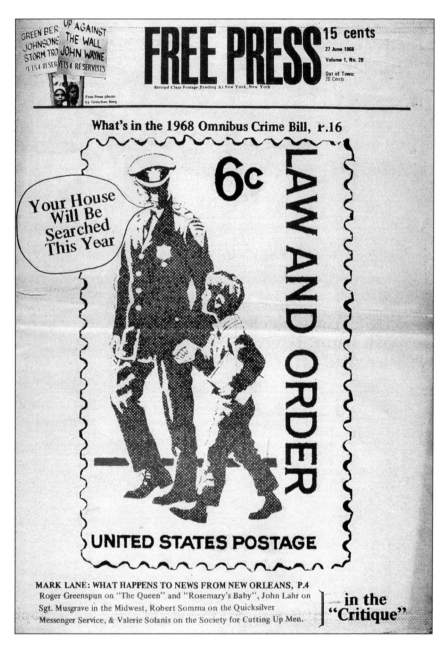

The first cover of the New York Free Press, *1968, that I ever worked on. I had no idea what I was doing.*

GROWING UP UNDERGROUND

A few weeks before my high school graduation in 1968, I walked uninvited into the dingy Upper West Side offices of the *New York Free Press,* a New York underground paper. Portfolio in hand, I was looking for a job as a cartoonist. Little did I know I would find a career.

For two years before this, I had been drawing cartoons vaguely in the manner of Jules Feiffer—panel-less sequences that were morose explorations of the human psyche, specifically my own adolescent fixations with sex and death. Some people said that I must not have had a very happy childhood, but all agreed that my cartoons were worth publishing. So as a sophomore in high school in 1966, I brought my cartoons to the office of the late Dick Hess, then art director of *Evergreen Review,* a slick leftwing bimonthly devoted to sex, politics, and culture, which regularly featured drawings by Ed Sorel, Robert Grossman, Paul Davis, and Seymour Chwast. I was almost sixteen years old and dreamed about drawing for this irreverent magazine (which, incidently, years later, I would art-direct in its twilight). Hess's secretary told me to leave the portfolio and come back the next day. Not only wasn't I offered a job, but God only knows whether Hess, or anyone else for that matter, looked at the work—there was no note, and the matted pictures were still in the order I had left them. Could it be that the only people who truly liked my artwork were friends and relatives? I was so disheartened that I decided not to go to an appointment that had been arranged for me the following week at the other most important magazine in my life, the *New Yorker*. My mom had a friend who had a friend who called some woman at the *New Yorker*, who actually called me back to make the appointment, which I cancelled and never rescheduled.

Disappointment fueled my art, forcing me to draw my innermost demons for over a year before attempting to take my stuff to the four underground papers that were based in Manhattan: the *East Village Other*, the *Rat*, the *New York Free Press*, and the *Avatar*. I went to the last first, because after learning what the word avatar meant, I decided to capitalize on the fact that most of my cartoons included a naked, autobiographical, Christlike figure whom I drew either in a state of crucifixion or in the throes of some other martyrdom. It turned out the people at the *Avatar* were indeed interested in my fixations, because the magazine itself was edited by a self-proclaimed Christ—a fellow named Mel Lyman, who in addition to being an avatar, hippie, jug band musician, and drug experimenter, was the megalomaniacal leader of a Boston commune with a chapter in New York. Since I hadn't read the magazine before going up to visit the New York office, I was slow to realize that virtually the entire content was devoted to how world and local events affected Lyman's life. Had I known that this was a cult, however, it probably wouldn't have made much difference, since these people actually wanted to publish my work—not just one drawing, but five of my very favorites in one issue.

As great as I felt, I realized all too soon that the *Avatar* was a little weird, even for me. After a second set of drawings was published in a subsequent issue, the editor wanted me to meet the great Lyman himself, but first I was told I'd have to shave my entire body and swear to some oath. My Bar Mitzvah was enough religious ritual for one lifetime, so I graciously declined and took my work to the *Rat*. Edited by Jeff Shero (now Jeff Nightbird), and art-directed by Bob Eisner (now Robert Eisner, design director of *Newsday*), the *Rat* staff had just finished a series of issues covering the May 1968 student uprising on the Columbia University campus, where police were called in to restore order and where, for the first time in New York, SDS (Students for a Democratic Society) flexed its muscles. A cover of *Rat* with a Nazi helmet covering Columbia's Low Library could be seen on many newsstands as well as wheat-pasted on countless post-no-bill hoardings around the city. The *Rat* storefront office near Cooper Square was a hotbed of activity when, without an appointment, I walked in with my portfolio.

Bob Eisner was exhausted after days without sleep but did not turn me away. He politely paged through my work saying nothing at first, until coming to a cartoon that showed a black man and a white man arm-in-arm, giving each other the bird. "Yep, that's racial equality all right. Can we use it?" he asked. I'm sure I said yes without skipping a beat, and I think I assigned him worldwide rights going into the next century. I was so excited when it came out a week later that I offered to hawk copies on the street. I sold twenty-five to passersby and ten to myself. But my *Rat* affiliation did not last long. "We like your stuff," said Eisner candidly, "but Shero thinks its too spiritual—have you tried taking it to the *Avatar?*"

Next I tried the *East Village Other.* This anarchic tabloid was not New York's first official underground paper (one might say that the *Village Voice,* founded in 1955, was), but it was the most infamous. It was the launching pad for many of the early Underground Comix artists, including R. Crumb, Spain Rodriques, Kim Dietch, and Gilbert Shelton. It was the home of the "Slum Goddess of the Lower East Side," a biweekly homage to the East Village's most desirable ladies. It always ran afoul of the law with its advocacy of mind-altering drugs and radical street actions, but was also a wellspring of counterculture criticism. Its memorable covers included a picture of General William Westmoreland, chairman of the Joint Chiefs of Staff, as a viper, President Lyndon Baines Johnson as Adolf Hitler, and on the occasion of the death of Vicar of the Army Cardinal Spellman in 1967, it ran an official photograph with the headline, "Congratulations on Your Promotion." While *Evergreen Review* represented the intellectual left, the *East Village Other* spoke to the youthful left, the hippies and yippies of my generation who ate up every puerile word and savage insult written or drawn on its pages.

If I had a career strategy, it was only that I was working my way up to be published in *EVO,* the cream of the undergrounds—the maker of legends.

Unfortunately, the editors, Walter Bowart and Alan Katzman, didn't think as highly of my work as I did of theirs. Our meeting was short and curt. Apparently, the staff was in a frenzy to get an issue out. "Leave your stuff, we'll call you," said Bowart while running through the storefront office located on the edge of Tompkins Square Park.

"Will you return it if you don't want to use anything?" I asked timidly. "Maybe," he shouted from the men's room in the rear, "I'm busy, okay!"

After about a week without word, I collected my stuff and went to the *Free Press*. Geography was one reason for not going sooner. How could a real underground paper be located on 72nd Street and Broadway? Real undergrounds were in the East Village. In fact, I rarely traveled above 23rd Street myself, except to go to school. The other reason was looks: the *New York Free Press* didn't look like an underground paper. It was too neat on the one hand, and too tabloidy on the other—a cross between the *New York Times* and the *National Star*. It didn't carry comix; it wasn't raucous in any way. And based on the two issues that I bought, it was primarily concerned not with the counterculture, but with proving that there had been a Kennedy assassination plot (Mark Lane was a contributing editor), with supporting Bobby Kennedy's presidency (I was a McGovern supporter), and with defaming most liberal politicians for being too soft on most issues.

The *Freep,* as it was known, was once a community newspaper owned by a covey of New York liberals until it was bought out by Grove Press, the publisher of *Evergreen*. It was then made a bit more radical, which alienated most of its traditional constituency. Soon afterward, Grove tired of supporting it and left the *Freep* staff to fend for itself. The *Freep*'s publisher was a musty Lefty and consummate failure named Jack; its editor was a thirty-three-year-old karate expert and nighttime bartender, Sam, who once edited a very prestigious arts magazine; its managing editor was Jim Buckley, who would later become the copublisher of *Screw;* and its art director was a tough-talking, beer-drinking Egyptian named J. C. Suarés, who later went on to be art director of the *New York Times* Op-Ed page, *New York Magazine,* and scores of other posts and positions. It was he who reviewed my portfolio on that first fateful visit.

A former contributor to Paul Krasner's the *Realist,* the most venerable and sacrilegious of the alternative gazettes, Suarés was art director, layout man, and principal cartoonist for the *Freep*. His caricatures looked exactly like David Levine's in the *New York Review of Books,* only done quickly in magic marker rather than exquisitely in pen and ink. In any case, Suarés had at least one drawing in every issue and was protective of his turf. He looked at my work, and between gulping down swigs from a quart bottle of malt liquor, he said, "Good shit but I can't use it. You want a mechanical job?"

I didn't know what he meant. Coincidentally, only a few days before, I had noticed the term "mechanical artist" in the classifieds of the *New York Times* and had asked my father its meaning. He knew about as much as I did. Now I was being offered a job doing them. "Sure," I said. "But what is it?" J. C. took me into the outer room, a large space with a huge typesetting apparatus (I soon learned it was an IBM MTS—a magnetic tape input that ran an electric typewriter with removable balls) and a few old desks where editors, writers, and a mechanical artist sat. Only the mechanical artist was there at that time, busily pasting down galleys of text and veloxes (of course this was all Greek to me). "This is a galley," said Suarés, pointing to the materials on a desk. "This is glue. This is a knife. This is a mechanical board. You cut the galley with the knife, paste it down on the board with the glue—now it's a mechanical. You want a job? $50 a week."

I accepted, unaware that I was replacing the woman who was already doing it, who Suarés had apparently fired that afternoon. Blissfully, I started the job two days later. Two weeks later, Suarés had left to start his own satirical magazine called *Inkling,* with offices in the Empire State Building—as far as I know, it never came out. Sam, the burly editor who looked exactly like a young Papa Hemingway, called me into his adjoining office for the first real meeting I'd had with him since I was hired by J. C. "Kid," he said, emphasizing the *i,* "You want the job, Kid?"

"Sure, but I really don't know enough, Sam," I said nervously.

"How old are you, Kid?"

"Seventeen."

"Good. You'll learn. You got the job. How's $40 a week?"

"But Sam," I said, mustering up some courage, "I'm supposed to be getting $50 for the mechanical job, although I haven't received anything in two weeks."

"Okay, $50, we'll raise it when you get more experience," he concluded. "Oh, by the way, I like your cartoons. Let's run them as part of the $50."

Needless to say, I was grateful for the job, his confidence in me, his wanting to publish my drawings (which I did in every issue under the rubric, "A Heller"), but I was totally ignorant about this business. Sam helped me bungle through the basics, until one day he said, "Kid, I want you to use a duotone on the cover."

"A what?!"

"Spend some time with the printer, he'll show you."

And so my graphic arts education began. On the days that I wasn't laying out the *Freep*—usually Sunday and Monday—I'd take a train out to the farthest Queens stop, where the printer who printed the *Freep,* the *Rat,* and *EVO* was located. While most of the guys there had no use for a snot-nosed kid underfoot, one of the strippers proceeded to teach me about tints, duotones, overlays, veloxes, and so on. Within a month I could order any printing trick by name—though I couldn't visualize the result.

Before his abrupt departure, Suarés taught me about type. Well, sort of. He used to set headlines in 11-point Times Roman on the MTST, which he'd send off to a stat house to be blown up to 600 percent. That was the display type he used. It was also my only concept of typography until I met a young artist, just off the bus from Kansas City, named Brad Holland, who introduced me to the work of Herb Lubalin and the wonderful world of smashed letterforms.

After my second month at the *Freep,* I'd been cocky enough to think I could produce my own magazine. Holland answered an ad that I had placed in the *Village Voice* calling for artists and writers to work on *Borrowed Time,* a new poetry magazine. Even though I really hated poetry, it seemed like the right thing to do. Holland arrived with a portfolio that was beyond beautiful, full of superb chiaroscuro fantasy drawings, plus a published illustration in *Avant Garde,* which for me had replaced all others as the best magazine of the era. He agreed to work for me for nothing, for what reason I'm still not certain, but instead of being a docile illustrator, he took command. After I'd assembled the editorial contents, cover, and back cover (my own illustration, which paled before Holland's work), he volunteered to help design the pages. He was shocked, indeed, that I had planned on using "Suarés type," and offered to photostat alphabets from the Photolettering Inc. catalogs and paste them together for me. He did meticulous mechanicals on the floor of this East 11th Street tenement living room/bedroom; and by example I learned that all I had previously learned was wrong. Holland illustrated almost a third of the pieces and came up with typographic solutions for a few others. It looked great. Too bad the content was less than inspired. Nevertheless, after it was printed, Holland and I sold over two hundred copies on the street in front of the Fillmore East and took in enough money to open a bank account together, intended to seed another issue. Unfortunately, we never did.

The account lay dormant for almost a decade before the money was turned over to the State of New York.

Meeting Holland, my elder by seven years, was one of the most critical events in my professional and personal life. I looked up to him as an artist and intellect. In a few short months he taught me more lessons that have stuck to this day than I could have learned in school. But I hated him, too. He was a tough taskmaster who did not dole out compliments readily. I desperately wanted him to tell me my cartoons were good, but he never did. Out of spite, I kept him from appearing in the *Freep,* even though his art would have been a major contribution—indeed a viable alternative to Underground Comix. "Sam said he only wants to use me," I would tell him, lying through my teeth. Moreover, I thought, Holland didn't need the *Freep;* he had just been hired by *Playboy* to do a monthly feature, and he was getting other work, too. I still wanted Holland to bless my own work and give me his uncritical approval for what I was doing. He never did. So one day, I decided not to draw again. A couple of months later, Holland said, "How come I don't see your cartoons anymore? Some of them were really good."

Although I forget my answer, I know my immediate response was satisfaction because somehow I thought that by not doing the cartoons, I was hurting Holland, who had hurt me. I'm certain today that there were other motives, but I hardly ever went back to drawing after that. Yet thanks to Holland, I did find an expressive outlet in design.

The *Free Press* was kind of open territory, as long as what I did fit the budget and editorial constraints. Since the budget was nil, I learned how to piece things together. Since editorially, Sam wanted a text-driven paper, not a visual one, I was restricted to playing with the two covers (front, and inside culture section). Since Sam did not really consider the *Freep* an underground paper, but rather alternative in a traditional sense of publishing what the mainstream press would not, there really wasn't much room for visual experimentation. Sam's goal was to develop the *Freep* into a muckraking paper, specifically concerned with city politics. Some of our best stories, written by Ray Schultz, a *New York Post* copyboy who fancied himself the next Jimmy Breslin, focused on corruption in the sanitation and police departments, and an exposé of the *New York Post* itself, which got him fired. We ran picture features showing "Red Squad" cops who posed as hippies or reporters at all the antiwar rallies. We ran endless reports on the

Kennedy assassination whose allegations would put the film *JFK* to shame. We had serious pieces on deficiencies in New York's education system and other bureaucracies by writers who went on to work in the mainstream press. And on the cultural end, Sam's experience at the arts magazine came in handy: Our critics included Eric Bentley, Brecht's translator in the United States; Roger Greenspun, who later became a *New York Times* critic; Gregory Battcock, a leading author and art critic; and R. Meltzer, a brash young music critic. Although, I'm still not convinced of the veracity of all our stories, taking jabs at the establishment was a lot of fun, and somehow I felt we were doing a more responsible job than the other "kick-ass" undergrounds.

Despite our best efforts, the *Freep* did not have a strong or loyal readership. We found this out every time we would run a nude woman on the cover. The first one was almost an accident. Our serious cover story on some scandal or other was never filed, and Sam moved a culture story about this oddball, erotic, happening artist named Kusama onto the cover. Kusama was the consummate publicity hound and provided any and all papers—over and underground—with lurid photographs of her living artworks, usually totally naked men and women debauching under Kusama's watchful direction. So we ran one not so terribly lewd photograph on the cover, and that week's sales skyrocketed. The following week, we ran a serious story, and sales dropped. After that, we ran a nude woman wearing a gas mask, and sales soared again.

It had been said that *EVO* enjoyed a relatively large circulation because of its sex classifieds. We believed it. No matter how good the stories or design, the *Freep* could only survive if we ran sexy (or sexist) covers, which was such a great blow for Sam that he decided to fold the paper. Coincidentally, at that same time, Sam got into a fight with Al Goldstein, publisher of *Screw,* and Jim Buckley, who was devoting more and more time in the *Freep* offices to *Screw,* which was enjoying amazing success. Resentful that *Screw* was doing well while the *Freep* was dying, Sam decided to start his own sex paper, the *New York Review of Sex,* and asked me to be copublisher and art director.

Having gotten a pretty good dose of publishing, having learned to love design and layout, and having decided to quit college to pursue this as a "career," I agreed. I mended my own psychological fences with Brad Holland, who became a regular contributor. I applied the lessons learned at Holland's feet to the design of the *NYRS,* gathered the money we got to start it up from our distributor, and proceeded to make a magazine that turned out to be my design graduate school. Though the *NYRS* was still underground, I was able to see light in the far distance. I knew that I would be doing something like this for the rest of my life.

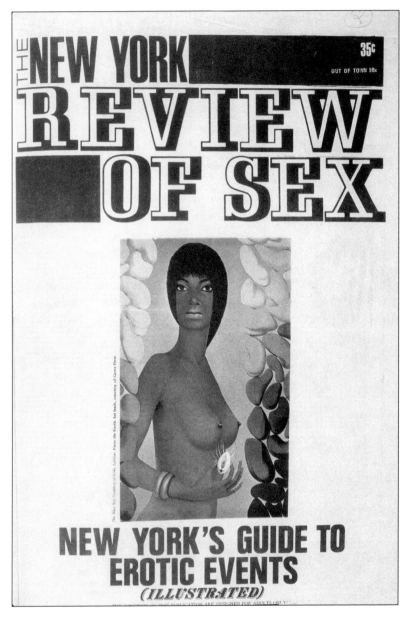

The first issue of The New York Review of Sex, *1969, with type cut out and pasted up from old type books.*

I WAS A SEVENTEEN-YEAR-OLD PORNOGRAPHER

At seventeen years old, I was a pornographer. That's how a young assistant district attorney described me to a sleepy Manhattan night court judge as I stood before him in the wee hours of the morning on July 3, 1968. I had been arrested the afternoon before, but because the DA's vice squad detectives didn't know in which downtown precinct to book me, we were too late for day court, and so I was held in Manhattan's Tombs until the night session began around 8:00. Since the docket was full of petty criminals, prostitutes, and drug dealers, I didn't go before the judge until two in the morning. Instead, I spent many hours being moved from one overcrowded cell to another—like passing through the digestive tract of the criminal justice system—until finally spit out into a brightly lit courtroom.

I was the art director, designer, and copublisher of the *New York Review of Sex (& Politics),* an odd mix of new left politics and sexploitation. I was pasting up our fourth issue when we received a telephone call. "That was the DA's office," said the office manager excitedly. "They said that you, Sam, and Jack (the editor and copublisher, respectively) were under arrest and should not leave the premises." Sam was on an errand and Jack had absconded with all the money in our bank account a week before. I broke into a cold sweat. I was alone and under age. I called our lawyer. He was in a meeting and couldn't be disturbed. "I'm about to be arrested," I told the secretary frantically. "I'll give him the message," she said calmly. Next, I called our distributor, a nasty little man whose relatives had been Murder Inc. mobsters during the thirties. His secretary said that he had been called by the DA's office and had left the premises. Finally, I called my father (I still lived at home). He was out, too. For godsakes, where was everyone? I told his secretary to tell him I was being arrested and would probably be home late for dinner.

The moment I hung up the phone, two detectives entered the office. Both looked surprisingly familiar. I had seen the young one on the TV news a few nights before talking about investigating the Mob in New York. The heavyset one had come by the office a week before to buy copies of the newspaper. He'd said he was a bookseller from Long Island. They showed their badges, read me my rights, and asked the whereabouts of my two partners. I told them I had no idea. I asked if I could go to the bathroom. They came with me while I tied my shoulder-length hair in a ponytail just in case the stories I had heard about goings on in jail were true. I asked if they wanted to handcuff me; they said no, unless I was planning an escape.

As I sat between them in the front seat of their unmarked car, they informed me that all the sex-paper publishers and distributors were being rounded up. "We figured you'd all be at Woodstock," said the heavyset one who had heard on the radio that the rock festival, which had begun that day, was already attracting thousands of people. "I would like to go," admitted the young one, but said he had to work. "I decided to work this weekend, too," I volunteered. They asked me exactly what I did. The question seemed innocent enough that to reply without a lawyer being present would not jeopardize my case. "I'm the art director," I said proudly. "What's that mean? You photograph the models?" asked the heavy one. "No, I design the format, pick the type, crop the pictures, buy the illustrations, paste up the mechanicals, and sometimes work the typesetting machine, and get paid very little in the bargain," I said.

Actually, during the time it took to find the booking precinct and then get down to the courthouse for arraignment, the young one and I had developed a good rapport. He told me that he really didn't want to arrest me, or any other art director; he was after the Mob. He hated the Mob, and pledged to disrupt as many of its operations as possible. "But we're not mobsters," I said. "Maybe our distributors are, but all newspaper distributors, restaurant suppliers, and private trash disposal companies are Mob-run. We're just trying to publish an underground paper that takes jabs at authority and hypocrisy." I told them that my Murder Inc. distributor had accused me of being the only person in New York who could make a sex paper fail. (Incidentally, the issue the cops were busting us on was called "Our Especially Clean Issue," in which the only vaguely hardcore sex photograph in the entire issue was an ad for *Screw* (four months earlier, I had been the first art director of *Screw*). Everything else was not only soft-core, but no-core: The hottest picture in the issue was a fully clothed woman in a raincoat sitting on a fire hydrant). Nevertheless, some citizen had complained to the DA's office about the all the sex papers, and that was impetus enough for the vice squad to take action.

When I reached the Tombs, a few of my elder colleagues from the other sex papers had already been processed and were ready to make their courtroom appearances. My arresting officers hastily tried to get me through the clogged system, but without success. When the court authorities found out I was still a minor (my eighteenth birthday was only days away), I was put through even more red tape before being allowed to appear in court. As a minor, I was eventually placed in a pen with the prostitutes, where, between scarfing down their bologna sandwiches and drinking Kool-Aid (that day's holding pen rations), they teased me and played with my ponytail until my name was called. When I entered court, I found that my distributor had provided a lawyer, and I was released without bail pending trial.

In the period between the arrest and the trial, I was arrested again in another roundup. This time I was eighteen, and the process was not as much fun. My elder partners and I were placed in a huge holding cell full of the flotsam, jetsam, and yeech of New York's streets (my partner Sam even tried bartering me for a few cigarettes, but mercifully without success). We learned that these roundups of publishers and distributors were intended to put us out of business by harassment, because the DA really had skimpy legal grounds for censoring our publications. No matter how sexist they were, the DA could not prove pornography. Indeed one of the indictments against *Kiss,* the sex paper of the East Village Other, cited an R. Crumb cartoon for obscenity. The case was thrown out of court, but only after costly legal battling.

After the second arrest, the *New York Review of Sex (& Politics)* was on its last legs. Our distributor gave us an ultimatum: that we either include enough hard sex to interest a viable readership, or fold. Our response was to add "& Aerospace" to the already cumbersome title, include even more political content, and ultimately call the publication the *NYRS&P (& Aerospace)*—not even mentioning sex in the title. Brad Holland designed one of the *NYRS&P* covers using an illus-

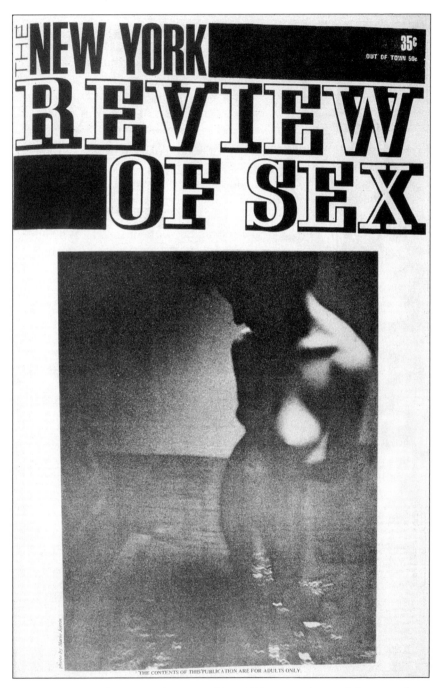

The second issue of The New York Review of Sex, *1969; I was embarrassed about sex so I published artsy art and photographs.*

tration that was so unerotic that the paper looked exactly like the unprofitable *New York Free Press* we'd been in before entering the sex trade. The distributor cut us off, and the paper died. Nevertheless, I was still under indictment. I still had to appear in court on felony charges. And I still faced a prison sentence if convicted. Art direction sure was a dangerous job.

By this time, we had a reputable lawyer who was paid by our former distributor. In fact, he later went on to defend Jean Harris and Claus Von Bulow (and lost both times). His strategy was to petition a three-judge panel prior to our initial trial on the grounds that the *NYRS&P* and *Screw* were unlawfully censored (citing prior restraint). The judges had to determine whether the DA was indeed harassing us, or, based on the content of the paper, had reasonable cause for confiscating issues and arresting principals. They were also to determine whether each issue could be reviewed by judges before warrants were issued, or if that was also unconstitutional. The legalities were complex, but fundamental. Somehow during the blitz of briefs and testimony, it was determined that the DA did not adhere to the law, and we were exonerated on all charges before going to criminal trial. Nevertheless the *NYRS&P* had folded, and I returned to art-direct *Screw*.

Winning this case meant that New York City and State authorities left the sex papers alone, and *Screw* took every opportunity to see how far that tolerance could be stretched. While the legal actions against *Screw* were minor during my two-year tenure, shortly after I left my stint as art director, the Feds indicted *Screw* in Witchita, Kansas (the hub of the postal service) for pandering through the mails. This was not taken lightly, since Ralph Ginzburg, former publisher of *Eros,* had been found guilty and imprisoned on similar charges.

Given my own experience, I knew that before *Screw* could be convicted for pornography it must be proven that it was void of any redeeming social value, which, without excusing its rampant sexism, it had in that it was a journal of cultural criticism pegged to sex. I knew that as art director I could help *Screw* pass muster if ever it was judicially scrutinized by maintaining a high level of design and illustration to offset the truly awful photography. Hence, I suggested that Push Pin Studios redesign *Screw* in 1971 (which they did, though badly) and also hired some of the best artists to do the exclusively illustrated covers— Brad Holland, Marshall Arisman, Ed Sorel, Mick Haggerty, Philippe Weisbecker, Jan Faust, Don Ivan Punchatz, John O'Leary, and so on.

Cover of Screw *illustrated by Marshall Arisman, 1972. Art instead of photographs on the cover made us seem respectable.*

(Doug Taylor even won an AIGA award for one of his covers.) Some of these were erotic, but most were very witty commentaries on sex and mores. I took a similar approach to inside art, too. Whenever I could, I'd replace bad photography with good illustration. My strategy was put to the test when, only a few months after I left *Screw* for the *New York Times,* I was subpoenaed to appear first before a Federal Grand Jury, and afterward as a hostile witness for the Witchita Federal prosecutor in the trial against *Screw.*

Unlike the Warren Commission, these proceedings can now be told: I was warned that if I refused to testify, I would be imprisoned for contempt; yet little did they know, I wouldn't have missed this for the world. When it came time for me to testify, the prosecutor (whose wife, for some reason, sat behind his desk in the courtroom knitting like Madame Defarge in *A Tale of Two Cities*) showed me large blowups of some of *Screw*'s more prurient pages taken from two or three issues. He asked me to explain how they had been put together, what contribution I had made to the makeup, and, most critical to his case, did I believe they had any artistic merit. I detailed the way type was set, the distinctions between typefaces, and the decisions that led to the design. I admitted that some pictures might be distasteful even to me, but that the entire publication had great artistic merit. While reminding the jury that I was a hostile witness, he tried to prove otherwise. Under cross-examination, *Screw*'s lawyer also brought forth blowup pages—which included illustration, most of which came from the same issues that had provided fuel for the prosecution. He asked what the drawing depicted, who had done the drawing, and what had the rationale been for using a drawing, not a photograph. Each question was a planned opening to wax poetical about the art, to describe the achievements of the artists (i.e., Brad Holland appears regularly on the Op-Ed Page of the *New York Times,* does covers for *Time* magazine, has been honored by the Society of Illustrators and the Art Directors Club, teaches at Pratt Institute, and so on). With each description of a distinguished artist, the case for redeemability was reinforced, and the prosecutor's case faded away.

The jury found *Screw* not guilty as charged after a short period of deliberation. The lawyers said that calling me as witness was a major mistake for the prosecutor, because my testimony solidly helped convince the jury to bring in a not guilty verdict. However, it was the last time I was involved with pornography. I had learned an invaluable lesson: Art direction can be dangerous when you mess with the law or play with taboos.

First issue of Mobster Times, *1972, I shot the cover with real bullet holes, but no one noticed.*

THE SOPRANOS AND ME

A drive through the New Jersey wetlands can be quite enjoyable, but not when the invitation comes as a threat from Sal, a hulk of a guy with reputed ties to the underworld, who ran a printing firm I worked with, and who was upset because I had hired some guys to go to a bindry in Jersey and tear up ten thousand magazine covers he had printed badly. "Stevie, Stevie," he said over the phone, "you can't do this, babe. You're costing me money."

"I'm sorry, Sal," I said with a quiver, but firmly holding my position. "The job stinks, and I just can't let it go through."

After a brief silence, he muttered, "Okay, let's take a ride to the bindry. I'll pick you up."

Fifteen minutes later, he pulled in front of my office in his sparkling white Caddy. I got in. He looked over and sneered. *What was I doing here alone with Sal going to Jersey?* I asked myself.

"Don't worry, Stevie," he replied as if reading my mind. "We'll settle this shit once and for all." And so began what I thought was the last car ride of my life.

You see, it was 1972, and I was the art director of *Mobster Times,* a magazine started by the publishers of *Screw,* for whom I was also art director, as a journal of satire (à la the *National Lampoon*) focusing somewhat on the political scandals that were beginning to brew during the Nixon administration (and also as a curiously vindictive response to *Screw*'s former art directors, who had fallen into disfavor when they'd left the *Screw* family and started a magazine called *Monster Times*). Nevertheless, it was a serious effort to make a topical humor magazine that focused on new trends in white-collar crimes, while appealing to an audience who savored true crime stories. It was also *Screw*'s first foray into nonsex publishing.

In fact, the first issue—which had the subtitle "Crime Does Pay" and whose editorial page showed photographs of *Screw*'s publishers and myself in Al Capone hats, mockingly pointing guns at the reader— was edited by a respected author of crime books. The issue included an interview with Gay Talese, who had just finished researching the life of Mafia kingpin Joe Bonano (and was about to write a book about the sex trade in New York); a story by Noel Hynd, who currently writes best-selling crime novels; an exposé of fake nuns who beg for money in the New York subways; a feature on Richard Nixon's brother's shady dealings with Howard Hughes; and a quiz to determine the world's greatest mobster: J. Edgar Hoover. But the tour de force was a review of the newly released movie *The Godfather,* a review purportedly written by soon-to-be-slain mobster Joey Gallo, as told to our publisher Al Goldstein. Our first cover was a sepia photograph of Al Capone (our mascot) shot with bullet holes (which I'd made myself).

Since *Screw*'s publishers believed that *Mobster Times* was as viable as the *National Lampoon* (which in 1973 was in its heyday), they wanted to avoid the *Screw* distribution setup and instead find a national distributor. A few were approached, but only Curtis, the venerable publisher of the *Saturday Evening Post, Holiday,* and scores of other household magazines, was interested. Actually, Curtis had overdiversified and fallen on hard times, and was looking for an easy income vehicle. Since we were producing the magazine entirely, Curtis had to put up very little money and agreed to take us on. But even with the promise of national distribution, we could not afford full-color printing or slick paper, so *Mobster Times*'s guts was printed on newsprint by *Screw*'s cheapo web press printer. We wanted the covers to be printed on glossy stock at Sal's shop. Herein the trouble begins.

Sal basically printed sexually sensitive material for which quality control was not a major issue. He didn't always print this kind of stuff, nor was he always wealthy. In fact, he used to do small, run-of-the-mill jobs and was on his way to debtor's prison when purportedly his business was "acquired" by—well, you get the picture . . .—who proceeded to keep the half-dozen multiliths working through the night and on week-ends printing a genre of printed matter known as T&A books (tits and ass). While I have no idea how it all worked, I assume the T&A was distributed by the new owners, who distributed other items as well. All I do recall is that whenever a grand jury was called to investigate strong-arm tactics and takeovers in the publishing and printing business, Sal would turn on his answering machine and take an extended vacation.

When Sal's business associate, whom we shall call Sir, learned that *Screw* was publishing another magazine that was going to be distributed by someone else, he called a lunch meeting at Umberto's Clam House—the very same restaurant where, a few weeks later, Gallo, who was somehow related to Sir, would be unceremoniously gunned down, initiating a yearlong gangland conflict. The conversation was as heavy as the food and began with Sir's menacing inquiry, "So what's this new venture you got?"

Before lunch, we had been worried that Sir would be more disturbed by the content of *Mobster Times*—with emphasis on the word mobster—than by the fact that he wasn't going to distribute it. "Its a magazine about Nixon and hypocrisy," I offered. "We didn't think you'd be interested in it."

"I'm interested in everything that's on the newsstand," said Sir, "especially when its produced by someone with whom I have a relationship. You sure this isn't another sex paper?"

I shook my head nervously. "Definitely not," I said impetuously. After all, I was only twenty-two years old, and since I did not have the good sense to get a respectable job, here I was at lunch with Sir, just a heartbeat away from making a jerk of myself. "This is about crime in high places," I continued, "like that J. Edgar Hoover guy, who has abused his power for decades, and Nixon, who's doing God knows what to make a mockery of our system, or—"

"Okay, I get the picture," interrupted Sir impatiently. "This is another one of those crackpot, commie, underground papers, right? That's what it sounds like. And you're right—I don't want anything to do with it."

"Unless it turns a profit?!" quipped Sal.

"Yeah, right," replied Sir, who, it turns out, had voted for Nixon.

"But what about the printing?" asked one of the publishers, "Can we print with you?"

"Only as a favor, and only at night. I don't even want to see that commie stuff in my shop," Sir responded in an annoyed tone.

I wonder whether, if *Mobster Times* had been devoted to the heroes of the underworld, Sir would have been more enthusiastic. Regardless, he did allow us to print at his shop, which saved us a bundle of money.

Still, we weren't out of the woods.

After putting the content and design together, we decided to take out ads in the *New York Times,* the *Daily News,* and the *Village Voice.* We printed posters and stickers using our mascot photo of Capone with the headline "Now There's A Magazine for Him, *Mobster Times*" (my idea), and I did a typographically elegant display ad that explained what we hoped to accomplish. At the end of the copy (and as an end mark for all our stories) I printed a black hand—cute, eh? The newspaper ads were costly—in fact, we'd only break even if we sold over a thousand subscriptions—and Curtis didn't spare a penny to help. The ads were timed to coincide with a massive (for us) publicity campaign that included a press conference, press release, and press package that would include promo copies of the magazine. Everyone was poised. I went to the printer to check the guts.

After a few hours of printing, I noticed a flat full of our covers. Sir was not kidding; they had been printed late at night, and they hadn't even me informed me so that I could watch the run. I cut the plastic ties and looked at the covers. Ugh! Not only had they been printed late at night, but it looked as if they had been done in total darkness. Every other cover was washed out, the black border surrounding the photograph was gray, and the sepia was dull red. I was furious! In a fit of pique, I called Sal: He was out. I called my publisher: He told me to destroy them.

"How?"

"Hire some guys."

I did. And so, two days later, the floor of the Jersey bindry was littered with thousands of torn *Mobster Times* covers. And I was sitting on white leather seats, listening to a Sinatra eight-track tape, on my way through the Jersey wetlands, possibly to a watery grave. For all I knew, Sal may have driven other smart-assed art directors to the same place.

Instead, we arrived at the bindry, where Sal looked at the mess and said, "Stevie, you're right, babe. It's my fault. I had a moron working that shift. I'm sorry, we'll reprint, and I'll eat it. But remember what I'm doin' here."

Second issue of Mobster Times *with Rembrandt homage by Brad Holland.*

Of course, I thanked him profusely. We drove back, and this time I was able to enjoy the natural wonders of Jersey's threatened swamps. But our troubles were still not over.

The *Daily News* and the *Voice* ads ran two weeks early, doing us no good at all. The *Times* ad ran on time, but the day the issue was to be released by Curtis, J. Edgar Hoover died. What timing! First, Joey Gallo had been killed right after we'd printed the guts, and then J. Edgar on the day we were to premiere with an insulting feature about the FBI's dearly departed leader. Needless to say, no one came to our press conference; and worse, the ostensibly conservative Curtis stopped distributing the issue, citing that it would be in bad taste to premiere it at this time. We heard from Sal that Sir was not too happy with the issue either, but for other reasons, and looked forward to seeing it die.

We published two subsequent issues. The second cover showed Brad Holland's parody of Rembrandt's Drapiers of the Syndics (a.k.a., The Dutch Masters), featuring J. Edgar, Nixon, Hitler, and other of the world's most reprehensible criminals. Inside, we ran a terrific piece called "The Misfortune Society Newsletter," which explored the horrible conditions within American prisons; an exposé on industrial espionage; and a calendar of great moments in crime. Unfortunately, Curtis couldn't or wouldn't get us good display on newsstands, and sales went nowhere. Moreover, despite our rather acute predictions of and smart-ass commentary on government wrongdoing, the last issue was published eight months before the Watergate hearings began, and most people, like Sir, refused to believe and would not support a publication that alleged such scandalous things.

Mobster Times died as it had lived, with hardly anyone noticing. But I wouldn't have missed it for the world.

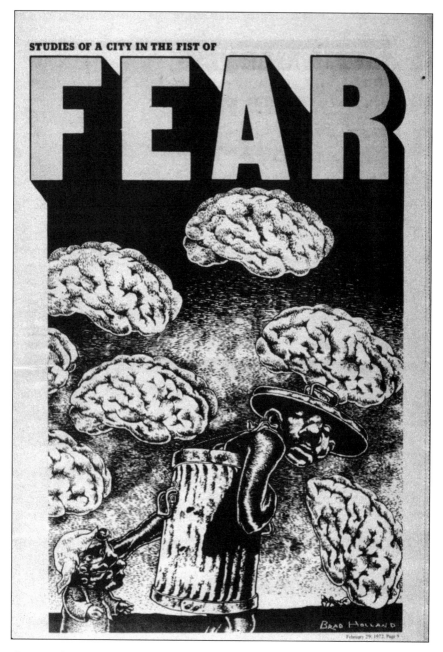

Cover of The New York Ace's *special section on "Fear" illustrated by Brad Holland, 1971. New York hasn't changed much, or has it?*

MY MENTOR

Whenever I write a book, I save the acknowledgments for last—not because I want to be sure I've included everyone who helped me with the project, but because for me the acknowledgments are the most enjoyable part. The acknowledgments in my first book, *Artists' Christmas Cards,* were longer than the entire introduction. Since it was my first book, I wanted to thank anyone and everyone who'd ever shown me the least bit of kindness and encouragement.

I've thanked a lot of people in the books that I've written and edited since 1979, but there is no one who deserved the thanks more in that first acknowledgments page than Brad Holland. Almost thirty-five years ago, in 1968, he became my first and—perhaps my only—real mentor. Although he was not the first person I met on my march toward careerdom, he was the first I found with a distinct vision of this then-mysterious field who was willing to share his ideas with a virtual stranger. While much of what I learned from him in those early days was technical—and obsolete today—the most important lessons, which will never lose currency, focused on the ethics of making art; how an illustrator, cartoonist, or art director can make a decisive contribution to a publication, the culture, or whatever. He showed me that an illustrator could be every bit as important to the visual arts as a painter or sculptor—even more so, owing to the potentially larger audience for an illustration in the mass media. While it sounds lofty, it was practical, indeed necessary, inspiration for a kid who wanted to be some kind of an artist and who stumbled by accident into a profession that was somehow about art. It was an important concept to hear, since for a few years prior to our meeting, as a student of Saturday classes at New York's Museum of Modern Art, I had been indoctrinated into believing the myth of high and low art—in which illustration, and commercial art in general, represented the latter.

I don't believe that many people in my position, without a commercial art education or professional connections, get the opportunity to meet the right person at the right time. Even my first publishing employer, although he opened a door, never imparted the practical information or philosophical foundation on which I could effectively build a career. I met Holland by accident, but it was the most fortuitous meeting of my life. Today, I continue to adhere to many of Holland's basic principals about the integrity of illustration and design. In fact, although long ago I developed my own precepts, Holland still possesses me—often I still feel him standing next to me, as I felt him so many years ago, judging my actions. It's an eerie feeling.

I met Brad Holland through an ad I placed in the *Village Voice* for contributors to a magazine I was starting with the Bar Mitzvah money set aside in trust for college (it had been turned over to me when I turned eighteen for me to do with as I liked). I was fulfilling a childhood dream—to publish my own magazine. The resulting publication, *Borrowed Time,* was unfortunately molded in my image and therefore lacked direction and a point of view, except that all the stories and poems I had chosen to publish reflected my own adolescent obsession with death and martyrdom. Holland was among forty prospective artists and writers who answered the ad.

At our first meeting in the basement apartment of a friend's brownstone on East 10th street, Holland arrived carrying the largest portfolio I had ever seen—equivalent to five black pizza boxes. He was tall, gaunt, and wore a short beard. He looked out of place in Greenwich Village, like a rube off the bus from points west of the city, and didn't pretend to be hip like me or the other artistes who had answered the ad. He spoke softly with a mid- or southwestern accent— I couldn't tell which at the time. He told me he was originally from Arkansas and had worked in Kansas City at Hallmark Cards. Throughout the entire hour we were together, he said little else but fixed his eyes exclusively on his work as I briskly turned over the large original pieces; he never once looked directly at me. He was twenty-four; I was seventeen. He was a pro; I was full of myself.

Who was I to be judging this exquisite work? I was a self-proclaimed editor, the first kid from my graduating class at Walden School to strike out in the real world, so impressed by my small success that I stunk of arrogance. "Good stuff," I told him, holding my awe in check at the sight of his meticulously rendered, chiaroscuro line drawings of surreal fantasies and vignettes. "I like 'em. But can you illustrate literature? Can you stick close to the text?" Literature, indeed! The stories I was about to publish were puerile at best. And be literal to the text? I had no idea what I was saying. Yet Holland agreed to be a contributor—and for no fee—so long as he maintained complete control over what he did. I agreed. "But, don't forget, I'm still the editor," I said.

"Sure you are," he replied.

Nevertheless, I was surprised that Holland actually returned a week later for a meeting I had called to explain the magazine to all the contributors. He listened quietly to my pedantic monologue about the "philosophy" of *Borrowed Time,* whatever it was. He stuck around until everybody left, at which point he said with what I then perceived was an air of superiority, "I'd like to help you design this thing."

"But I already have an art director." I was referring to an old high school buddy who did what I then considered to be the best drawings anyone had ever done (I later learned they were copied from Aubrey Beardsley).

"He doesn't know shit about making a magazine," said Holland confidently. "I'm sure he won't mind if I help out. And frankly, you don't know much about putting a magazine together, either, so I'd like to be involved at least where my drawings are concerned."

His words pierced my protective confidence like harpoons. "What do you mean? I am the art director of the *New York Free Press!* I do too know what I'm doing."

Holland just smiled and said he'd be back.

I wasn't sure I wanted him after that, but he was curiously persistent. He was also correct about my "art director," who admitted to me a few weeks later that design was not his métier and resigned his post. By default, I allowed Holland to take over. We transferred our operation from my friend's brownstone apartment to Holland's East 11th Street tenement. The first thing he did was to introduce me to typography.

Holland was right about me, too. I knew less than nothing and didn't want to admit it. I had energy, ambition, and chutzpah, but no knowledge about type, typefaces, or type designers. At the *Free Press,* Suarés had taught me to blow up 11-point Times Roman Bold to 600 percent as my display type. I had no sense that types came in families, styles, and weights. I didn't even know how to make a good mechanical. This is how Suarés had taught me when I'd started at the *Free Press:* "This is a galley. This is glue. This is a knife. This is a mechanical board. You cut the galley with the knife, paste it down on the board with the glue—now it's a mechanical." Mine were quite crude, and dirty. Holland showed me how it was really done. In fact, he would do meticulous mechanicals on the floor of his apartment. Using Herb Lubalin as his model and *Avant Garde* magazine as an example (where, incidentally, his first illustration had been published), he showed me the expressive nuances achieved by smashing, overlapping, and otherwise allowing type to speak.

I was also pissed. Ignoring reality, I resented the implication that I was a know-nothing. I rejected any knowledge that did not flow in and out of me through the intervention of another person. I hated that he was so much better than I was. Yet I wasn't stupid. I knew that what Holland was giving me was the equivalent of hours of school. Moreover, he was doing all this work for free for my magazine. I was torn between feeling gratitude and anger.

In addition to being the editor of *Borrowed Time,* I was also an illustrator/cartoonist. The *New York Free Press* was running one of my satirical drawings in each issue under the heading, "A Heller." My drawings were crudely rendered, mostly of Christlike figures without genitals in various stations of angst. I wanted to be Jules Feiffer and so focused in on personal turmoil as my primary theme. At that time I had never seen an Illustrators Club or Art Directors Club annual—I didn't even know they existed until Holland showed them to me—so I'd never had to compare my talents to those who were making a living at this. When I saw Holland's work for the first time, I prayed that he was an exception to the rule, for I could never compete with his competence and imagination. I guess I resented him more for his talent than for his superior attitude and arrogance, which would often emerge when I'd argue with him about something we were doing together. I resented him so much that even as we worked together almost every day for five months on *Borrowed Time,* I kept him from being published in the *Free Press.* "The editor doesn't want anyone but me," I insisted, lying through my teeth. I thought he believed me, because he rarely challenged my assertion. He later confided that he'd known all along what I was doing and simply hadn't wanted to make waves.

Even as my envy percolated, I truly admired Holland's vision. I listened in rapt attention as he told me about bouts and duels with editors and art directors over matters of principle. He religiously stuck by his rule never to render someone else's idea, but to find a better, if not more personal, solution to the problem. He was adamant even at the expense of losing a job. I thought his determination was courageous, though foolhardy. Yet, I remember the days when it paid off, when something without equal was published in a national magazine or on a book jacket. I understood that Holland was not only fighting against the conventional wisdom that an illustrator was the extension of an art director's hands—or worse, an editor's hands—but trying to change the traditional method of narrative and sentimental illustration celebrated by the Society of Illustrators to something more expressive. Indeed, he entered all the annual competitions in order to break through the old-boy network. He once confided in me that he would either win or he'd quit—there was no middle ground. I remember the first piece accepted into the Society of Illustrators—I was so proud of him, though jealous too.

I desperately wanted to have Holland's talent; the frustration of being limited by own limited abilities was too painful. I couldn't draw realistically if my life depended on it. Holland could. I couldn't come up with the visual metaphors that seemed so natural to Holland. Yet I continued to draw my little cartoons, and tried to get them published with some success in various undergrounds. I also took my work to Lubalin at *Avant Garde* and Ken Deardorf at *Evergreen Review* (where Holland was being published and where years later I was art director), but both art directors politely rejected them. More important to me, however, was earning Holland's approval of what I was doing. I wanted his validation that my works in general, but specifically my drawings, were good. Since he failed to say so in as many words—at least I never heard him say it—I decided not to draw anymore.

Sounds childish now, but I presumed that since I couldn't compete with Holland, and since I liked being an art director anyway (I found an expressive outlet playing with type and images), I'd just stop doing one and emphasize the other. I also figured that if I stopped drawing, I'd be hurting him, not me. It used to work, I thought, when I was mad at my parents. In fact, six months after I had stopped publishing my drawings, I met Holland in the street and he innocently asked, "How come I don't see your drawings anymore?"

"I decided to stop doing them," I said with a sharp, ironic edge to my voice.

"Too bad, some of them were really good," he said.

My revenge seemed sweet. He did like them, after all. And now, because he was so stingy with his compliments, I was never going to do them again. So there! And I rarely drew again after that. I had given Holland power, but I had abused our relationship. Yet a new relationship did take hold. As an art director I felt I was under his watchful eye, but I was not in direct competition with him. In fact, as an art director of a number of other undergrounds that Holland contributed work to (the *New York Review of Sex,* the *East Village Other, Screw,* and the *New York Ace*), I was actually better equipped to apply some of the lessons I learned from him to my job, such as giving license to artists and redefining illustration and design problems so that personal solutions were possible.

By 1974, when I moved from the undergrounds to the job of art director of the *New York Times*'s Op-Ed page, Holland had already been a regular contributor there for some time. Introduced to the *Times* by J. C. Suarés, he was producing powerful graphic commentaries on social and political issues. That Holland was working for the *Times* made getting the job on my own merits very sweet indeed. The Op-Ed page was the most important illustration outlet in America, and being selected to be its art director at twenty-four years old, after having worked almost exclusively on underground and sex papers, was the epitome of my career. Yet the sum total of my knowledge at that time focused on underground comix and underground papers, so again Holland became my active mentor, introducing me to a legacy of acerbic graphic commentary from nineteenth and early twentieth century Germany, France, and the United States. This area was the underpinning of my early writing on the history of satiric art and periodicals.

As I matured, my relationship with Holland seasoned. Over time we became equals, though I still get a bit nervous when I think about how he might critique all that I do. These days, we don't see each other often, but our bonds will never be broken. Over the years I've had many close friends and supporters among the artists, writers, and editors I've worked with, but none have had such a fundamental impact on the way I think about and practice in this field. Without Holland,

C 23

Lisbon's Shrinking Nest Egg

By C. L. Sulzberger

FOREIGN AFFAIRS

The Poppy Whose Sap Is Anti-Life

By Charles B. Rangel

Drugs Whose Flowers Are Life

By Stephen L. DeFelice

Separating American Messages

By Frank Stanton

frankly, I'm not sure whether I would have ever started studying satiric art, which led directly to my interest in design history. I doubt if I would be writing about illustration and design history had it not ultimately been for Holland's mentoring. He is such linchpin that I know that my life would be completely altered if we had never met, or if we had met at a different time and place.

INDEX

BOOKS FROM ALLWORTH PRESS

The Education of an E-Designer edited by Steven Heller (paperback, 6¾ × 9⅞, 352 pages, $21.95)

The Education of a Graphic Designer edited by Steven Heller (paperback, 6¾ × 9⅞, 288 pages, $18.95)

The Education of an Illustrator edited by Steven Heller and Marshall Arisman (paperback, 6¾ × 9⅞, 288 pages, $19.95)

Business and Legal Forms for Graphic Designers, Revised Edition by Tad Crawford and Eva Doman Bruck (paperback, 8½ × 11, 240 pages, includes CD-ROM, $24.95)

AIGA Professional Practices in Graphic Design: The American Institute of Graphic Arts, edited by Tad Crawford (paperback, 6¾ × 10, 320 pages, $24.95)

Graphic Design History edited by Steven Heller and Georgette Balance (paperback, 6¾ × 9⅞, 352 pages, $21.95)

Graphic Design Timeline: A Century of Design Milestones by Steven Heller and Elanor Petit (paperback, 6¾ × 9⅞, 288 pages, $19.95)

Graphic Design and Reading: Exploration of an Uneasy Relationship edited by Gunnar Swanson (paperback, 6¾ × 9⅞, 240 pages, $19.95)

Looking Closer 3: Classic Writings on Graphic Design edited by Michael Bierut, Jessica Helfand, Steven Heller, and Rick Poynor (paperback, 6¾ × 9⅞, 304 pages, $18.95)

Looking Closer 2: Critical Writings on Graphic Design edited by Michael Bierut, William Drenttel, Steven Heller, and DK Holland (paperback, 6¾ × 9⅞, 288 pages, $18.95)

Looking Closer: Critical Writings on Graphic Design edited by Michael Bierut, William Drenttel, Steven Heller, and DK Holland (paperback, 6¾ × 10, 256 pages, $18.95)

Design Literacy by Steven Heller and Karen Pomeroy (paperback, 6¾ × 9⅞, 288 pages, $19.95)

Design Literacy (continued) by Steven Heller (paperback, 6¾ × 9⅞, 296 pages, $19.95)

Sex Appeal edited by Steven Heller (paperback, 6¾ × 9⅞, 296 pages, $18.95)

The Swastika: Symbol Beyond Redemption? by Steven Heller (hardcover, 6 × 9, 176 pages, $21.95)

Careers By Design: A Business Guide for Graphic Designers, Third Edition by Roz Goldfarb (paperback, 6 × 9, 232 pages, $19.95)

Please write to request our free catalog. To order by credit card, call 1-800-491-2808 or send a check or money order to Allworth Press, 10 East 23rd Street, Suite 510, New York, NY 10010. Include $5 for shipping and handling for the first book ordered and $1 for each additional book. Ten dollars plus $1 for each additional book if ordering from Canada. New York State residents must add sales tax.

To see our complete catalog on the World Wide Web, or to order online, you can find us at *www.allworth.com.*